MAR

& FRANKENSTEIN

MARY SHELLEY

& FRANKENSTEIN

The Fate of Androgyny

WILLIAM VEEDER

The University of Chicago Press
Chicago & London

WILLIAM VEEDER is professor of English at the University
of Chicago. He is the author of *Henry James—The
Lessons of the Master: Popular Fiction and Personal Style
in the Nineteenth Century* and co-editor of *The Art of
Criticism: Henry James on the Theory and Practice of
Fiction,* both published by the University of Chicago
Press.

THE UNIVERSITY OF CHICAGO PRESS, CHICAGO 60637
THE UNIVERSITY OF CHICAGO PRESS, LTD., LONDON

LIBRARY OF CONGRESS CATALOGING IN PUBLICATION DATA

Veeder, William R.
  Mary Shelley & Frankenstein.

  Bibliography: p.
  Includes index.
  1. Shelley, Mary Wollstonecraft, 1797–1851.
Frankenstein. 2. Androgyny (Psychology) in literature.
3. Sex differences (Psychology) in literature. 4. Split
self in literature. I. Title. II. Title: Mary Shelley
and Frankenstein.
PR5397.F73V44 1984   823'.7   85-14141
ISBN 0-226-85225-3
ISBN 0-226-85226-1 (pbk.)

For
Maisie
and
Willy

Contents

CONTENTS

Did you read in the *Times* that Shelley left on his table a bit of paper with a blot on it and a flung down quill? Mary S. *had a glass case* put over same and carried it all the way to London *on her knees.* Did you ever *hear* such rubbish!! That's her final give away for me. Did she keep it on her knees while she ate her sandwiches—Did everybody know? Oh— *didn't* they just. I've done with her.

Katherine Mansfield

. . . perhaps he is already planning a poem in which I am to figure. I am a farce and I play to him, but to me this is all dreary reality.

Mary Shelley

But what mortal can cope with a creature of his dream? The imagination creating the enemy is already vanquished.

Ambrose Bierce

Introduction

> Alas, we know not what we do when we speak
> words.
>
> Percy Bysshe Shelley

I CAME TO MARY SHELLEY THE WAY MOST READERS DO, THROUGH *Frankenstein*. And like many recent readers I saw the novel in basically oedipal terms. At least for a while. Each rereading increased my sense that much of the text was not explained or was flat-out contradicted by the Oedipus. In this reaction I was participating, I see now, in the recognition by psychoanalytic critics that their praxis had to become more delicate in its readings and more intricate in its paradigms.[1] My own reading of *Frankenstein* is not finally psychoanalytic. I have been helped by Freud and Lacan, and by their many explicators and fellow practitioners; I draw upon such concepts as the negative Oedipus, and partake in the recent interest in fathers absent and present. But the psychological model ultimately most helpful to me lies outside strictly Freudian purlieus; it comes from Mary Shelley's own fiction and life. The fact that Mary Shelley appears now in a discussion of method indicates the evolution of this book. It has become primarily about *her*. My attempt to understand *Frankenstein* has led me to Mary's* life and other writings, and to her husband Percy's life and work.

Reading *Frankenstein* in context is of course not new. Mary Shelley herself gave to the biographical genesis of her novel a prominence and specificity rare in our fiction. Critics have followed her lead. As early as 1928 Church wondered how Mary could name the monster's first victim after her beloved son William. "Miserable delight in self-torture" (101), he concluded. More sympathetic and sophisticated biographical critics have, particularly in the last two

---

*The very act of referring to the Shelleys is difficult. "Mary and Shelley" is obviously sexist, while calling her "Shelley" is particularly confusing in a book where the poet is mentioned often. I will use "Mary" and "Percy" whenever the two authors appear in proximity.

1

decades, read *Frankenstein* in terms of birth trauma and primal scene, and have expanded on earlier examinations of a daughter's tangled ties to father and mother.[2] The success of these contextual approaches is part of the larger success which critics have had with Romantic texts and authors since the waning of New Critical prohibitions against biographical, intentional, and psychoanalytic approaches. What I want to do is to integrate context and text in ways which cast new light upon both *Frankenstein* and its author. My book, as I have said, is finally about Mary Shelley herself.

Her mother, Mary Wollstonecraft, sounds the keynote. "Those compositions only have power to delight, and carry us willing captives, where the soul of the author is exhibited, and animates the hidden springs."[3] Mary Shelley's novels vary widely in originality, in execution, and especially in power, but they all reflect her lifelong concern with the psychological ideal of androgyny and its opposite, bifurcation—the harmonious balance of traits traditionally considered masculine and feminine, and the desolating polarization of these traits. Mary's fiction reflects her involvement with the era's most androgynous poets, Shelley and Byron, as they bifurcated repeatedly into extremes of willfulness and weakness. The fact that androgyny and bifurcation can also characterize woman is recognized by Mary Shelley in herself and in women around her, and is dramatized too throughout her fiction.

Of Mary Shelley's seven novels, *Frankenstein* is her most powerful examination of the psyche, but also her most difficult. Readers have for generations found aspects of the novel inchoate and bizarre. That biography can help solve some of these problems does not mean there is any easy one-to-one equivalence between Mary's life and art. Victor Frankenstein is in no way a simple stand-in for Percy Shelley. Though I, like Fleck, Ketterer, Small, and other critics, see strong connections between Victor and Percy, I implicate Byron and Godwin as well, and I stress Frankenstein's differences from these biographical figures, because the ultimate source of the power of *Frankenstein* lies beyond biography. Mary Shelley has laid bare psychological workings timely for readers today because perennial in human beings. Moreover, Mary not only relates to *Frankenstein* as author examining male conduct, but also projects herself into the text in diverse roles. What Wexelblatt says about the murder of Elizabeth—"Mary subconsciously played all three parts in that climactic scene: killer, victim, and observer" (109)—is true in even more intricate ways throughout *Frankenstein*.

Biography offers additional light upon aspects of the *Frankenstein* text which have attracted, yet resisted, close scrutiny: for example, the creation and nature of the monster; the motives for his killings, particularly of little William; and Victor's relations with women. Biography also helps directly with problems which critics have tended to overlook—the role of Ernest, and the reason for and the formal placement of the death of Alphonse Frankenstein. More generally, attention to Mary's life helps to create an analytic ambience in which aspects of her text reveal additional significances—the character and role of Margaret Saville, the events of the wedding night, and the nature of the novel's women, especially Elizabeth.

Approaching *Frankenstein* contextually involves me in Mary Shelley's other novels as well as her life. All three components— the life, the masterpiece, the later fiction—illuminate one another. The very schematicness which limits Mary's later novels as art highlights the interplay of androgyny with bifurcation and the interaction of women with men which figure importantly in her life and her masterpiece. In turn, the contrast in intricacy between *Frankenstein* and its successors prompts us to return to Mary's life and seek deeper for the causes of her decline as a novelist, while at the same time we see in the later novels a continuity of concerns and a shaping of formal elements which increase our appreciation of them.

My contextual approach has resulted in a book which does not fit into traditional genre categories. It combines close analysis and biography with an overview of Mary's career. Ultimately what I hope to give a sense of is the *drama* of Mary Shelley, the special splendor of a woman who could without exaggeration call her life "romantic beyond romance" (*J* 186, 11 Nov. 1822) and could write one of the influential novels in our language. All my pages aim toward the last few, where I attempt to define the special darkness of Mary's vision at its most valuable—how she could in *Frankenstein* be both conservative and subversive, acolyte and assassin, how she could be Mary Shelley.

*

My contextual approach raises other questions which I should take up now. One concerns intentionality, about which I may seem cavalier to some readers. Not only do I not work through those objections which deconstructionists and others have raised to the very possibility of authorial intention, I do not distinguish absolutely between Mary's conscious and unconscious processes in creating *Frankenstein*. What an author did or did not intend on any level of the psyche is a question which vexes any psychological study.[4] An answer unsatisfying with even the most perfect works—that the artist saw some and did not see all—is especially unsatisfying with a lumpy performance like *Frankenstein*. I agree with students of psychoanalysis that a literary text is composed of at least *two* voices, and that distinguishing conscious from unconscious is often difficult. As the artist is both voices, so both voices express what the artist intends on different levels to say. What *Frankenstein* says has proven powerful for nearly two centuries, and the sources of that power are the focus of my close analysis. I am less interested in whether Mary Shelley is fully, or even partially, conscious of the multilayered effect of an image or word or event or pattern than in whether the formal element does indeed have that effect. When I say "Mary sees" or "she knows," I mean that in creating the form which produces a particular effect she knows what she is doing in the only sense that matters.

Intentionality may become an issue in a different way when readers encounter the intricacies I argue for in *Frankenstein*. "Could Mary Shelley possibly have intended *that*?" will be a way of asking, "Could she possibly be that sophisticated an artist—capable both of imagining so complex a situation and of manipulating technique so adroitly?" To this perfectly proper question I have only the answer that seeing is believing. We readers are predisposed to respect claims for intricacy in a text of Percy Shelley or Emily Brontë because these authors have already entered the canon. Whether Mary Shelley "could possibly be that sophisticated an artist" depends in part upon how sophisticated we are willing to consider her. Excellent recent criticism has increased considerably the status of *Frankenstein* as an imaginative and technical performance, but Mary Shelley has by no means escaped completely the caricature which has plagued her since 1818—that she was an inept neophyte who chanced upon a myth. Thus when I ask of *Frankenstein* the kind of question conventional enough with established masterpieces—why is Ernest Frankenstein not killed along with the rest of his family?—readers may react immediately (as they would not with *Wuthering Heights*) and answer that, odds are, Mary Shelley simply forgot about Ernest, as most critics do. When I see significance in the names Felix De Lacey, Safie, and Caroline, or ask why the murders occur in the order William-Justine-Henry-Elizabeth-Alphonse, I will be straining readers' credibility by the very questions, let alone by answers that posit a consistent shaping control—conscious or unconscious or both—by Mary Shelley. My best justification is coherence. I ask my readers to do for Mary Shelley what they do for more canonical writers—to put aside preconceptions about ineptitude and to see whether the claim for a specific textual moment fits into a coherent view of the scene, the novel, and the artist. My book aims above all to see *Frankenstein* as the coherent product of a sensibility's life-long preoccupation with certain themes and words and processes.

Another group of readers will be concerned about my fairness to the Shelleys, especially to Percy. The evenhandedness essential for any scholarly undertaking is particularly difficult to sustain with the Shelleys, who have sparked fierce controversy for generations. The acrimony cannot be attributed simply to the feistiness of readers attracted to the Shelleys. Mary and Percy are partly responsible. They are so diverse psychologically, are capable of so extreme a range of emotions and actions from the benign to the homicidal and suicidal, that partisans tend to simplify them by insisting upon one personality trait as the entire character. For example, the legend of Mary Shelley, fostered by her daughter-in-law, Lady Jane, and perpetuated by biographers through Grylls and Leighton, makes Mary's devotion to Percy perfect and her fiscal privations dire. Massingham's counterattack—that these are exaggerations derived from Mary's own self-pitying view of herself, and that she in fact quarreled terribly with Percy and enjoyed relative financial security after 1822—goes too far in the other direction. "She possessed an unlimited capacity for self-deception" (218). Especially since the same mistake was made by Matthew Arnold about Percy Shelley ("a superhuman power of self-deception" [179]), I will try to avoid extreme positions.

Evenhandedness is difficult to achieve, however, for several reasons. Sources for the Shelleys' lives require careful sifting. Trelawny is prey to hyperbole and bias; Hogg is guilty of altering correspondence potentially embarrassing to himself; Medwin is pathologically prone to factual error. All three men, however, draw upon immediate experience which cannot be discounted entirely, and all three write at times with obvious conviction. I have sifted each source with care, seeking corroboration wherever possible from more reliable contemporary sources or from the Shelleys themselves. But the Shelleys themselves, as often as not, make matters *more* difficult. What are we to think, for example, when Mary tells Percy to "get your hair cut in London" (*MSL* 1:32, 26 Sept. 1817) or to "change your cap and jacket" (Trelawny 1:109), when she reprimands him for being no judge of flannel and says that "he can't be trusted with money" (*MSL* 1:39, 5 Oct. 1817; Trelawny 1:121)? We have arguably only the unseemly side of sublunary life, a nagging wife prevented by domestic trivia from keeping to the fore her husband's true worth, his poetic achievement. But a poet's trivia may be enormous for a poet's spouse. The ineptitude for which Mary nagged Percy contributed to the deaths of their children Clara and William, and to the perpetual turmoil of their household.

Being fair to Percy Shelley is particularly difficult because I must try to see him both "as he was" and as Mary did. The two viewpoints can never be separated completely, of course, since many of the Shelley legends derive ultimately from her. But I must attempt to separate fact from fancy. Certainly some of the myths dismissed long ago by Shelley scholars should be banished for all readers. The ineffectual angel, for example. As early as 1863, Thornton Hunt drew upon personal experience to insist that "grit" underlay Percy's "outward appearance and weakness. . . . His own ability to grapple with practical affairs was very great" (189, 190). No ineffectual angel could have impressed such men of action as Byron and Williams. Trelawny attests to Shelley's marksmanship (1:29), Hogg to his horsemanship (2:8), Peacock and Leigh Hunt to his prowess as hiker and rower (Peacock 65). Negotiating Mary's *Frankenstein* contract, Percy is a hard-nosed professional; he proves admirably decisive when he packs Mary in ice to save her from bleeding to death during her miscarriage at Lerici. The leitmotif sounded by Holmes as disasters rain down is moving indeed: "once again Shelley fought back."

I want to stress Percy's capacity for action because I will make much of Mary's exasperation at his ineffectuality. Being fair to Shelley is so difficult because the standard criticisms of him are at once apt and simplistic.[5] He was jejune, solipsistic, and homicidal, even as he was sophisticated, enormously gifted, and humane. Sincerity is not at issue. Shelley was a sincere feminist who indulged in macho fantasies; he sincerely loved his children and home, yet he fled both; he sincerely abominated sexual profligacy, but was also powerfully attracted to it. Percy Shelley was a ferociously bifurcated man whose passionate needs resulted sometimes in coherent action and sometimes in pandemonium. His power of self-analysis was substantial, but his power of self-deception was at least as great, because his sincere humanism could not always control destructive impulses and his puritan capacity for shame often hid himself from himself.

Insofar as I will bring up old charges against Percy, it is not to point an accusing finger but to direct the reader to what Mary is pointing at. That my book looks at Mary's experience through Mary's eyes does not mean I privilege her viewpoint to the extent of assuming that what she sees in men is factually "true," whereas what Percy sees in women is only self-satisfying fantasy. Of course Mary's vision satisfied psychological needs too. But the attempt to understand those needs requires me to highlight certain aspects of Shelley's art and life. I refer quite often, for example, to his early work and fragmentary texts—not because I imagine they constitute Percy's major achievement aesthetically but because they display features relevant to Mary's characterization of Frankenstein. I necessarily emphasize Percy the husband as seen by Mary the wife, or rather, Percy the man as seen by Mary the woman. And even here the going is tricky. Henry Clerval, as well as Victor Frankenstein, "is" Percy Shelley. Many readers have noted that Mary locates in Henry all the best of her husband. She splits Shelley into "good" and "bad" characters because, as I will argue in chapter 2, she can deal with him, and with herself, by facing at any one time only a part of either. She holds up to nature not a mirror but shards of a mirror (hence the cover of my book). What makes this fragmenting technique difficult for the critic is that it precludes, or at least circumvents, evenhandedness. Henry for all his excellences is not at the center of *Frankenstein*. He abides in exemplary isolation. However much Mary on one level wants to be fair to Percy, she cannot give parity to his two sides, or to her two views of him. Victor Frankenstein does not reflect equally the benign and the lethal aspects of Percy Shelley because *Frankenstein* is not an evenhanded event. Insofar as the marriage with Percy is happy, Mary does not need to express it in fiction.

This brings me to Mary Shelley's character, and the interpretative challenges which it poses. Mary uses fiction therapeutically because she is caught in a double bind: she has an emotional range as great as her husband's, but she is less inclined to express aggressive emotions openly. I say *less* because Mary as an adolescent did battle with her fractious stepmother, and as an adult did give way to irritability (Thornton Hunt among others recalls "her temper being easily crossed" [189]). But overall, Mary Godwin, particularly in her early years, reveals few counterparts to the wild moments of Percy Shelley. Her natural shyness, accentuated by her chill upbringing in William Godwin's library, inclines her to express her feelings psychosomatically. The paralysis which numbs her arm in 1812 vanishes when she escapes London for the liberation of rural Scotland and the orthodoxy of Isabel Baxter's family. This difficulty in han-

dling violent emotions, this combination of the need to express and
the tendency to repress (which psychologists call the approach-
avoid syndrome), characterizes the adult Mary Shelley too, as she
knows well.[6]

> . . . though I can rein my spoken words—I find
> all the woman directs my written ones & the
> pen in my hand I gallop over fence & ditch
> without pity for my reader—ecce signum!
> (*MSL* 1:333, 29 June 1825)

The violence implicit in "rein" and "without pity" appears more
openly when Mary feels herself embattled. Express-repress becomes
attack-retreat.

> I received your letter tonight I wanted one for
> [attack] I had not received one for almost two
> days, but [retreat] do not think I mean anything
> by this my love—[attack] I know you took a
> long walk yesterday so you could not write.
> (*MSL* 1:5, 3 Nov. 1814)

> [attack] You dont say a word in your letter—
> you naughty love to ease one of my anxieties
> not a word of Lambert of Harriet of Mrs. Stuart
> of money or anything. . . . but [retreat] my love
> do not be displeased at my chattering in this
> way for you know the expectation of a letter
> from you when absent always makes my heart
> jump. (*MSL* 1:6, 3 Nov. 1814)

> [attack] oh how I long to [be] at our dear home
> where nothing can trouble us neither friends or
> enemies—[retreat] dont be angry at this [at-
> tack] you know my love they are all a bad set.
> (*MSL* 1:6, 3 Nov. 1814)

These passages were written during Mary's first months with Percy.
Her anger will rage forth more openly in the years to come, as I shall
discuss soon. What I want to establish now is that the complexity
evident in these early letters characterizes all aspects of Mary's subsequent life. Her private prose, her later novels, her relations with
men, and *Frankenstein* all display Mary's need to express and her
tendency to repress. This express-repress penchant is particularly
significant because it also characterizes Mary's protagonist Victor
Frankenstein, and her husband Percy Shelley. Both men's silences
foster the chaos which their words could avert, and their confes-
sions occlude what they ostensibly avow. Thus our task as readers

of *Frankenstein* is doubly difficult: the author is expressing much of her own anger covertly; and her protagonist, like her husband, is doing the same thing with emotions which she sometimes shares and often reprobates. *Frankenstein*, and Mary's other pieces of public and private prose, must therefore be read with attention to silences and indirection, and to meaning as a thing of levels. Only through patient delicacy can we deal evenhandedly with Mary Shelley.

*

The Shelleys are also hard to write about because they attract audiences as diverse as themselves. Readers familiar with *Frankenstein* may know little about Mary Shelley's life and other fiction, and little of her husband beyond various myths and anthology pieces. Factual information essential for these readers will be old hat to experts on Mary and Percy, while my biographical interpretation of the Shelleys and my attention to Mary's later fiction—particularly in chapters 1 and 2—may seem excessive to critics concerned primarily with *Frankenstein*. I can only remind diverse readers that I am studying the Shelleys as well as *Frankenstein*, and ask of each audience patience with the others.

Anyone wishing more information on the Shelleys may consult appendixes A and B. Now I must present two essential biographical facts. The general reader may not have a sense of just how incompatible the supposedly blissful Shelleys were; the scholarly reader may date their discord late in the marriage, when in fact it was surfacing in the *Frankenstein* months of 1816–17.

First, the Shelleys' declarations of incompatibility. Percy says in 1822, "I only feel the want of those who can feel, and understand me . . . Mary does not" (*PSL* 2:435, 18 June). Mary says in 1819, "We have now lived five years together; and if all the events of the five years were blotted out, I might be happy" (*J* 122, 4 Aug.). We need not go so far as Trelawny's claim that Mary "did not understand or appreciate" Percy (1:229) to recognize the couple's fundamental disagreements about society and convention, Platonism, philosophy in general, perfectionism, poetry, and "victory." An extraordinary emblem of the continuity of Mary's disinclination to Shelleyism appears when we put together vignettes from Claire Clairmont and Trelawny which date from the first and the last months of the Shelleys' life together.

> On our way to Pontarlier [during the 1814
> elopement, Claire records], we came to a clear

running shallow stream, and Shelley entreated the Driver to stop while he from under a bank could bathe himself—and he wanted Mary to do the same as the Bank sheltered one from every eye—but Mary would not—first, she said it would be most indecent, and then also she had no towel and could not dry herself— He said he would gather leaves from the trees and she could dry herself with those but she refused and said how could he think of such a thing.[7]

At sunset the whole population of men, women, and children [at Lerici in 1822, Trelawny notes], took to the water. . . . We occasionally did the same, Shelley especially delighting in the sport. His wife looked grave, and said "it was improper." Shelley protested vehemently against the arbitrary power of the word. . . . Then turning to his friend, he continued, "At Pisa, Mary said a jacket was not proper, because others did not wear them, and here it's not proper to bathe, because every body does. Oh! What shall we do."

The Shelleys disagree fundamentally because Mary was never essentially a radical. What Massingham says derisively—"by nature submissive to and doctrinaire on behalf of the common acceptances, she was by accident of birth and marriage swept into the great movement of revolt whereof her father was the crabbed lawgiver and her husband the inspiration" (195)—can be restated with the sympathy warranted by Mary's situation. She is caught between powerful polar forces. She grows up with Godwinite radicalism, but she also partakes of the rising countertide of conservatism which establishes several decades before Victoria's ascension the values now termed Victorian. These polar forces impact so strongly upon Mary because they reflect her personal self-division.[8]

On the one hand she sympathizes with certain radical, or at least liberal, causes: increased education for women, relief for the poor, compassion for the fallen woman, freedom for the politically oppressed. On the other hand, Mary Shelley displays the self-division which characterizes most nineteenth-century feminists of both genders as well as their less radical contemporaries. Very few people are, like Elizabeth Cady Stanton, philosophically radical across the board. Many who campaign, for example, for woman's right to em-

10

ployment will not support the suffrage crusade, and both groups tend to maintain (at least publicly) a healthy distance from Free Lovers and Birth Controllers. The parental wellsprings of Mary's own radicalism are similarly self-divided. Godwin privately violates his public prohibition against wedlock by entering the institution himself and by disowning his daughter for not following suit. Mary Wollstonecraft directs radical reform to conservative ends. "Make women rational creatures, and free citizens, and they will quickly become good wives and mothers" (264).

Small wonder, then, that Mary Wollstonecraft Godwin is not the thoroughgoing radical whom Massingham expected her to be and whom some critics today make of her. In her well-known journal confession, Mary Shelley insists that she is not a feminist.

> With regard to "the good cause"—the cause of the advancement of freedom and knowledge, of the rights of women, & c.—I am not a person of opinions. . . . Some [people] have a passion for reforming the world; others do not cling to particular opinions. That my parents and Shelley were of the former class, makes me respect it. . . . I was nursed and fed with a love of glory. To be something great and good was the precept given me by my Father: Shelley reiterated it. Alone and poor, I could only be something by joining a party; and there was much in me— the woman's love of looking up, and being guided, and being willing to do anything if any one supported and brought me forward— which would have made me a good partisan. But Shelley died, and I was alone. . . . If I have never written to vindicate the rights of women, I have ever befriended women when oppressed. (204, 205, 206, 21 Oct. 1838)

With equal candor Mary admits to what Trelawny and Massingham deride her for—cherishing orthodoxy's ideals of a stable home life with each spouse fulfilling the role prescribed by the theory of complementary spheres. "The sex of our [woman's] material mechanism makes us quite different creatures [from men]—better though weaker" (*MSL* 2:98, 11 June 1835). Better though weaker: what could be more conventional? Throughout her public and private prose, Mary Shelley distinguishes the sexes in terms of traditional traits. Men are more active and assertive, capable of courageous and even generous acts, but strongly prone to cruelty, insensitivity, and predation. Women are the opposite. Though able at times to act decisively, they are largely passive, adaptive, patient, pure, selfless, tireless, intuitive.[9] How deeply Mary responds to woman's traditional traits is manifest by their proliferation in her fiction.

> A true feminine love of home . . . feminine love of order . . . feminine tenderness . . . the feminine delicacy of her mind and manners . . . feminine prudence . . . feminine aptitude . . . feminine tact . . . with feminine instinct she read her heart . . . those peculiarly feminine virtues.

> Her quick woman's wit . . . woman's wit . . . a woman's tact and keen penetration . . . a woman's tact and a woman's zeal . . . the generosity and pride of woman . . . woman's softness . . . woman's grace . . . a woman's heart . . . a woman's heart and sensibility . . . Endurance is the fate of woman . . . she was all woman, fearful of repulse, dreading insult . . . her woman's fears . . . her woman's fears, tenderness, and weakness . . . all woman in her tender fears. (*Lodore* 2:267, 282; *Valperga* 2:48; *Falkner* 1:160; *The Last Man* 24; *Falkner* 2:114; *Perkin Warbeck* 3:253; *The Last Man* 301; *Perkin Warbeck* 1:71; *Valperga* 3:239; *Perkin Warbeck* 1:93, 2:28, 251; *Falkner* 2:203, 250; *Lodore* 2:272; *The Last Man* 131; *Lodore* 2:40; *Perkin Warbeck* 2:134, 3:205, 213; *Falkner* 2:198.)

Mary Shelley thus partakes in what Welter has called the cult of True Womanhood.[10] Maintaining that woman's highest office is to be the mother or wife of a great man, Mary insists in both her public and her private prose that "women . . . have no public career—no aim nor end beyond their domestic circle. . . . my sex has precluded all idea of my fulfilling public employments . . . there is no greater annoyance than in any way to be brought out of my proper sphere of private obscurity" (*Lodore* 3:297; *MSL* 1:367, 5 Jan. 1828). Mary Shelley does not, therefore, seek to overthrow the patriarchy. She does, however, partake of what recent scholars have called "domestic feminism." As I will show in chapter 1, she espouses self-consciously the basic goal of the women's movement from 1750 to 1914—to improve woman's lot by both curbing male extremism and confirming female otherness. Now I want to stress the conservative side of her brand of feminism—the desire to please dominating males. First Godwin, then Percy and Byron. By her public prose and in her private life Mary seeks to compensate Godwin for not being the son he wanted, to provide Percy with the "antitype" he craves, and to convince Byron she is the intellectual he can never really take her for. *Frankenstein* grows in part from Mary's frustration at failing to satisfy any of these men.

Incompatibility, moreover, dogs the Shelleys not only because they disagree about fundamental issues, but because Mary cannot, will not give in and become a mere reflection of her spouse. Percy likewise will not, cannot change substantially. He modifies some of his more extreme intellectual stands by 1822, but the obsessive continuity of Shelley's life, which Dowden tries dutifully to deny, is confirmed when Dowden himself admits that the disastrous Wales harbor project "was the history of the expedition to Dublin repeated in another shape" (1:320). Dowden locates the commitment to perfectionism as early as 1812; Medwin establishes Shelley's interest in Plato in the Eton years; Brown dates the antitype theory from about the same time. The fascination with science begins even earlier, and the relentless changes of residences precede Mary considerably.[11] More importantly for her, the aspect of Percy's personality which affects Mary most directly, his relations with people, shows little real change. He endangers his first daughter, Ianthe, by subjecting her to the same type of long carriage journey that will kill his daughter Clara five years later. The need to place a buffer between himself and his beloved begins on his first honeymoon, when Shelley invites Hogg to stay with him and Harriet in Edinburgh; it reappears at the end of his life when he insists that the captivating Jane Williams and her husband share the Shelleys' small quarters at Casa Magni; and it persists through the years from 1814 to 1822 as he espouses Claire's disruptive presence in the household. What Medwin said of Shelley's penmanship was, Mary learned, true of everything Percy laid his hand to: "His hand was very early formed, and never altered" (373).

Granted that personalities so unchanging and so incompatible lead to the anger which Mary volleys forth in 1822, is discord already alive enough in the *Frankenstein* months of 1816–17 to generate the hostility which I find in the novel? To answer this question about what some biographers have called the Shelleys' "garden days" at their Marlow home,[12] we must trace the incompatibility back to its beginnings in 1814. Even a biographer as well-attuned to the Shelleys' discords as Cameron can say that "the October to December letters of 1814 show the first glow of enthusiasm" (2:363). They also show the first cracks in the foundation, as the attack-retreat sentences quoted above indicate.

> I had not received one [letter] for almost two days . . . . You dont say a word in your letter— you naughty love to ease one of my anxieties not a word of Lambert of Harriet of Mrs. Stuart of money or anything. . . . how I long to [be] at our dear home where nothing can trouble us neither friends or enemies.

Already in 1814 Mary's irritability finds the targets which will provoke her to outbursts in 1822—Percy's failure to keep in touch, his absences from her side, the bedeviling outside forces. The ardor of new love and the anxiety of vulnerability (living with a married and impecunious outcast whose pregnant wife is intent upon reclaiming him) keep Mary's attack instinct in check in 1814. But by 1816 irritability emerges prominently. After the suicides of Harriet and Fanny "had taken their toll. . . . [Mary] looked haggard . . . for the first time in her life she was dressing carelessly. . . . She was often waspish, too" (Gerson 103). Gerson insists that Mary's irritability did not extend to Percy, but Holmes sees the situation less sentimentally. "This nagging, carping side of Mary's personality gradually emerged through her craving for complete emotional security, which Shelley's temperament could never satisfy" (378).

More than the suicides weighs upon Mary by 1816–17. There are money troubles, Percy's continued ill health, and what inevitably affects a socially conscious person, ostracism. Marriage vows do not legitimize Mary in the eyes of the local gentry, who know of Percy's scandalous reputation and wonder openly at his Marlow menage— *two* women (Claire plus Mary), each with a child (Byron's Allegra and Shelley's William). Moments of peace and closeness there are, of course, but that Mary has still not found fulfillment with Percy is expressed not only in the 1820 ring inscription, "the good times will come," but also in her 1817 question, "ought we not to be happy?" (Gerson 103). Years later, Mary will call going "to Marlow—no wise thing at least" (*NL* 226, 20 Mar. 1822).

Another source of Mary's dissatisfaction is Percy's own discontent. Long before his "To Mary Shelley" poems of 1819 confirm a substantial rift in the relationship, Shelley's early verse signals the opening of that rift. "Yes, all the faithless smiles are fled . . . The glory of the moon is dead" ("To——" 25, 27). This is 1815, six years before Percy will use moon imagery in *Epipsychidion* to argue that Mary has been frigid from the first. Even the laudatory moon image of 1814, "my mind without yours is dead & cold as the dark midnight river when the moon is down" (*PSL* 1:414, 28 Oct.) restricts Mary's influence to "mind." Did Percy feel from the first that her head ruled her heart? He certainly adds to their elopement the emotional Claire Clairmont. By 1817, at the very time that Mary is writing *Frankenstein*, Percy is writing his great love poems to Claire, the Constantia lyrics. In the months after *Frankenstein*, Shelley's pen indicates how troubled marital relations are. As the young wanderer in "The Coliseum" who comes upon Mary and Godwin in the guise of adoring daughter and blind wise man, Percy tells them through art what he cannot yet bring himself to say in life. "Nor have I ever explained . . . the difference which I perceive between my language and manners, and those with whom I have intercourse" (*JS* 6:306).

I therefore question Cameron's conclusion that the Shelleys "up to the period of the final crisis . . . had an affectionate but not a passionate relationship, which Mary apparently found satisfying but Shelley did not" (2:304). How satisfied could Mary be, knowing that her husband was unsatisfied with her as a woman? And she did know it. Her later protestation that "had one been more alive to the nature of his feelings . . . such would not have existed" (*CP* 510) is just that—protesting too much. Mary knows Percy's feelings because she reads his early poems and she lives intimately with him. Thus to her irritability and dissatisfactions is added anger, anger at charges of coldness from a man to whom she had surrendered with abandon and whose criticisms and womanizing helped generate whatever coldness she did exhibit. The result is not yet the open hostility of 1822. Mary in 1817 still wants desperately to save the marriage. What occurs initially, besides flareups, is indirect: a literary dialogue between authors. After *Alastor* presents a man unable to find a woman to satisfy him, *Frankenstein* locates the source of such dissatisfaction within the male. Shelley then replies. His unpublished review of *Frankenstein* makes Victor the victim (see appendix C). Then the maniac in *Julian and Maddalo* shows the castrating effects of women like Harriet (who make the husband ashamed of conjugal passion) and like Mary (whose *Frankenstein* emasculates a protagonist named with Percy's pseudonym, Victor). It is after Mary in 1817 has revealed in her *Frankenstein* manuscript the horrors of her Victor that Percy rejects her nickname for him,

"Elfin Knight," and, addressing her directly in the dedication to *The Revolt of Islam*, proclaims himself "victor Knight" (3). His *Prometheus Unbound* then confirms the superiority of Shelleyism, particularly of the philanthropic idealism attacked so strenuously in Victor Frankenstein and Robert Walton. And finally, *Frankenstein's* implication of Percy in monster-making with fire and clay is countered in *The Witch of Atlas*, where a benign creature is made from "fire and snow" (321). All in all, the Shelleys' marriage even before 1818 subverts Grylls' piety that "in essentials Mary and Shelley were at one" (xiii). Essentials is just where the Shelleys were at odds.

*

I will outline the stages of my argument in some detail because my book is as unconventional in its shape as in its genre. The combining of biography, close analysis, and overview precludes beginning with *Frankenstein*; even the sections devoted primarily to the novel are forced by its intricacies to supplement close analysis with biographical and contextual materials.

Mary Shelley & Frankenstein examines Mary and her fiction in light of the psychological model that she and Percy looked upon as ideal, the androgyne. Particularly for Mary, androgyny has three stages. Within the individual psyche, it means the balance of "masculine" and "feminine" traits. Since no individual can effect a perfect balance, the true androgyne for Mary Shelley is the couple. A man and a woman complement one another, each providing what the other lacks, and together constituting a complete intercourse. Complementarity and androgyny are associated inextricably for Mary Shelley. The ultimate integration is then possible: the couple becomes part of the community, achieving solidarity with mother and father and with the other women and men who extend family relations. *Frankenstein* examines these three stages, and my book examines Victor at each stage.

Focusing upon the first stage, the psyche itself, part 1 is predominantly biographical. Chapter 1 presents the ideal of androgyny as Mary and Percy define it and as he and Byron embody it. I trace five forces which help shape Mary's particular version of androgyny: the traditions of the androgyne itself, of Eros, Agape, feminism, and sentimental fiction. Here and throughout I minimize Freudian and Lacanian terminology and use primarily the concepts of the Shelleys themselves, along with the traditional Eros and Agape. Chapter 2 describes Mary's response to the fact that Percy (and Byron) cannot sustain their ideally androgynous moments. In their attempt to escape death and achieve immortality, Promethean men undergo bi-

16

furcation: their masculine and feminine traits polarize into willfulness and weakness. Chapter 3 studies this turmoil as it is reflected in the early pages of *Frankenstein*—in Robert Walton's opening frame and in Victor's creation of the monster.

Part 2 examines the social workings of androgyny—union with the complement and integration with the community. I continue in this section to use biography to supplement textual analysis, because the lives and works of Mary and Percy Shelley remain so fruitful a context for Frankenstein's obliquities. Chapter 4 traces Victor's relations with Elizabeth, his mother, and by extension, womankind. Chapter 5 concentrates upon men, particularly fathers. Here examination of the psyche joins with study of the plot, since criticism must explain not only why Alphonse dies, but also why his death is placed last among the family fatalities.

Part 3 addresses questions raised by the argument so far, especially the role of women in *Frankenstein* and the final vision of Mary Shelley. Chapter 6 introduces the feminine psyche. Dissenting from the critical consensus that Mary's female characters are simple stereotypes, I present her women and herself in light of the ideal of androgyny and the threat of bifurcation. Mary cannot pretend that women are immune from destructive urges or that her anger—her participation in those urges—is restricted to men. Her antagonism towards her stepmother Mrs. Clairmont, her stepsister Claire, and even her half-sister poor Fanny Imlay, and her mix of untoward desires for Godwin, surface in *Frankenstein* amid her indictment of Prometheanism. With these complications in place, I turn to the end of *Frankenstein*. Victor and Robert in the closing frame and the "good" survivors throughout *Frankenstein* reflect the novel's sustained tension between domestic orthodoxy and diurnal realities, between the value and the viability of Mary's ideals.

Frankenstein's continuing power after nearly one hundred and seventy years derives in large part, I believe, from the fact that the psychic intricacies which it traces are enduring features of human beings in our culture. Shakespeare before Mary Shelley and Victorian and modern novelists after her reveal what she experienced in her Promethean contemporaries and inscribed in her masterpiece— that men who destroy their women castrate themselves, that sons who castrate their fathers destroy themselves, that narcissism is a mode of suicide, that thanataphobia also leads to suicide, that true manliness requires a strong component of the feminine, even as macho rejection of the feminine assures effeminacy. Throughout my book I note Mary's ties to writers past and future, because only an

17

appreciation of the general force of her particular insights can do justice to their enduring power.

I also see Mary Shelley in light of one of women's studies' most basic questions today. Is there a special thing called woman's literature which is produced by a special thing called woman's unique sensibility, or do women writers function like their male counterparts in drawing upon common traditions and conventions, and upon experiences that are similar, if not identical? This question, unanswered today and possibly unanswerable, is posed by Mary Shelley with a poignant intensity which makes her as representative of woman confronting her profession as she is of women confronting men. Mary, like all writers, draws upon common traditions (Dante, Milton) and conventions (gothic, sentimental), and upon experiences of androgyny and bifurcation which she insists are ideals for and threats to both sexes. Mary also, however, sees herself peculiarly isolated as a woman. However different Shelley is from, say, Byron and Polidori, the men of Diodati are similar in ways which exclude Mary. She remains as an adult what she was in Godwin's library, the onlooker, critic, judge. Mary further emphasizes her specialness as a woman by insisting that will and weakness, however common to both sexes, operate differently in woman. They do not prevent her from achieving the moral superiority which for orthodoxy is the compensation of her gender.

*

Defining the sections of my book is far easier than thanking those who have contributed to it. Students who helped prepare the manuscript: Heather Blair, Lukass Franklin, Adriane LaPointe, and particularly John Wright. Colleagues who advised upon specific issues: Gregory Colomb, Elizabeth K. Helsinger, Gwin J. Kolb, and Stuart M. Tave. Colleagues and friends who from hectic lives took out the time to read a manuscript ultimately shorter because of the length of their patience: Linda DeCelles, Lorna Gladstone, Suzanne Gossett, Gordon Hirsch, Randolph Woods Ivy, C. A. Kasper, Michael Pownall, Lisa Ruddick, Jeffrey Stern, Ronald R. Thomas, and Joyce Wexler. Colleagues whose repeated ministrations earn them now only the repayment of more words from me: James K. Chandler and David Williams, who without audible sighs heeded a second call upon their skills; Paul J. Emmett, who remains the finest reader of fiction I know; Susan M. Griffin, rigorous scholar and generous friend, whom it has been my privilege to watch fulfill the promise of her student years; Richard Strier, whose insistence upon the needs of readers was ever accompanied by a warm awareness of my own needs; James Rieger, whose assistance began by providing the *Frankenstein* text upon which this project depends and ended by providing for my text a delicate, canny commentary which drew upon a life's devotion to Mary and Percy Shelley.

And finally, two special thanks. To Gordon M. Ray of the John Simon Guggenheim Foundation, for his encouragement at the beginning of this project. And to my wife, Professor Mary Harris Veeder, who assisted at every phase of my work while advancing her own career and retaining her sense of humor.

I

Self

And from singing I changed my mind to crying.
                                        Nelly Dean

1

Androgyny

A great mind must be androgynous.

Coleridge

MARY SHELLEY'S PARTICULAR VERSION OF ANDROGYNY DRAWS UPON five intellectual currents which sweep into the Romantic period: the traditions of the androgyne itself, of Eros and of Agape, of feminism, and of fiction.

> Human nature was originally one and we were whole, and the desire and pursuit of the whole is called love. (*The Symposium* 193B)

Plato here sums up the millennia-old belief of peoples West and East that disintegration characterizes our condition, and that reintegration constitutes our mission. Myths have consistently seen God as the supreme male-female, whose first creations were comparably androgynous. In the *Upanishads*, Atman "caused his self to fall into two pieces, which became a husband and a wife" (O'Flaherty 311); in the Old Testament, "God created man in his own image, in the image of God created he him; male and female created he them" (Gen. 1:27). Ever since the splitting of the androgyne caused, so the myths tell us, mankind's fall into history, we have sought to escape back out of time by reuniting our riven halves. Androgyny is thus a cosmic dream as well as a psychic ideal and a social goal.[1] By striving to achieve in the psyche an ideal balance of the traits traditionally considered masculine and feminine, we can best prepare ourselves for union with an other in marriage and for relations with others in society. We may even achieve the millennium—returning earth to paradise, returning ourselves to the primal oneness, becoming (again) like unto God.

We seek these psychic, social, and cosmic unions, as Plato said, through love. What Plato did not say is what "love" means. In Western culture, two types of love have endured in opposition, generating controversy and attracting acolytes, for twenty centuries: Eros and Agape. In defining them I will draw upon Anders Nygren, Denis de Rougemont, and Martin D'Arcy, not only because *Agape and Eros, Love in the Western World,* and *The Mind and Heart of Love* remain indispensable texts on love, but because their particular formulations, especially D'Arcy's, describe with uncanny accuracy the two types of love that Mary Shelley and Percy Shelley espoused in their lives and dramatized in their art.

Eros goes through two distinct historical stages. At both stages, mankind is seen as cursed with a double nature: the soul caught in the unclean fetters of matter seeks liberation into the divine beyond. In the era of Eros before Plato, in the Orphic and Dionysiac mysteries, liberation is achieved through abandonment and ecstasy, "through a self-surrender, a form of the espousals with the dark goddess. . . . a madness that takes one out of one's self and ends in a complete surrender of all that one is" (D'Arcy 84, 227). Then comes stage two.

> It was an event of immense importance in human history when Plato in his doctrine of Ideas effected a synthesis of Greek rationalism and Oriental mysticism. . . . For both of them [Plato and the mysteries] salvation means the deliverance of the soul from the prison house of the body and the senses, and its restoration to its original heavenly home. . . . In the mystics, the soul's salvation is attained through initiation, purification, and ritual observances, while in Plato it is through philosophy. (Nygren 166, 167)

Though Plato himself was neither hostile to marriage nor enamored of death, both of these aspects of the pre-Platonic Eros find expression in Platonism, and reappear, as Eros does, in neo-Platonism, and Gnosticism, in the troubadors, and in the Tristan story of Wagner. "The dark passion draws the lover away from all that is earthly and living to seek death. . . . it despises the law-abiding and reasonable morality—marriage, for example. . . . the troubadours scoffed at the marriage bond which the Cathars called the *iurata fornicatio*" (D'Arcy 35, 114; de Rougemont 85).

Agape differs from Eros on all counts because Agape grows from the Incarnation. Once God becomes flesh and dwells among us, mankind need not reject the mundane for any dark Dionysiac goddess or bright Platonic form. Rather than seeking to escape from time into the absolute, Agape "made the best of time and of the present" (D'Arcy 84). Agape neither craves death nor contemns marriage.

> Eros rushes to the funeral pyre of all that is finite. . . . but in Christianity this process is inverted and death is swallowed up in victory. . . . the symbol of love is no longer the infinite *passion* of a soul in quest of light, but the *marriage* of Christ and the Church. (D'Arcy 46; de Rougemont 169)

Agape and Eros each lead the lover to a union of masculine and feminine, but, expectably, the two unions differ fundamentally. Agape produces an androgyny based upon equality. Since God is one with humankind through the Incarnation, there can be no opposition between "love of 'neighbor' and the love of God himself. . . . Agape accepts the other" (D'Arcy 39, 47). Marriage is the model: what is true in society is true in the psyche. The feminine, whether as wife or as trait, attains equal status with the masculine, because the lover can become integral only by acknowledging the integrity of the beloved as other.

> Married love wants the good of the beloved, and when it acts on behalf of that good it is creating in its own presence the neighbor. And it is by this roundabout way through the other that the self rises into being a person—beyond its own happiness. Thus as persons a married couple are a mutual creation, and to become persons is the double achievement of "active love." (D'Arcy 47)

Eros, on the other hand, produces a union of masculine and feminine which some scholars have called androgynous but which is based upon inequality, not equality. Whether the inferior element is the masculine or the feminine depends upon whether the Eros is Dionysiac or Platonic, whether the love is self-surrendering or self-projecting. In the Dionysiac Eros, the lover surrenders himself passively to the goddess, who is all-active and all-determining. There can be no equality in such a union, because the lover is contaminated by his unclean world and the beloved is beatified beyond body. Then, "Eros after Plato consisted of a desire to have and to possess. . . . the very fact that Eros is acquisitive love is sufficient to show its ego-centric character" (D'Arcy 97; Nygren 180). In Platonism the masculine becomes dominant, because the intellect can now recognize the good consciously and seek it actively. "The correlation of desire with self-perfection is therefore complete. . . . What was Dionysiac has become Apolline, the feminine and the clinging [has become] the most masculine and self-assertive" (D'Arcy 97, 84). Now the feminine is neither the dominating divinity of the Dionysiac Eros nor the integral other* of the Christian Agape, but a projection of ego-centric masculinity. She becomes either the feminine aspect of himself, or Love itself. In either case, there is no real marriage.

> Eros does not really wish that there should be
> two in love; one of them must cease to be. . . .
> It belongs to the nature of this passion that its
> victim should be in love not with any physical
> love object, but with love itself. . . . he is in
> love with love. (D'Arcy 47, 35, 219)

If the troubador lover abased himself before the eternal feminine in best Dionysiac fashion, the Romantic heir of the ego-centric Eros "like Narcissus gazes into the water to see its [Eros'] own sad love. . . . [Nineteenth-century Eros] had a narcissistic quality of self-love, as when Tristan cares more for his ideal of love than for Isolde when she is with him" (D'Arcy 45, 69).

*

The tradition of the androgyne thus enters the Romantic period associated with two quite different types of love, Eros and Agape, woman as goddess-projection and woman as integral other. Percy Shelley is given to both types of love and both views of women. Mary Shelley is not. She cleaves fiercely to Agape, and to woman as other. Before we can fully understand her inclinations here, we must define two other forces which help shape her as woman and writer. One force is primarily social, the other literary. Both, like androgyny, Eros, and Agape, are concerned with integrating masculine and feminine.

The change in woman's social status between 1750 and 1914 can be seen as a single drive—often balked, and never thoroughly uni-

---

*"Other" as a term applied to woman has several quite distinct meanings. I do not intend the negative connotations: woman as object to be dominated because she is seen as part of the realm of things which exist for the male's use; or woman as incomplete because she is seen as castrate and thus characterized by absence, unlike the phallic male who alone constitutes presence. I use "other" throughout this book to mean integral. Ontologically woman (like man) exists independent of any perception of her; her being is not projected upon her or derived from anyone outside her.

fied—toward a two-part goal. "The men must become more like women, and the women more like angels." That the speaker here is Sarah Josepha Hale seems to pose an immediate problem. How can the editor of *Godey's Ladies' Book*, the arch-apologist for orthodoxy,[2] sum up a feminism which includes radicals like Mary Wollstonecraft, who said derisively that "weak women are compared with angels" (93)? Hale can speak for feminism because orthodox and radical positions cannot be contrasted schematically.

Within orthodoxy's apparently homogeneous and complacent ranks there developed a substantial group of "domestic feminists" dedicated to winning the autonomy necessary for an integral identity.[3] Radicalism in turn continued to be attracted to traditional ideals. For example, the rationalist tradition from Wollstonecraft to Mill agrees with domestic feminism about woman's basic nature and role.

> The rearing of children . . . has justly been insisted on as the peculiar destination of woman. . . . make women rational creatures, and free citizens, and they will quickly become good wives and mothers. (Wollstonecraft 280, 264)

> When a woman marries, it may in general be understood that she makes choice of the management of a household, and the bringing up of a family, as the first call upon her exertions, during as many years of her life as may be required for the purpose. (Mill 179)

Wollstonecraft also celebrates what is the ideal of domestic feminism and the embodiment of conjugal androgyny—complementarity.

> I have then viewed with pleasure a woman nursing her children. . . . I have seen her prepare herself and her children, with only the luxury of cleanliness, to receive her husband, who returning weary home in the evening found smiling babes and a clean hearth. . . . a couple of this description, equally necessary and independent of each other, because each fulfilled the respective duties of their station, possessed all that life could give. (215)[4]

Thus despite certain persistent differences between domestic and radical feminists (particularly over woman's active campaigning for reform), Wollstonecraft can provide for Hale's "angel" sentence a gloss which indicates both the basic continuity of feminism from 1750 to 1914 and the importance of androgyny during those years.

Why must men "become more like women"? Wollstonecraft answers for a century and a half of feminists: "Men are certainly more under the influence of their appetites than women; and their appetites are more depraved by unbridled indulgence and the fastidious contrivances of satiety" (207). What makes a feminist—radical or domestic—is the conviction that "it is vain to expect virtue from women till they are in some degree independent of men" (213). The need for improvement in women which Wollstonecraft's "till" and Hale's "must *become* like angels" attest to is documented by Wollstonecraft extensively. But she and Hale and feminists radical and domestic all agree where the primary responsibility for unangelic sensualism lies. "I will venture to assert, that all the causes of female weakness, as well as depravity . . . branch out of one grand cause—want of chastity in men" (208). The consequence for women is inescapable. "Till men are more chaste women will be immodest" (192). Equally inevitable is woman's two-part goal—to develop the feminine, and proceed to curb the masculine. Developing the feminine, in turn, means both helping men to liberate the feminine component in themselves androgynously and helping women to gain control over their domestic and social existences.

Helping men to achieve an androgynous balance of gender traits in the psyche entailed a redefinition of masculinity itself. Wollstonecraft indicts traditional male roles as, paradoxically, emasculate. Soldiers are trained in "the school of *finesse* and effeminacy [rather] than of fortitude" (219). Rakes are impotent, "dragging from one scene of dissipation to another the nerveless limbs that hang with stupid listlessness" (213). Wollstonecraft's cure for such male dysfunction is "modesty . . . that soberness of mind which teaches a man not to think more highly of himself than he ought to" (185–86). Virtue knows no gender, so that traits traditionally considered feminine are proper for men too. "Chastity, modesty, public spirit, and all the noble train of virtues on which social virtue and happiness are built, should be understood and cultivated by all mankind" (210).

Indicting as emasculate the machismo which warrants male license, and espousing the androgyny which curbs such license, are continuous features of feminism and of fiction from the eighteenth century to the twentieth (and will be essential to my interpretation of *Frankenstein*). Wollstonecraft's particular singling out of Jesus

Christ as ideally "modest" (186) foreshadows the development of the androgyny argument in the century after her death. Victorian Christianity revives the ancient view of Jesus as the model androgyne, the "Logos-Sophia, the union of Word and Wisdom, male and female" (Hoeveler 10). Tennyson, for example, celebrates "the character of our Lord, that union of man and woman, sweetness and strength" (Killham 260). Many mid-century Christians go further and, reacting against the harshness of the patriarchal Jehovah, emphasize the "feminine" Jesus who said "Blessed are the meek, for they shall inherit the earth" (Matt. 5:5). Welter, Douglas, and others document this attraction of Victorian Christians to the "submissive, meek and forgiving" Jesus who had, like woman, suffered at the hands of "man" and who was, again like woman, characterized by "patience and forbearance" (Douglas 126, 127).[5]

> One clergyman, writing in 1854 on "The Woman Question," not content with asserting that the "womanly element predominated" in Christ, likened woman very specifically to the Messiah: "She must open the long disused page of the beatitudes among us, for manly energy rots among its husks, having dismissed reproving meekness and poverty of spirit. Let woman offer them an asylum; let her rise and take the beautiful shape of the redeemer." (Douglas 110)

As this passage indicates, some Christians move beyond Jesus as woman to woman as Jesus. In England

> the Reverend James E. Smith . . . believed in a female Messiah and the "Doctrine of the Woman," that is, that salvation would come from the feminine in contrast to the earlier salvation Christ had brought. Socialist and Owenist journals were constantly expounding the theory of the gradual ascendancy of "woman-power," a civilizing influence which would counteract the growing horrors of industrialism. (Hoeveler 270)

In America, Mother Ann Lee of the Shakers, Jemima Wilkerson, and later Mary Baker Eddy announce themselves as the new Messiah. More important, many Christians who do not go so far as to expect a woman God do look forward to Woman's Era. Thomas Wentworth

Higginson proclaims that "there are thousands to-day who are looking out of their loneliness, their poverty, or their crime, for the NEW AGE, when Women shall be truer to themselves than Men have ever been to Woman; the new age of higher civilization, when moral power shall take the place of brute force, and peace succeed to war" (Farnham 2:425). For such apocalyptic feminism, Eliza W. Farnham provides a Darwinian basis in *Woman and Her Era* (1864).

> Life is exalted in proportion to its Organic and Functional Complexity; Woman's Organism is more Complex and her totality of function larger than those of any other being inhabiting our earth; therefore her position in the scale of Life is the most exalted. . . . the nobler Organic Life of Woman, coming into the scale of Forces above instead of below . . . must replace, in the world of motive and action, (as springing from human relations), force with persuasion; iron will . . . with the gentle rule of love (1:26, 2:445–46).[6]

Also under way by the 1850s is the other aspect of "developing the feminine"—woman's determination to gain control over her life by curbing traditional male prerogatives.[7] The domestic feminist concentrates upon "increasing [her] autonomy within the family" (Scott 131). Paramount here is that "sexual control of the husband by the wife" (Scott 123) which Wollstonecraft dreamed of. Woman increasingly insists upon limiting the number, and determining the interval, of her pregnancies. This insistence combines with economic pressure on husbands (particularly in the last quarter of the century) to produce startling results: the birthrate drops in America by fifty percent and in Britain by twenty-five percent between 1800 and 1900.

Since control of male license is also needed outside the home, feminists more radical than their domestic sisters take up the challenge of applying woman's virtues to man's world. Again Wollstonecraft is a forerunner. She insists that woman's virtue cannot remain cloistered. Women must "render their private virtue a public benefit. . . . the most salutary effects tending to improve mankind might be expected from a REVOLUTION in female manners" (223, 284). How can women qualify to do this? "Women are more chaste than men" (189). Particularly in the years after 1865 when the Abolitionist Movement had given women in America (and to a lesser extent in Britain) exposure, experience, and confidence, feminists are ready to attack what Wollstonecraft had originally targeted: the double standard. Unlike the woman's movement in the 1960's, the movement after 1865 seeks not to win for women the sexual freedom available to men but to "require of men the same standards of purity previously demanded of woman alone" (Pivar 7).

There is continuity, rather than disjunction, between this more radical public feminism and its domestic counterpart, because the public feminism involves, as Freedman says, "the extension, rather than the rejection, of the female sphere" (518). Espousing an ideal very like—and in some cases based upon—androgyny, The Purity Crusade and the movements for prohibition, female ministry, prison reform, and suffrage all attempt to use woman's angelic qualities to reform excesses caused by unlicensed masculinity.[8] This attempt is in fact an exercise in cultural logic. If woman is so superior morally, as the culture endlessly proclaims, why is she not superintending the governance of society? Why, in effect, is androgyny not a political as well as a conjugal and psychic ideal?

*

Mary Shelley, as both her mother's daughter and a domestic feminist, believes that sexual warfare will end only when feminine virtues curb masculine excesses. She is particularly open to this view because she encounters it in the fiction, as well as the politics, of her day.

Fiction's ties to feminism and androgyny have been discussed in terms of individual authors, particularly of the nineteenth century; and *Pamela* has frequently been associated with the new cult of motherhood in the eighteenth century.[9] But I believe that there are more essential and far-reaching connections between fiction, feminism, and androgyny. Like feminism, the novel begins as a serious force around 1750. Like feminism, the novel of Fielding and Richardson espouses the androgynous ideal. Novelists from 1750 to 1914 dramatize repeatedly the two imperatives of feminism: that male propensities to extremism must be tempered by female capacities for moderation, and that woman in the process must be acknowledged as an integral other. To outline this aspect of fiction's evolution briefly, I will begin with Fielding and Richardson.

The great proposal scene in *Tom Jones* sets male grossness off against female excellence, and then insists upon man coming up to woman's standard.

> "The delicacy of your sex [Tom tells Sophia]
> cannot conceive the grossness of ours, nor how
> little one sort of amour has to do with the

heart."—"I will never marry a man," replied
Sophia very gravely, "who shall not learn re-
finement enough to be as incapable as I am myself of making such a distinction." (877)

Tom has in the past been all too capable of making and acting upon
the distinction between lust and love. But that he is capable now of
moderating his passions is indicated when Squire Western suddenly
bursts into the room and cries "with his hunting voice . . . 'To her,
boy, to her, go to her'" (878). Western represents the gross masculinity that Tom is now beyond.

What has transformed Tom is the preceding scene, the androgynous moment with Sophia before the mirror. Responding to
her request for a guarantee of his constancy, of his rejection of that
"distinction" between lust and love which distinguishes gross man
from excellent woman, Tom proclaims:

> "I will show you, my charming an-
> gel" . . . seizing her hand and carrying her to
> the glass. "There, behold it [the guarantee]
> there in that lovely figure, in that face, that
> shape, those eyes, that mind which shines
> through these eyes. . . . You could not doubt it,
> if you could see yourself with any eyes but
> your own." (877)

Tom can see himself with eyes other than his own because he is
blessed with more than one pair of eyes. Sophia in the mirror is the
feminine, better half of himself projected outward as ideal. The
"mind which shines through [her] eyes" is the tempered consciousness by which the feminine is characterized and of which
Tom Jones is capable. Thus, in seeing Sophia's eyes in the mirror,
Tom is seeing himself at his best, and is seeing himself see himself
at his best. The visual component of morality has already been established by Fielding in the dedication: "An example is a kind of
picture, in which virtue becomes, as it were, an object of sight."
Tom's example is Sophia. The ideal of women becoming more like
angels, and men more like women, is thus realized. Sophia is expressly called "angel" (877). And Tom expressly pledges to become
like her. "I will be all obedience to your commands" (877).

In *Pamela*, a transformation similar to Tom's occurs when Mr. B
eschews his role of phallic predator and accepts the role of devoted
husband. Also similar is the method of transformation: morality is

again visual. Mr. B is won over not by hearing Pamela's protestations or by feeling her resistant arms, but by reading her letters. In accepting Pamela's epistolary interpretation of events, Mr. B takes on her moral perspective. The emphatic femininity of this perspective is stressed by the physical location of the letters: they are within Pamela's skirts. As emanations of feminine sexuality, the letters establish more than the hegemony of love over lust. Pen is penis in this marriage.

This does not mean, however, that Richardson and Fielding equate morality with woman. Each author creates a male virgin, because each insists upon purity as the ideal for both genders.[10] Sir Charles Grandison androgynously "combin[es] his mother's virtue with his father's spirit" (Kinkead-Weekes 312). Sir Charles uses her virtue "to transform the characteristics he inherits from his father, redirecting them to moral ends. When the self-centredness of Sir Thomas is removed from his high 'spirit,' it becomes moral courage" (317). Joseph Andrews is Fielding's virgin male, whose rejection of Lady Booby's advances recapitulates the triumph of Joseph over Potiphar's wife in the biblical exemplum of male purity. Virtue in Fielding is genderless because, as Tom Jones demonstrates, the man must *develop* his feminine aspects, not assimilate a woman's. Long before the mirror scene, Tom is "feminine" enough to weep with pity. That he is, in fact, generous and sympathetic to a fault is his real problem. He lacks not feminine traits but proper control over them. What Sophia represents, as her name implies, is wisdom. Extremism in the cause of goodness is no virtue. But, fortunately for humankind in Fielding, goodness and control over it are inherent in us all.

So is otherness. As men must develop their feminine traits, women must develop their masculine, active side. Sophia is more than a projection of Tom Jones; she has a life of her own outside the mirror. The assertiveness required to leave home and travel through England's rural and urban wilds establishes Sophia as a being with her own path to follow. Functioning outside woman's sphere enables her, in turn, to return to it with greater efficacy and be a good wife to her comparably improved lover. An integrity like Sophia's is also achieved by Pamela. She refuses to be assimilated into Mr. B's erotic fantasies and remains independent until he accepts her conditions for sexual union. She is thus more than the new mother: she is the prototype of the domestic feminist who insists upon her autonomy in the orthodox setting of hearth and home.[11] Both Pamela and Sophia enter wedlock as integral others. Their marriages reflect the androgynous balance of gender traits which Richardson and Fielding consider the psychic ideal.

Fiction advocates this ideal for the next century and a half. Jane Austen, for example, believes that each gender needs both head and heart to function adequately as adults, although she, like Mary Shelley, keeps her women decidedly feminine and her men reliably manly. *Pride and Prejudice* presents in Elizabeth and Darcy a complementary pair who learn from one another because each possesses qualities lacked by the other; *Persuasion* shows how much pain this process of education may involve, as Captain Wentworth overvalues the martial virtues and must be taught that Anne has been stronger than he. The particular need to control male excesses is dramatized in the Austen novel published the same year as *Frankenstein*. *Northanger Abbey* features men given to stereotypic extremes. Their intense pride of possession—General Tinley's garden is "unrivaled in the kingdom" and John Thorpe's liquor "is famous good stuff. . . . You would not often meet with anything like it" (178, 64)—is particularly serious because one of the things which these men try to possess is woman. John changes Catherine's plans without consulting her; General Tinley makes up to her fervently when he assumes her an heiress; and his son Captain Tinley seduces Isabella out of boredom. The violence inherent in such possessiveness erupts when John swears savagely at his horses, when General Tinley dismisses Catherine abruptly upon discovering her relative poverty, and when Captain Tinley abandons Isabella.

In contrast to these violent males is the Reverend Henry Tinley. "Henry drove so well," Catherine observes, "so quietly—without making any disturbance, without parading to her, or swearing at [the horses]" (157). Control of the horses reflects balance in the psyche. Henry says wryly but accurately, "I will prove myself a man, no less by the generosity of my soul than the clearness of my head" (112). Besides possessing the "feminine" trait of generosity, Henry is conversant with fabrics, enjoys dancing and novels, and is not ashamed to say so. He thus achieves a balance which allows him to woo Catherine tenderly and yet oppose his father's mistreatment of her manfully. "He steadily refused to accompany his father into Herefordshire . . . and as steadily declared his intention of offering her his hand. The general was furious in his anger, and they parted in dreadful disagreement" (248). Eventually the general is required to give in, ostensibly because his daughter's marriage into great wealth "threw him into a fit of good-humour" (250), but actually because Jane Austen insists that the cleric's true manliness prevail over the general's machismo. She has already, after all, established where true phallic adequacy resides. Salisbury cathedral with its "well-known spire" towers up visible for "twenty miles" (194), while the general's towerless home is "so low . . . that she [Catherine] found herself passing through the great gates . . . without having discerned even an antique chimney" (161).

The most important depiction of the androgynous male between *Sir Charles Grandison* and Jane Austen occurs in a novel by Mary Shelley's father. *Caleb Williams* opens with a protagonist patterned consciously upon Sir Charles.[12] The androgynous Count Falkland is feminine in appearance and manner, "a man of small stature, with an extreme delicacy of form. . . . The graces of his person were enhanced by the elegance of his deportment" (5, 19). Lest there be any question about Falkland's manliness, however, we are told expressly that he is "elegant without effeminacy" (20). His actions prove it. Falkland's wit has "vigour" (19); his presence inspires "awe" (5). Godwin confirms Falkland's androgynous nature by showing masculine and feminine traits balancing in this "delicate, gallant" man (10). Falkland's "compassionate and considerate" side complements his "stateliness and reserve" (6). His most androgynous conduct occurs at the most dire moment in book 1, when fire threatens Emily's life and the village's survival. Falkland saves the day by directing operations "with a voice of grand, yet benevolent, authority" (43).

Godwin's ultimate intention in *Caleb Williams* is not to imitate *Sir Charles Grandison*, however, but to criticize it. Godwin acknowledges the value of the male androgyne, but he questions whether female traits can in fact curb male passions. Falkland suddenly loses control and commits a murder cowardly as well as terrible. He responds to physical humiliation at the hands of the coarse Barnabas Tyrell by stabbing Tyrell in the back. Backstabbing manifests the feminine and the masculine at their worst extremes—as "woman's way" (proceeding by stealth and guile rather than direct confrontation) and as machismo (retaliating violently rather than enduring patiently). Thus the gender traits which had initially been balanced androgynously now undergo polarization. Falkland throughout the rest of the novel oscillates between extremes of passivity and activity, of paralytic lethargy and furious rage. Since Caleb Williams also tends to polarization—periods of near paralysis are followed by outbursts of frenetic energy—we see Godwin questioning the ideal of androgyny in the face of incursions from the unconscious.

In her later novels Mary Shelley, like Jane Austen, idealizes the androgynous man, but, as blood is thicker than water, her greatest novel is more like *Caleb Williams* than like *Northanger Abbey.* *Frankenstein,* as we shall see, goes beyond establishing the value of androgyny, and asks whether that ideal is viable in a world where "romantic" males incline more to Eros than to Agape. Though she does not use the terms Eros and Agape, Mary knows well what they represent. The lover as ego-centric and the beloved as his self-projection she has encountered in Plato before she ever meets Percy Shelley. As for Agape, the secularism of Godwin's later life should not lead us to underestimate his daughter's acquaintance with, and deep commitment to, orthodox Christianity. Mary knows the liturgical calendar well enough to speak of March 25th as "Day of Our Lady, the Virgin Mother of God" (*J* 42, 1815). She espouses throughout her life the love of neighbor which is Agape ("I have ever befriended women when oppressed" [*J* 206, 12 Feb. 1839]), as she espouses both the ideal of wedlock and the hope of heavenly peace. She also knows, of course, the other traditions which I have described. Feminism she encounters through her mother's writings, and through the writing and conversation of her father, husband, and circle. She finds androgyny in Plato, Genesis, and Percy, and in the fiction of Richardson, Fielding, and Godwin.

These influences, plus the impact of a daily existence which I will discuss soon, produce two cardinal beliefs of Mary Shelley. First, that the male Eros in both its Dionysiac and its ego-centric forms is the chief cause of unhappiness in life. Both forms of Eros allow the male to disregard persons as they are, and to reconfigure life as he pleases. Woman as either subsuming goddess or mental projection ceases to be other and becomes object. Death prevails, as husbands exert their wills with impunity and kings indulge their fantasies in war.

Mary Shelley also believes that the male Eros *may* be controllable by the androgyny of Agape. To understand Mary here we must recognize how much of the power traditionally credited to the androgyne does not interest her. She always said she was not philosophical, and nothing proves it better than the mundane quality of her particular version of androgyny. She is not, for example, obsessed with the cosmos. She does not expect androgyny to return earth to paradise or to return her to the primal oneness. Rather than aspiring to become God, she believes that such messianism is a regressive egotism which has allowed men to make themselves into willful children and to make life into hell on earth. Mary neither seeks death with rapturous self-surrender nor flees from it into some perfect dream. She, like Jane Austen, abhors perfectionism. She is determined to wring from the present as much happiness as is possible to severely limited creatures under severely limiting circumstances. By striving toward an androgynous balance of gender traits in the psyche, she hopes to qualify herself best for the marriage which constitutes Agape. The couple is the ultimate androgyne for Mary Shelley, because neither sex alone can effect a perfect balance of traits. What one spouse cannot achieve, the other will provide, so that through complementarity—orthodoxy's testament to difference—the couple attains the balance forever denied to the individual. By keeping her women womanly and men manly, Mary avoids that unsexing of humanity which feminists were forever accused of. Another danger she does not worry much about: that the androgyne will become what Girard calls the "monster of no difference" and what Shakespeare warns against in the Falstaff plays. Gender traits in Falstaff, rather than balancing, blend into a promiscuous formlessness which threatens the vast father-mother with moral amorphousness and requires Henry V to banish him so that order and roles may be reimposed. Another type of amorphousness is the asexual androgyne which Blake envisions when he demands that "sexes must vanish & cease / To be" (*Jerusalem* 92:13–14). Mary cannot imagine life without gender. And so she, unlike her husband, is not tempted toward any version of the sexlessness which allows angels in *Paradise Lost* to interpenetrate completely.

Ultimately, Mary Shelley's version of androgyny reflects the practical viewpoint of a woman pregnant five times in her eight-year relationship with a man who was initially married to another woman and who was perpetually vexed in his amatory and financial and domestic and familial and legal and professional affairs. Agape, androgyny, complementarity—these for Mary Shelley are ideal enough to transform life into something worth living, and are practical enough that they just might work. Let us begin trying to understand Mary's life and art by studying how she experienced actually, joyously, the ideal of male androgyny at its best.

THE ANDROGYNOUS MALES
What does Mary Shelley find attractive in men?

> He [Procter] is not well and that interests me
> also—as I told you [Leigh Hunt] before I have

always a sneaking kindness for these delicately
healthed Poets.—Poor Keats I often think of
him now. . . . I have always a sneaking (for
sneaking, read open) kindness for men of literary and particularly poetic habits who have
delicate health; I cannot help revereing [sic] the
mind, delicately attuned, that shatters the material frame, and whose thoughts are strong
enough to throw down and dilapidate the walls
of sense and dikes of flesh that the unim-
aginative contrive to keep in such good repair. . . . He [Velluti] is a gentle graceful angelic being—too much the reverse of coarse
natures to be relished by them—If he has not
all the boasted energy of that vain creature
man he has what is far better, a strength all his
own, founded on the tenderness & sympathy
he irrisistibly [sic] excites. (*MSL* 1:279, 3 Nov.
1823; 1:280–81, 27 Nov. 1823; 1:345, 23 June
1826)[13]

All this seems consonant with the Shelley legend—Mary as acolyte
of angelic men. But legends rarely tell the whole story. As Percy
never pretended to be an ineffectual angel, Mary's actual standard
for males precludes the effeminacy usually associated with ethere-
ality.[14] The "strong . . . strength" which "excites" her "irrisistibly" in Procter and Velluti is one of several "manly" qualities that
she celebrates in her public and private prose.

His manly features . . . his manly breast . . .
manly guardianship . . . his manly heart . . .
manly sports . . . his manly sun-burnt com-
plexion . . . manly fortitude . . . manly figure . . . not so devoid of manliness as to be de-
stitute of fortitude . . . [tastes] more manly
and dangerous than theirs . . . "Be a man . . .
we shall triumph yet" . . . his manly guidance . . . a manly generous spirit . . . he was
manly enough to feel "that a man's a man for
all that" . . . manly endurance . . . manly habits . . . his manly father . . . a manliness of
thought . . . [features] manly and interesting . . . [brow] manly and expansive . . . the
manly wish to protect the oppresed . . . manly
fortitude . . . manly virtues . . . manly
hearts . . . the manly shout . . . the manly

form . . . so frank & manly a spirit . . . it is
more manly & natural to desire to be in arms
& in danger. (*Perkin Warbeck* 1:30, 136–7,
146, 209; 2:40, 198; 3:337; *Lodore* 1:8, 21, 76,
81, 117, 175; 3:142, 147, 209; *Valperga* 1:69,
71, 79; 3:62; *Falkner* 1:41, 128; *The Last Man*
22, 122, 276, 297; *MSL* 2:156, 6 June 1842;
202, 20 Sept. 1843)

Although Mary Shelley rejects any "coarse . . . vain" extreme of
masculinity, she is unquestionably attracted to a very traditional
erectness in men.

[Perkin was] so blooming, and so frankly
erect. . . . Perkin would have stood erect and
challenged the world to accuse him. . . . The
Mariner, yet more weatherbeaten, thin to emaciation, but stood erect. . . . the Yorkists erect
with renewed hopes. . . . some erect and manly
spirits still remained, pillars of state. (*Perkin
Warbeck* 2:109, 299, 3:43, 1:120; *The Last Man*
41)

The erect male is attractive because, upright in all respects, he can
provide the support traditional in oak-ivy relationships. The intense
need for support which Mary reveals in her fiction (the word "support" and support situations recur obsessively) is made explicit
when she admonishes Robert Dale Owen about even so resolute a
woman as the pioneer feminist Fanny Wright. "Do not imagine that
she is capable always of taking care of herself . . . we [women] have
all in us—& she is too sensitive & feminine not largely to partake in
this inherent part of us—a desire to find a manly spirit whereon [to]
lean" (*MSL* 1:366, 9 Nov. 1827).

What attracts Mary Shelley is thus a complicated blending of
traits traditionally divided between the sexes. The male must be
erectly supportive in a traditional manly way and yet capable of the
"tenderness & sympathy" attributed conventionally to womankind. The conventionality of this attribution is what Mary Shelley, like Fielding and Richardson, insists upon. To temper his potentially "coarse" masculinity the man needs traits associated with,
but not restricted to, women. Lionel in *The Last Man* learns to control his "savage revengeful heart" by submitting to the "sweet benignity" of Adrian (17). "All my boasted pride and strength were
subdued by the honeyed accents of this blue-eyed boy" (18). Lionel
can soon achieve the true masculinity which harmonizes male and

female traits. "My manly virtues did not desert me . . . but all was softened and humanized" (22).

The balancing of traditionally male and female traits is an androgynous ideal which Mary Shelley tests out in every novel from *Frankenstein* to *Falkner*. In *Perkin Warbeck*, DeFaro is a ferocious mariner whose muscles are like "iron" and whose brow "lowered over eyes dark as night" (2:264, 1:196); but "when he smiled, his soft mouth and pearly teeth, softened the harshness of his physiognomy. . . . he looked gentle and kind . . . [protecting his daughter] with feminine gentleness" (1:196, 2:204). Mary's thoroughly adequate males range in age from the boy Alfred in *The Last Man* ("an upright, manly little fellow, with . . . soft eyes" [164]) to the old Hermit in *Valperga* ("the gentlest and most amiable of mortals . . . fearless and independent" [3:95]). But the fullest embodiments of the ideal are young adults. One is Perkin Warbeck, in whom "a sweet regard and amiable grace, / Mixed with manly sternness did appear" (1:186). Another is Adrian, who surpasses the ostensibly hardier males in *The Last Man*. Unlike Ryland, whose macho cry "Every man for himself" (177) reveals unmanly fear, Adrian knows that true virility is fostered by and reflected in "the benevolent and social virtues" (222). Thus Adrian transcends traditional male heroes—warriors and politicians—precisely because his combination of gender traits qualifies him for leadership as machismo alone could not. "'I cannot lead on to battle. . . . But I can be the first to *support* and guard my country . . . I can bring patience, and sympathy.' . . . [his was] a devotion and sacrifice of self at once graceful and heroic" (185, 179, 223; my italics).

Mary Shelley called her life "romantic beyond romance" (*J* 186, 11 Nov. 1822), and nothing proves her point better than the fact that her ideal of androgynous manhood materializes right before her eyes, twice. Once in the person of Lord Byron. Though his reputation for macho escapades makes Mary initially apprehensive, Byron's other, feminine side charms her immediately. "How mild he is! how gentle! so different from what I expected."[15] Feminine traits ("ever gentle, merciful, generous") blend with manly appearance and "powerful mind" (*J* 80, 28 May 1817) to establish Byron as admirably androgynous. "There is strength and richness as well as sweetness" (*MSL* 2:29, 19 Jan. 1830). Especially because his verse features androgynous males (Sardanapalus, Don Juan, and Tiresias), Byron becomes for Mary Shelley a reference point for other men. The English traveler Robert Finch, for example, has "the dear Corsair expression half savage half soft" (*MSL* 1:68, 26 Apr. 1819). Even after intervening years qualify Mary's enthusiasm for Byron, she speaks well of the dead by reaffirming his basic androgyny. "Beauty sat on his countenance and power beamed from his eye" (*J* 194, 15 May 1824).

Byron's combination of feminine and masculine traits allows him to satisfy a two-fold need in Mary Shelley. She can be open with one so tenderly sympathetic, and she can be dependent upon one so capably strong. When Mary as a shy but ambitious apprentice has known Europe's most famous author for only a few weeks, he assures her that "you and I . . . will publish ours [ghost stories] together" (Buxton 14). When Mary as a distraught widow needs help after Shelley's death, "L B is to me as kind as ever . . . in the only instance that I called on him for action he complied with my request in the kindest and fullest manner" (*MSL* 1:208, ? Dec. 1822). How completely Byron can satisfy Mary is established when the ghost story project has flowered into *Frankenstein* and Percy writes to Byron that "it has met with considerable success in England; but she bids me say, 'That she would regard your approbation as a more flattering testimony of its merit'" (*PSL* 2:13, 28 Apr. 1818).

Mary's other androgynous male is of course Percy himself. Casual acquaintances like the Irish *litterateur* Count John Taafe recognize immediately that blend of gender traits, that "unquenchable courage contrasting strangely with his feeble frame and girlish voice" (Buxton 173) which lifelong friends like Hogg know well. "Shelley was full of spirit and courage, frank and fearless; but he was likewise shy, unpresuming, and eminently sensitive" (1:280). What these and such other contemporaries as Trelawny, Medwin, Peacock, Captain Kennedy, Williams, and Rogers say about Shelley[16] is in fact what he says about himself. The great autobiographical moment in the dedication to *The Revolt of Islam*, when the young poet achieves his identity, defines that identity androgynously: "I was meek and bold" (36). The adult version of this poet-self appears in "The Coliseum." "Over [the stranger's face] . . . was spread a timid expression of womanish tenderness and hesitation, which contrasted, yet intermingled strangely, with the abstracted and fearless character that predominated in his form and gestures" (*JS* 6:300).

Shelley knows of androgyny not only through the egg/yolk metaphor of Plato and the Adam/Eve division in Eden, but also through the hermetic androgyne of Paracelsus and the alchemical tradition.[17] That he shares Mary's commitment to the combining of gender traits is indicated throughout his non-autobiographical writings. Her admiration for the "manly" is echoed in his own early use of the word ("his manly limbs," "his manly frame" [*Queen Mab* 3:8, 77]), even as he seconds her distaste for feminine and masculine extremes. He finds in the statues of Antinous an "effeminate sullenness" and attacks priests as "unmanly" (*JS* 6:299; 7:16). The opposite fault, an extreme masculinity, Shelley criticizes in the "monstrous & detestable" statuary of Michelangelo (*PSL* 2:80, 25 Feb. 1819) and in the poetry of Michelangelo's contemporary, Ariosto. "[He] delighted in revenge and cruelty. . . . where is the gentle seriousness, the delicate sensibility, the calm and sustained energy without which true greatness cannot be?" (Medwin 262). They are in Godwin's fiction, which Shelley praises for its androgynous "union of delicacy and power" (*JS* 6:219).

These traits are also to be found in Shelley's own art. Machismo is rejected in *Islam* when Laon refuses to respond violently to the violent men who overwhelm him. "There are no sneers upon his lip which speak / That scorn or hate has made him bold; his cheek / Resolve has not turned pale,—his eyes are mild" (4471–73). This ideal of psychic cohesion—mirrored in Laon's idyllic intercourse with Cythna—is espoused throughout Shelley's literary career. In the early *St. Irvyne*, Wolfstein is a "towering" male with "features beaming with somewhat of softness" who charms Eloise; soon there appears the "towering" Ginotti-Nempere, who androgynously offers the susceptible Eloise "gentle violence" and speaks with such a "fascinating tenderness" that "the softness of his accents" spellbinds her (*JS* 5:144, 174). The good man in Shelley's first major poem, *Queen Mab*, is rightly defined by Dowden as androgynously "resolute yet meek, gentle but of unalterable will" (1:343). By the *Frankenstein* months of 1816–17, Percy is presenting the male ideal in an androgynous Hermit (like Mary's) who, "grand and mild," speaks with "sweet and mighty" eloquence (*Islam* 1401, 1505). Amid "soft looks of pity" he can "dart / A glance as keen as is the lightning's stroke" (1465–66). In the period after *Frankenstein* Shelley achieves his most powerful and celebrated expressions of the androgynous ideal. Prometheus' union with Asia establishes heterosexual love as an emblem of psychological completeness. The comparable union of the lovers in *Epipsychidion* then evokes Shelley's famous image of the hermaphrodite ("Fragment" 57).

As Mary is attracted to androgynous males like Byron because they satisfy basic needs, Percy too finds androgyny efficacious. "Such strength is in meekness" (*Prometheus Unbound* 2.3.94) that the very salvation of the world is possible through androgyny. The androgynous Witch of Atlas with her "gentleness and power" (48) can save humanity from itself because s/he has united the halves of the self in love. First s/he creates an Hermaphrodite who

> . . . seemed to have developed no defect
> Of either sex, yet all the grace of both,—
>   In gentleness and strength its limbs were
> decked,
> . . . .
> And she would write strange dreams upon the
> brain
>   Of those who were less beautiful . . .
> . . . .
> . . . all his evil gain
>   The miser in such dreams would rise and
> shake
> Into a beggar's lap . . .
> . . . .
> And timid lovers who had been so coy
>   They hardly knew whether they loved or
> not,
> Would rise out of their rest, and take sweet
> joy.
>   (330–32, 617–18, 621–23, 649–51)[18]

For ordinary mortals to apply androgyny to social life requires the openness to feminine influence which Mary required of her males. "I must," Percy says, "become in Marys [sic] hands what Harriet was in mine" (*PSL* 1:414, 28 Oct. 1814). For males in general, Shelley defines several sources of feminine influence. One is poetry, which has traditionally "softened" men (*JS* 7:116). Another is love: "[it is] superfluous to explain how the gentleness and the elevation of mind connected with these sacred emotions can render men more amiable, and generous and wise" (*JS* 7:128). The final source is woman herself. Cythna, whose androgynous "spirit strong and mild" (951) distinguishes her from "the strong and the severe" tyrants in *Islam*, educates Laon about the wrongs of women. "This misery was but coldly felt [by Laon], till she . . . endued / My purpose with a wider sympathy" (982–84). The man's psyche, educated by its feminine component, can expand perceptually and emotionally until he reaches that paramount feminine state, the sympathetic.

Laon also becomes an effective spokesman for that feminism which allows Shelley to apply the androgynous ideal to contemporary society. Woman is necessarily man's equal once the feminine aspects of the psyche equal the masculine in importance.

> Never will peace and human nature meet
> Till free and equal men and women greet
> Domestic peace.
>
> *(Islam* 994–96)

To appreciate the cohesiveness of Shelley's feminism we must recognize that equality, absolute equality, was not what most early
feminists argued for. J. S. Mill's popularity today obscures the fact
that what we admire in him—his insistence upon gender equality—
was by no means the majority position in 1868, even among those
who revered *The Subjection of Women.* Most feminists took the
other line and, like Mary Shelley, viewed the sexes in terms of complementarity, of the *differences* between men and women. Although this view insists that woman receive equal respect, it can
lead in practice to condescension and inequality. Woman is credited
with the quiescent virtues least useful to, and the compensatory
traits most convenient for, males in an acquisitive, competitive society. Shelley's rejection of complementarity emphasizes "the error
which confounded diversity with inequality of the powers of the
two sexes" *(JS* 7:129). Only by insisting that a woman, like Cythna,
can possess all the necessary masculine traits (she enters battle rid-
ing a horse and wielding a sword) can Shelley assure women true
respect and fair treatment. Once he has based the timeless world of
the psyche upon the equal value of male and female traits, he can
insist with inexorable consistency that the diurnal world of eco-
nomics and politics come into line.

A practical, efficacious concern for the welfare of his neighbor is
what warrants enrolling Shelley (and to a lesser extent Byron) on the
side of Agape. Shelley of course spent considerable energy inveigh-
ing against institutional Christianity. But he also distinguished
Christ from Christianity, linking Him repeatedly with the pagan
exemplar, Socrates. More important, Shelley put Agape into practice
again and again. The "feminine" traits of generosity and sympathy
which characterize his most androgynous moments enable Shelley
to perform beautiful acts of *caritas.*

> Marlow was inhabited . . . by a very poor popu-
> lation. The women are lacemakers, and lose
> their health by sedentary labour, for which
> they were very ill paid. The Poor-laws ground
> to the dust not only the paupers, but those who
> had risen just above that state, and were
> obliged to pay poor-rates. The changes pro-
> duced by peace following a long war, and a bad

harvest, brought with them the most heart-
rending evils to the poor. Shelley afforded what
alleviation he could [providing money and
blankets]. In the winter . . . he had a severe attack of ophthalamia, caught while visiting the
poor cottages. I [Mary] mention these things—
for this minute and active sympathy with his
fellow-creatures gives a thousandfold interest
to his speculation, and stamps with reality his
pleadings for the human race. (*CP* 157)

Despite propensities to Erotic narcissism which I will discuss in
chapter 2, Shelley is capable of seeing love as Agape, as other-di-
rected. "Love . . . is that powerful attraction towards all that we
conceive, or fear, or hope beyond ourselves" (*JS* 6:201). In this frame
of mind he can see woman as more than a self-projection, as "equal,
yet unlike" (*Epipsychidion* 358). Shelley can, moreover, recognize
and condemn his own propensity for Erotic solipsism.

What a strange being I am, how inconsistent,
in spite of all my bo[a]sted hatred of self—this
moment thinking I could so far overcome
Natures [sic] law as to exist in complete seclusion, the next shrinking from a moment of solitude . . . seeking any thing rather than a continued communion with *self*. (*PSL* 1:77–78, 8
May 1811)

Shelley at one point even contrasts the loves which I have been calling Eros and Agape. "A love which is self-centered self devoted [sic]
self-interested" cannot match the love "which seeks the good of all;
the good of it's [sic] object first, not because that object is a minister
to *it's* pleasures" (*PSL* 1:173, 11 Nov. 1811 ?).

This love for the other as other expresses itself practically in
Shelley's lifelong generosity. He subscribes handsomely to the
Treath Mainr embankment fund which would reclaim from the sea
farmland for the Welsh poor. Among numerous loans to friends,
none does Shelley more credit than the money he continues to furnish Godwin when the older man is savagely berating him for living
out of wedlock with Mary. And we must not forget that it is on a
journey to assist the beleaguered Hunt family that Shelley dies at
Lerici.

*

That Mary Shelley should find so androgynous a male irresistible
is not surprising. She sees in Percy's letters "tenderness, and gener-

osity, combined with manly views," and she sees in him personally "the most impassioned, and yet the purest and softest heart that ever yearned for sympathy" (*JS* 5:xiv, viii). Over and over the now familiar terms recur. On the feminine side, "gentle sympathies. . . . gentle and cordial goodness . . . warm affection and helpful sympathy" (*JS* 5:vi; *CP* ix); on the masculine, "lofty aspirations. . . . eagerness and ardour. . . . active endeavours" (*JS* 5:vii; *CP* ix, 836). In her most eloquent passage celebrating the androgyne as ideal male, Mary finds in Percy

> that modesty, that forebearance, and mingled meekness and resolution that, in my mind, form the perfection of man. "Gentle, brave, and generous," he describes the Poet in Alastor: such he was himself, beyond any man I have ever known. (*JS* 5:xv)

2

The Self Divided

The recipe for love is this,
That first we must divide you.

Goethe

The world becomes at last only a realized will—
the double of the man.

Emerson

I Am He Who Is
Thou art she who is not.
The Eternal Father to St. Catherine of Siena

And the soul afraid of dying
That never learns to live.

"The Rose"

ANDROGYNY PROVES MORE OFTEN TO BE THE IDEAL THAN THE REALITY
for Mary Shelley, because Percy Shelley (and Byron and Godwin)
prove more devoted to Eros than to Agape. Mary's men, despite truly
loving and life-fostering moments, are prone to the opposite—to a
self-indulgence which uses woman rather than bonds with her, and
which seeks death not life. Mary responds to Erotic indulgence with
actions taken and forgone, with words and silences, in private and
public prose. *Frankenstein*, her paramount response, is so intricate
that I have sought in the Shelleys' lives and art for help in understanding the causes and effects of Eros. Contextual work now will
allow me in succeeding chapters to face more adequately the various
controversies over *Frankenstein*. Is Victor heroic or homicidal? Is
Elizabeth at best hopelessly perfect and at worst unattractively helpless? I will begin by defining the psychic bifurcation which is Eros'
alternative to Agape's androgynous balance; I will then offer a tenta-
tive explanation of this bifurcation, and will study Mary's response
to it in her life and later fiction.

47

BIFURCATION
Percy Shelley accepts the body/soul dichotomy basic to Eros.

> 'twas a sight
> Of wonder to behold the body and soul [of
> Ianthe]
> The self-same lineaments, the same
> Marks of identity were there:
> Yet, oh, how different! One [the soul] aspires
> to Heaven,
> . . . .
> The other, for a time the unwilling sport
> Of circumstance and passion, struggles on;
> . . . .
> Then, like a useless and worn-out machine,
>   Rots, perishes, and passes.
>   (*Queen Mab* 1:144–48, 152–53, 155–56)[1]

Despite moments of sensual exultation, Shelley frequently responds
to body like the Platonists, neo-Platonists, and Gnostics, who "consider . . . the soul imprisoned in the body" (D'Arcy 60). In his early
years, Shelley laments for Ahasuerus "imprisoned for ever in this
clay-formed dungeon" (Hogg 1:195); in his last year, Shelley laments for Ariel "Imprisoned . . . In a body like a grave" ("With a
Guitar, To Jane" 38–39). Eros' consequent disgust with "the un-
cleanliness of this world" is echoed both in Shelley's late nausea at
"this dunghill of a world" (*PSL* 2:211, 7 July 1820) and in his early
question, "Are we but bubbles which arise from the filth of a stagnant pool, merely to again be reabsorbed into the mass of its corruption?" (*PSL* 1:201, 10 Dec. 1811). Nausea extends inevitably to
human beings. As Eros "despised man and recked so little of his
personal worth that it would willingly dissolve him in the divine
essence" (D'Arcy 39), Shelley, despite philanthropic endeavors, reduces his neighbor repeatedly to an animality which he can readily
dispense with.

> All the sounds of Nature harmonize; they
> soothe: it is only the human animal that is dis-
> cordant with Nature and disturbs me. . . . The
> oyster that is washed and driven at the mercy
> of the tides appears to me an animal of almost
> equal elevation [to an Irish mob] in the scale of
> intellectual being. . . . [The Gisbornes] are the
> most filthy and odious animals with which I
> have ever come in contact. . . . my father was

> so civil to all of them [guests]—to animals I re-
> garded with unmitigated disgust. . . . [a ball-
> room is] the magnet of apes asses geese. (Trel-
> awny 1:104; *PSL* 1:267, 8 Mar. 1812; 2:243, 29
> Oct. 1820; Hogg 1:207; *PSL* 1:192, 24 Nov.
> 1811)

From this view of neighbor to an outright rejection of marriage is a short step, for Shelley as for Eros. Though Shelley can at his best feminist moments criticize marriage for its enslavement of woman, his invectives against the institution are often virulent enough to indicate less humane sentiments as well. "I could not endure the bare idea of marriage even if I had no arguments in favor of my dislike—but I think I have" (*PSL* 1:80, 9 May 1811). Arguments here rationalize a distaste for marriage so elemental that Shelley before eloping with Harriet feels "ineffable sickening disgust" when he—in the Westbrooks' very house—contemplates the "hateful detestable . . . fetter" (*PSL* 1:80, 8 May 1811). The violence evident here translates into action on the day of the elopement with Harriet when Shelley, flinging across the street empty oyster shells from breakfast, "repeat[s] over and over to Charles [Grove] with an ironic sigh: 'Grove, this is a *Shelley* business'" (Holmes 79). Irony recurs when Percy describes sarcastically his second wedding, with Mary. "The ceremony, so magical in its effects, was undergone this morning" (*PSL* 1:525, 30 Dec. 1816).

Shelley is so intensely Erotic that he displays both Dionysiac and Platonic propensities. Traits which Nygren described in historical progression—"Dionysiac has become Apolline, the feminine and clinging [has become] the masculine and assertive"—can coexist psychologically, as D'Arcy astutely recognizes. "[Eros'] two extremes of egotism and self-abandonment are closer bedfellows than one might think" (224). They are, however, less amically paired than "bedfellows" might suggest. The "masculine" and "feminine" traits which balance ideally in the androgyny of Agape—bedfellows indeed—tend under Eros to bifurcate into ego-centric willfulness and self-abandoning weakness. First one extreme, then the other holds the Erotic man in thrall. At one moment he manifests a Dionysiac "clinging" dependency; at another moment, an Apolline "assertive" dominance. At the passive extreme he becomes effeminate, displaying lethargy, paralysis, ineffectuality, indifference; at the hyperactive extreme he displays machismo, predation, cruelty. I will examine each extreme in Shelley, who described himself during the *Frankenstein* months with words applicable to Caleb Williams,

Count Falkland, and Victor Frankenstein as well. "My feelings at intervals are of a deadly & torpid kind, or awakened to a state of such unnatural & keen excitement" (*PSL* 1:572, 7 Dec. 1817).

D'Arcy defines the ego-centric Eros as "a Will-to-have" (71). Nygren agrees. "It should be especially noted that even where Eros seems to be a desire to give it is still in the last resort a 'Will-to-possess'" (176). Although Percy Shelley at times offers effective critiques of willfulness and exemplary alternatives to it,[2] he also espouses will with a passion evident to his contemporaries. "Shelley believed," says Medwin, "that mankind had only to will, and that there should be no evil, and [there] would be none" (213); "Shelley believed," says Mary Godwin, "that mankind had only to will that there should be no evil, and there would be none. . . . in youth he had read of 'Illuminati and Eleutherarchs,' and believed he possessed the power of operating an immediate change in the minds of men and in the state of society" (*CP* 271, 551). In youth, Shelley had also read words of Godwin which he quoted throughout his life: "There is nothing which the human mind can conceive that it may not execute" (*CP* 335).

The Erotic will which Mary Shelley presents in her protagonists from Frankenstein to Falkner appears in Percy Shelley's art (his marital life I will take up later) in three stages. Initially Shelley tends to equate will and efficacy. "Whatever his [Wolfstein's in *St. Irvyne*] will might determine, his boldness would fearlessly execute" (*JS* 5:124). This belief in the congruence of will and power informs Shelley's early political documents, *An Address to the Irish People* and *Proposals for an Association*, and continues more or less intact in 1813 in *Queen Mab*: "When the power of imparting joy / Is equal to the will, the human soul / Requires no other heaven" (3:11–13). I say *more or less* because the word "when" here implies that power and will are not necessarily congruent. Frustrated in his first attempts to apply his will to social life—his trip to Dublin to foster Catholic emancipation and his support for the Treath Mainr embankment in Wales—Shelley feels firsthand the intransigence of reality. The effect upon his poetry is suggested in *Queen Mab*'s "when" and is evident in his work up through the *Frankenstein* months.

Shelley continues to insist upon the power of active will that "renovates the world; a will omnipotent" (*Islam* 1035), but now he faces the inevitable question. Why has this will not perfected society?

> "Ye princes of the Earth, ye sit aghast
> Amid the ruin which yourselves have made,
> ....
> Who, if ye dared, might not aspire to less
> Than ye conceive of power."
>> *(Islam* 4351–52, 4362–63)

Shelley thus rejects Maddalo's dark belief that "men change not" and are "baffled" (*Julian and Maddalo* 115, 130). Julian can deny that "man be / The passive thing you say" (160–61) and can still explain human failure. We let it happen. We, like *Islam*'s princes, allow a gap between will and power, timidly fearing to effect our desires.

> ". . . it is our will
> That thus enchains us to permitted ill—
> We might be otherwise—we might be all
> We dream of happy, high, majestical.
> Where is the love, beauty, and truth we seek
> But in our mind? and if we were not weak
> Should we be less in deed than in desire?"
>> *(Julian and Maddalo* 170–76)

Over and over, Shelley criticizes citizens "bent / Before one power, to which supreme control / Over their will by their own weakness lent" (*Islam* 731–33; see also *A Proposal for Putting Reform to the Vote, JS* 6:63–64; *The Mask of Anarchy* 184–87; *Rosalind and Helen* 608–9, 1644–45; and "Ode to Liberty" 244–45.)

In his last years Shelley continues to believe in the power of active will and in man's responsibility for misery, but he is forced by disasters personal and political to relocate will in a larger, more reliable force.

> the one Spirit's plastic stress
> Sweeps through the dull, dense world,
> compelling there
> All new successions to the forms they wear.
>> *(Adonais* 381–83)

A decidedly (if unconsciously) Hegelian confidence in victorious will grows from Shelley's belief in the course of history. "In the great morning of the world, / The Spirit of God with might unfurled / The flag of Freedom over Chaos. . . . Freedom, so / To what of Greece remaineth now / Returns" (*Hellas* 46–48, 82–84). Belief in the ultimate victory of righteousness does not, of course, make

51

Shelley's late verse sanguine about present-day situations. As Laon and Cythna cannot sustain their newly founded paradise and are destroyed by tyranny, so *Hellas* ends before final victory is achieved, and *The Triumph of Life* breaks off with folly rampant. Nonetheless, ultimate victory is assured. At times Shelley transfers the triumph from the earthly to the sublime realm, as in the deifications of Laon and Cythna and of Prometheus and Asia. At other times he persists in his belief that will can be efficacious here on earth. "I feel persuaded that you are capable of the greatest things, so you but will." Shelley is doing more here than patronizing Keats (*PSL* 2:221, 27 July 1820); he is violating his own dictum that poetry is precisely *not* "a power to be exerted according to the determination of the will" (*JS* 7:135).

That Shelley was prey not only to ego-centric willfulness but also to the opposite extreme—Dionysiac weakness—was equally clear to his contemporaries.

> He was a climber, a creeper, an elegant, beautiful, odoriferous parasitical plant; he could not support himself; he must be tied up fast to something of a firmer texture, harder and more rigid than his own, pliant, yielding structure . . . he always required a prop. (Hogg 2:46)

Hogg here is making into a general condition what was a momentary, if recurrent, inclination in Shelley, but this exaggeration does not warrant our denying the inclination altogether.

> It's amusing [says Timothy Webb] to note Hogg's suggestion that Shelley was in need of support, if one has read the letters which passed between Shelley and Hogg, or if one remembers how in the most tangible of all senses, Shelley supported so many of his friends. . . . Hogg's need to patronize his gifted friend, to loosen Shelley's hold on reality, to exaggerate his weakness, can be traced not only to his own egotism and his crude standard of common sense but it [sic] also connects with Hogg's latent homosexuality. (8)

That there are psychological reasons for a biographer to stress one aspect of his subject does not deny the existence of that aspect. Shelley, given to Agape *and* to Eros, supported his "neighbors" generously *and* felt frequent need of support himself, as manifold sources besides Hogg attest.

In his writing, Shelley cannot espouse weakness as directly as he does will, but weaknesses of both body and conduct appear with authorial approbation (or at least without clear-cut criticism) throughout his work. Bodily weakness, for example, characterizes protagonists whom many readers have recognized as Shelley self-portraits. Compare Shelley "emaciated, and somewhat bent" (Medwin 233) with his "emaciated" Verezzi in *Zastrozzi* (*JS* 5:10) and his "bent" warrior in "Ghasta" (26). These figures, plus the increasingly debilitated Poet in *Alastor*, the lover in *Epipsychidion* "stumbling in my weakness" (251), and the "frail Form" with "feeble steps" of *Adonais* (271, 277), all resemble the debilitated Frankenstein in ways I will discuss in chapter 3. The question now is what physical weakness means to Shelley.

The assertion that Verezzi's "form . . . though emaciated, displayed the elementary outlines of exquisite grace" (*JS* 5:299) shows obvious authorial admiration. How does Shelley react when the narrative sets the weak body in motion, when his look-alike's "enfeebled form" proves "insufficient to support the conflict" (*JS* 5:6)? Verezzi's collapse into coma and suicide is accompanied not by moral evaluation, but by conventional moralizing. Chesser is correct that what masks as Verezzi's "remorse for yielding to the siren" is in fact "paralysis" (28). Nothing in *Zastrozzi* indicates Shelley's willingness to pierce through that mask and explore why such paralysis occurs, why males find it impossible to maintain "support." Instead, Shelley describes Verezzi's suicide in terms of the ecstatic escape characteristic of the Dionysiac Eros. "He raised the dagger which he still retained, and, with a little smile of exultation, plunged it into his bosom" (*JS* 5:88).

Shelley's apparent ambivalence toward his characters' passivity cannot be dismissed as a flaw typical of apprentice work. It persists throughout his career, as the critical controversies over *Alastor* (1815) and *The Witch of Atlas* (1820) show. Is the Poet in *Alastor* an ineffectual failure who never achieves the object of his quest because he is a self-deceived solipsist; or is he a valuable visionary who is destroyed because the soul demands what the mundane world cannot provide? Likewise, is the hermaphrodite in *The Witch of Atlas* a wondrous projection of the artistic imagination, or a parody of it, lying ineffectually passive throughout most of the poem? In the long-standing controversies over these poems, each camp possesses solid textual evidence; we are confronted here not with ambiguity rich in meaning, but with Shelley's recurrent refusal to deal decisively with a passivity which he knows is inadequate but sympathizes with deeply.

*

Erotic bifurcation is of serious concern to Mary Shelley because it affects both Percy's view of the beloved and his ability to sustain androgyny. When Shelley is under the sway of the ego-centric Eros, he views the beloved as a self-projection. The word "narcissistic" echoes throughout Nygren's description of the Platonic Eros, and narcissistic is what Shelley has often seemed to critical readers and biographers. Compare D'Arcy's statement that in the ego-centric Eros "the correlation of desire and self-perfection is complete" (97) and Shelley's statement that "so intimately are our [his and Mary's] natures now united, that I feel whilst I describe her excellencies as if I were an egoist expatiating upon his own perfections" (*PSL* 1:402, 4 Oct. 1814). Shelley's wry tone can modulate, but not fully obliterate, the egotism here. A sentence which begins with the couple sharing agency, and thus primacy, as subject ("our" natures) proceeds to separate the couple into Percy as agent-subject ("I . . . I . . . I") and Mary as object of his perception. By the end of the sentence Mary ceases to exist altogether. She is absorbed entirely in Percy, as the perceived object becomes "her excellencies" which become "his own perfection" which he expatiates upon. Shelley of course recognizes at times that the true lover is not "an egoist expatiating upon his own perfections." He says in 1814, "I never before [Mary] felt the integrity of my nature, its various dependencies, & learned to consider myself as an whole accurately united rather than an assemblage of inconsistent & discordant portions" (PSL 1:403, 4 Oct.). Even here, however, the unity that Percy perceives is not *with* Mary. She helps him recognize the essential cohesion of himself.

Critics of Shelley's narcissism have found ready evidence in both his poetry—

> I never thought before my death to see
> Youth's vision thus made perfect . . .
> . . . .
> At length, into the obscure Forest came
> The Vision I had sought through grief and
> shame.
> . . . .
> I knew it was the Vision veiled from me
> So many years—that it was Emily.
> (*Epipsychidion* 42–43, 321–22, 343–44)

How many a one, though none be near to love,
Loves then the shade of his own soul, half
seen
In any mirror.

(*Prince Athanase* 251–53)

and his prose—

> There is something within us which, from
> the instant that we live, more and more thirsts
> after its likeness. . . . We dimly see within our
> intellectual nature a miniature as it were of our
> entire self, yet deprived of all that we condemn
> or despise, the ideal prototype. . . . The discov-
> ery of its antitype;[3] the meeting with an under-
> standing capable of clearly estimating our
> own . . . this is the invisible and unattainable
> point to which Love tends. (*JS* 6:201–2)

That Shelley also has moments of self-*less* love is incontestable, as I
have shown. But critics who attempt to refute the charge of narcissism by arguing that Shelley's women consistently achieve an
equality consonant with his feminism and with Agape prove only
how problematic such an argument is. Brown, for example, calls
Shelley's most emancipated heroine, Cythna in *Islam*, "fully the
equal of the male [Laon]" (181). Holmes agrees (401). But is she? "As
mine own shadow was this child to me, / A second self" (874–75).
Cythna exists less as an autonomous being than as a reflection of
Laon. "Visions [she has] that were mine. . . . [I] in hers mine own
mind seeing" (927, 948). Although Cythna does enlighten Laon
about woman's sufferings, the educating process is not fully reciprocal. Predominantly he is the teacher and she the pupil. "This
beloved child thus felt the sway / Of my conceptions" (937–38).
(Cythna is Laon's "little" sister, not his twin, in the original *Laon
and Cythna*.) So when Cythna in *Islam* does go forth "bearing the
lamp / Aloft which thou [Laon] hast kindled in my heart" (1055–
56), she acts chiefly as his instrument.

> "Methinks, it is a power which thou
> bestowest,
>   Through which I seek, by most resembling
> thee,
>   So to become most good and great and free."

(1020–22)

Though momentarily successful in her holy war against tyranny, Cythna as warrior remains a projection of Laon. She christens her newly metamorphosed self *Laone!* Laon, needless to say, never renames himself Cythno.

Ultimately, woman does not exist for the narcissistic Shelley. What Nygren says of the ego-centric lover, "he is in love with love" (219), Shelley says about himself. "I love love" ("Song" 43). The repeated escapes from this unclean world in Shelley's love poetry constitute, in fact, an escape from the beloved herself.

Woman might seem to fare better when Shelley oscillates from the ego-centric to the Dionysiac Eros, for then he surrenders himself to the all-ravishing power of the beloved as goddess. The swoonings away in his poetry—"I am dissolved in these consuming ecstasies. . . . [Cosimo] faints, dissolved into a sea of love" ("To Constantia, Singing" 31; "Fiordispina" 25)—indicate Shelley's propensity for self-abandonment. He further indicates this by his readiness to adopt the role of the courtly lover, despite Brown's argument to the contrary:

> Steering clear of . . . courtly flattery, Shelley committed himself from the outset to the goal of full sexual equality. Hogg recalls a dinner party attended by the two friends during the Oxford period at which Shelley spoke "with great animation" in defense of women's character and abilities in spite of the gentlemanly condescension and sneers of his dinner companions. (177)

Granted that Shelley does in moments of sincere feminism insist upon woman's equality, we encounter something quite different when we read Hogg's actual description of the dinner party.

> After dinner there was some port wine, and much conversation; it rolled chiefly on the superiority of women. Bysshe spoke with great animation of their purity, disinterestedness, generosity, kindness, and the like. (1:302–3)

Rather than establishing "full sexual equality" here, Shelley is intoning the litany of traits which have traditionally established woman's "superiority." He can thus in best courtly fashion abase himself before the beloved, "being now, by all the laws of knighthood, captive to a ladys [sic] request," and can attest to "this chivalric submission of mine to the great general laws of antique

courtesy, against which I never rebel, and which is my religion"
(*PSL* 2:335, 15 Aug. 1821).

Such homage may seem to indicate the beloved's puissance, but
feminists from Wollstonecraft on have argued that woman-the-god-
dess is actually as much a creation of the male as woman-the-projec-
tion. In both cases an individual woman is reconfigured to constitute the perfection which the male cannot find or effect in reality.
In neither case is the beloved the equal of the lover. This is particularly serious for Mary Shelley, because gender equality is essential
not only to her role as Percy's beloved but also to her ideal of androgyny. In Eros either the male or the female is subordinate, so that
husband and wife cannot both achieve the integral otherness essential to the couple as androgyne, and masculine and feminine elements in the psyche cannot achieve the equality essential to androgynous balance. Percy's alternative to Mary's ideal of traditional
androgyny is a form of psychological hermaphrodism which I will
relate to Frankenstein's monster in chapter 4. Now I must take up
the question inevitable at this point in my characterization of Percy
Shelley. Why does a man so capable of androgynous union succumb
so repeatedly to bifurcation? Why does Eros war with Agape in
Shelley, and in Victor Frankenstein?

I am particularly chary of offering a simple answer because the
mystery inherent in any human psyche is respected, rather than explained away, by Mary Shelley. *Frankenstein* provides only the materials from which readers may construct explanations. And each
explanation, needless to say, will be personal and partial. My own
explanation will remain incomplete until the end of chapter 7, and
even then it will reflect Mary's continued sense of bafflement. Pro-
visionally, let me say that common sense, supported by recent psy-
choanalytical work, allows some generalizations about Erotic conduct. Willfulness is a compensation for a sense of weakness, so that
feelings of vulnerability lead the male to act invulnerable, and fears
of effeminacy prompt him to attack the feminine. These generalizations, however, do not explain *why* the Erotic male feels vulnerable.

Nor does a cultural line of argument—that men choose bifurcation over androgyny because western civilization makes them uneasy about conduct which may be construed as effeminate and encourages them in both of Eros' loves, the macho and the courtly.
This explanation does not account for the fact that our culture has
celebrated androgyny for centuries, and that world culture has given
it an honored place in myths. Particularly during the Romantic period, the tempering of masculine conduct by the feminine was highly

esteemed. A cultural explanation is further limited by its tendency to conclude that the Romantic man is *essentially* Erotic and that androgyny is only an aberration from, or cover for, his *real* propensities. (This is analogous to the old-school Freudian tendency to valorize one act at the expense of others: x and y exist only as screens for z.) For Shelley and the Romantics, androgynous moments are every bit as real and sincere as Erotic ones. When Mary Shelley says of Victor Frankenstein that "such a man has a double existence" (23), she means it. Conscious and unconscious, Agape and Eros, androgyny and bifurcation: Romantic men are difficult to understand precisely because neither of their existences is simply a screen for the other. If it were, Mary Shelley would have suffered less. She invested so much in Shelley and Byron because they warranted it. Men essentially coarse she knew in legion and dispensed with instantly.

Why does the Erotic male feel so vulnerable? He is, I believe, obsessed with death. (Even here an unanswerable question arises immediately: is an obsession with death what makes Shelley behave Erotically, or does he begin with Erotic propensities which seek fulfillment in death?) Androgyny and Agape involve the acceptance of mortality. They direct human efforts toward making as much as possible of a communal life defined ultimately by the common fact of death. Romantic men capable of androgyny cannot sustain an acceptance of mortality. Shelley is obsessed with man's "clay-formed dungeon" not only because the body is a dungeon, but because *his* body is clay. He knows that he will die literally as well as swoon away figuratively. When he asks, "Are we but bubbles which arise from the filth of a stagnant pool, merely to again be reabsorbed into the mass of its corruption?" (*PSL* 1:201, 10 Dec. 1811), he is afraid that the answer to his ostensibly rhetorical question is a very real "Yes, we are 'corruption' and will rot away." The consequence of the refusal to accept mortality is that men splendidly full of life prove incapable of living. Dinnerstein calls this *"playing out our death-denying impulse through life-denying enterprise"* (227). So extreme is the Erotic male's sense of vulnerability that he loses psychic balance. His masculine side rages into frantic activity: "I will not die." His feminine collapses into paralyzed ineffectuality: "I cannot live."

The pull of his feminine extreme toward death makes the Erotic male all the more determined to sustain individuation in the face of engulfment by woman. The beloved threatens to subsume the lover either by so enthralling him that he loses his will to function outside her, or by implicating him in the reproductive cycle that leads inevitably to death. Paradoxically, woman's power to enthrall, and her implication in the womb-tomb cycle, prompt the threatened male to attempt to possess her absolutely. Eros' desire "to possess . . . permanently" is, Nygren sees, a direct response to the threat of death. "Love is therefore always the desire for immortality" (180). Encouraged by the culture both to see woman as death and to react possessively to the threat, the Erotic lover may turn the beloved into a self-projection, or he may deify her as love itself. Either way, she has been reduced to a male construct, and thus to the male. The Erotic man escapes woman by making love to himself.

Narcissism is thus the ultimate defense against mortality. But ironically "the love of love itself has concealed a far more awful passion . . . the desire for death" (de Rougemont 46). Narcissism is fatal not only because it removes the lover from the community, which alone fosters life, but also because it is self-destructive. Confronted with the arduous (and from the Erotic viewpoint doomed) attempt to sustain individuation, the Erotic lover forgoes the extreme male response—resist!—and gives in to the extreme female response—succumb! "As morning dew, that in the sunbeam dies, / I am dissolved" ("To Constantia, Singing" 30–31). The Shelley who fears engulfment also longs to be "dissolved." The paradox defined by Otto Rank—that thanataphobia leads ultimately to suicide—is confirmed by D'Arcy: "The goal of Eros is death" (54).

BIFURCATION AND MARY SHELLEY'S LIFE

Frankenstein is produced not by the bifurcation of Erotic males, but by Mary Shelley's response to that bifurcation. Her response of 1816–17 will, I hope, gain in clarity by being seen in the context of her marital life and her private prose. I will begin with male will and weakness as they afflict Mary's marriage.

What she had to contend with is indicated by Trelawny, whose pride in being mulish ("a strong taint of the mule in my blood" [2:8]) gives special force to his admission that "those who knew us [himself and Percy] decided that Shelley's will was the most inflexible." How Shelley's will operates in personal, as opposed to political or ideological, situations is attested to by Trelawny with the insistence of conviction.

> He took no notice of what other people did. . . . nothing could make him pause for an instant when he had an object in view. . . . Shelley never wavered, he was unalterable. . . .

> he overbore all opposition in those less self-
> willed. (1:xvi, 105, 132, 156; see also Hogg
> 1:468, 2:168; Merle 704; Dowden 1:23.)

What Shelley himself said was, "I always go on until I am stopped, and I never am stopped. . . . *I* like the god of the Jews set myself up as no respecter of persons" (Trelawny 1:100; *PSL* 1:150, 16 Oct. 1811).

One person constantly endangered is Mary herself. Besides her well-known catalogue of grievances—Percy's intricate involvements with other women, his restless change of residences, his part in the deaths of Clara and William, his flights from home, his disdain for punctuality and society—there are the subtler applications of will, the salt in the wounds. Writing home during travels around Italy, Percy asks, "well my dearest Mary are you very lonely? Tell me truth my sweetest, do you ever cry?" (*PSL* 2:33, 18 Aug. 1818). Can this possibly be what White calls it—Shelley's attempt "to improve her spirits" (2:29)? Especially since Percy asks later, "Am I not like a wild swan to be gone so suddenly?" (*PSL* 2:40, 22 Sept. 1818)?

Many of the communications in *Frankenstein* work like this, the acid pill beneath the sugar coating. Mary learns about male will from reading such missive missiles as Percy's entry in their common journal on December 19, 1814.

> Hear of a woman—supposed to be the daughter
> of the Duke of Montrose—who has the head of
> a hog. (30)

The date of the entry signals the drama behind the scenes. By December of 1814, Mary's strange relationship with Jefferson Hogg has begun; she soon has an "odd dream" about him (*J* 30); their letters are erotic by January 1815; and by April 26 Percy is mentioning the two men sharing "our common treasure" (*PSL* 1:426). Although he ostensibly has encouraged the relationship, Percy in his journal entry of December 19 reflects his ambivalence. He is putting down for Mary to read: woman is pig. And, with an inescapable play upon "Hogg," he is calling a male rival (who has already tried to seduce *Harriet*) a swine and is converting him into a woman!

Mary experiences Percy's will in a different form when he treats her as condescendingly as he did Harriet. Compare his responses to both wives' additions to his letters. With Harriet he says, "I have filled my sheet before I was aware of it. . . . She desires to add something. I have scarcely room for her" (*PSL* 1:174, 11 Nov. 1811). That he scarcely has room for Harriet is true in several senses; that he finally will have no room for her at all is reflected in this letter too. It closes without poor Harriet ever getting to add her "something." The more forceful Mary manages to get in her two cents worth, but Percy does not always value her somethings more highly than that. "Mary will talk gossip, and send you the Indian air" (*PSL* 2:403, 31 Mar. 1822). (In a postscript to one of *her* letters Shelley asks, "I wonder what makes Mary think her letter worth the trouble of opening" [*NL* 145–46, 8 May 1820].) The same intellectual patronizing which prompted Percy to ask the now abandoned Harriet to "consider how far you would desire your future life to be placed within the influence of my superintending mind" (*PSL* 1:396, 16 Sept. 1814) occurs with his more gifted second wife. "I wish she were as wise now as she will be at 45, or as misfortune has made me" (*PSL* 2:218, 19 July 1820). Mary herself feels that Percy encouraged her writing "not so much with the idea that I could produce any thing worthy of notice, but that he might himself judge how far I possessed the promise of better things hereafter" (*F* 223).

Responding in her private prose to Percy's willfulness, Mary reveals the express-repress instinct which I discussed in the introduction. She embeds assertive moves among conciliatory, even self-effacing ones. "Tell me shall you be happy to have another little squaller? You will look grave on this, but I do not mean anything" (*MSL* 1:15, 5 Dec. 1816). Mary cannot resist pressing for the very domesticity which she fears will destroy her union with the man who complained that "in a house there is no solitude" (Trelawny 1:104).[4] How carefully she asks, "what did my love think of as he rode along—Did he think about our home, our babe and his poor Pecksie? But I am sure you did and thought of them all with joy and hope" (*MSL* 1:14, 5 Dec. 1816). The very asking of the question signals her fear of a negative answer, and two questions signal a double fear—that Percy was not thinking of home, and that, if he had, his thoughts would have been bad. Mary takes no chances; she credits him with the "joy and hope" which *must* be in his heart. The "but" reflects her anxiety, since it is illogical—if she is indeed sure. "Did he think? I am sure you did." There is no need for a "but." It is the sole surfacing of an otherwise repressed doubt. "Did he think? I doubt it. But I must be sure you did." The expression "poor Pecksie" shows Mary's readiness to abase herself to a diminutive status; evoking "home" and "babe" before mentioning herself asserts that she cannot be rejected without a repudiation of culturally sacred entities.

In these examples, Mary's anxiety is sufficiently strong that the other aspect of her express-repress instinct—anger at Percy's willfulness—is controlled better than she can manage regularly in her private prose. Compare her version of an 1814 episode and Claire's.

> Shelley calls on her [Harriet], whilst poor Mary and Jane [Claire] are left two whole hours in the coach. Our debt is discharged. Shelley gets clothes for himself. Go to Stratford Hotel; dine and go to bed. (Mary Shelley's *Journal* 15, 13 Sept. 1814)
>
> Shelley meets Voisey & go to Harriet's—Wait there for him two hours—Gets dark Part with our kind Boatman—Shelley returns—Drive to Stratfor[d] Hotel, Oxford Street. Dine & go to Bed. (Claire Clairmont's *Journal* 42)

Mary's "two whole hours," rather than Claire's "two hours," suggests how much longer the wait seems to the woman whose lover is ensconced with his pregnant wife. Less inevitable, but symptomatic, is the hostility "poor" Mary feels toward that lover. She never mentions what Claire establishes emphatically—that "Shelley returns"—but focuses instead upon the upshot of his return. Money. Since Claire is not implicated in the debt, she refers to it only in terms of a "part[ing]" and emphasizes the "kind Boatman." There is no boatman for Mary. There is only the debt which she shares with Shelley ("our") and the new possessions which she does not share. "For himself" is redundant after "Shelley gets clothes," but it is not superfluous. It indicates that Mary's point, however unfair, is less about individual need than about what she sees as Percy's selfish will.

Resentment grows throughout the rest of 1814, and in the process Mary develops a style in her private prose to reflect Percy's inexorability.

> Shelley and Clara set out all day to heaps of people . . . Shelley and Clara walk out, as usual, to heaps of places . . . Clara and Shelley go out together . . . Shelley and Clara . . . are out, as usual, all morning . . . he and Clara go to Longdill's . . . Clara and Shelley go to Tahourdin's . . . Shelley and Jane go to Garnerin's lecture . . . Shelley and Clara out as usual . . . Shelley and Jane go out . . . Shelley and Clara

go to Garnerin's . . . Shelley and Clara go sev-
eral places and then take a long walk . . . Shell-
ey and Clara set out . . . Shelley and Clara out
all day . . . Shelley and Clara out all day . . .
Shelley goes with Clara to Mrs. Peacock's . . .
Shelley and Clara go out about a cradle . . .
Shelley and Clara go to town . . . Shelley and
Clara go after breakfast to town . . . Shelley,
Hogg, and Clara go to town . . . Shelley and
Clara go to town . . . Shelley and Clara go to
Longdill's . . . Shelley and Clara walk part of
the way with Charles Clairmont . . . Shelley
and Jane walk . . . Shelley and Clara go out . . .
Clara goes out with Shelley . . . Shelley and
Clara walk to the Exhibition . . . Shelley goes
out with his friend . . . Shelley and the lady
walk out . . . (*J* 28 [four times], 29 [twice], 32,
34 [twice], 35 [twice], 36 [three times], 37, 39
[three times], 40 [twice], 41 [twice], 44 [twice],
46 [four times].)

Concentrated between December 5, 1814, and May 12, 1815, these
excerpts from a journal anything but garrulous do not seem to me
what Moers calls them, "chilly and laconic" (94). Only by reducing
language to formula can Mary speak at all. She is caught between
express and repress, between anger at Shelley's walks with Claire
and fear at his walking out with Claire. Mary can escape complete
repression and purge her resentment only by expressing herself with
such control that resentment cannot become anarchic. What she
said of her public prose is even truer of her private: "You see how
cautious & cold I am in my expressions *to be printed*, in comparison
with the real warmth that is obliged to find unworthy exit in cut &
dried phrases" (*MSL* 1:345, 23 June 1826).

Since Percy's willful vagaries increase substantially by the time
of *Frankenstein*, Mary cannot always sustain the express-repress
pattern and withdraw the resentment that has surged forth. "I almost think of writing my letter over again as the enclosed is so wild
I fear you will not attend to it" (*MSL* 1:38, 2 Oct. 1817). But the very
mention of rewriting the letter indicates that the repressive reflex is
still compensating for the expressive. It continues to operate in the
private prose—at least to the extent that Mary's dissatisfaction is
rarely expressed wildly. "Climate . . . has destroyed my two children" (*MSL* 1:74, 29 June 1819) seems not to blame Percy. But "my,"
rather than the "our" of the poor Pecksie letter, makes loss hers

alone. Excluded from the possessive adjective, Percy, whose impulsiveness and lethargy contributed to the deaths of both children, becomes part of the non-me, and thus part of the slaughtering climate. "When Shelley came to Italy, I said all is well if it were permanent; it was more passing than an Italian twilight" (J 159, 4 Aug. 1821). Again there is no "we." "Shelley came" establishes that the agency, and thus the responsibility, are his. Mary is once more set off as victim, and judge.

Whether Mary is being entirely fair with her "my" and "Shelley came" is questionable. But the countervening facts, that Percy did love the dead children and did ask Mary about Italy, are lost sight of amid her obsession with male inexorability. She comes not only to agree that Shelley is "no respecter of persons," but to believe that the Erotic male generally is "like the Hebrew God," a force of absolute will. The distance between Mary and Percy which we sense when she refers to "the peculiar views and sentiments which he *believed* to be beneficial to the human race" (*CP* 410; my italics) is unmistakable when she says, "Shelley believed that mankind had only to will that there should be no evil, and there would be none. It is not my part in these Notes to notice the arguments that have been urged against this opinion, but to mention the fact that he entertained it" (*CP* 271). If Mary really wished not to call our attention to the arguments against Percy's opinion, she would not do so. About the Percy of 1815, Mary says, "This is neither the time nor place to speak of the misfortunes that chequered his life. It will be sufficient to say that, in all that he did, he at the time of doing it *believed* himself *justified* to his own conscience" (*CP* 30; my italics). It is sufficient because Mary's emphasis is clear. Her words stress less Shelley's actions than his belief in those actions, less his fate than his will. Her emphasis upon temporality ("at the time of doing it") implies that retrospection might alter evaluation. The mercurial are prey to whim. "Justified" suggests the justification by faith in the self which made Shelley see himself as unacknowledged legislator of mankind, and womankind.

*

For an immediate sense of how Percy's other extreme, his weakness, affects Mary's life, compare her conventional belief that women "desire to find a manly spirit whereon [to] lean" and an ominous event on the elopement. During the channel crossing Mary tries to rest in Percy's lap, but his "knees . . . were unable to support her" (J 4, 28 July 1814). Then, on the overland journey, the donkey purchased for the women must be given over to "Shelley, [who] having sprained his leg, was obliged to ride all day" (*J* 7–8, 11 Aug. 1814).[5]

Percy's physical woes worsen with time, and Mary is sincerely concerned for him, of course. But increasingly her response becomes mixed. Formulae reflect the grind of nursing, while they control self-pity enough to prevent Mary from feeling disloyal.

> Shelley very unwell . . . Shelley is not well . . . Shelley unwell . . . Shelley very unwell . . . Shelley is very unwell . . . Shelley is not well . . . Shelley is not well . . . Shelley is not very well . . . Shelley very unwell . . . Shelley unwell . . . Shelley unwell . . . Shelley is not well . . . Shelley unwell . . . Shelley is very unwell . . . he is very unwell . . . Shelley unwell . . . Shelley unwell . . . Shelley not well . . . Shelley is not well . . . Shelley not well . . . Shelley very unwell . . . Shelley not well . . . Shelley is not well . . . he has been very unwell lately & is very far from well now . . . Shelley is by no means well . . . Shelley is far from well . . . (*J* 17, 23, 29, 31, 41, 63, 69, 75, 82, 91 [twice], 92, 97, 120, 124, 128, 129, 134 [twice], 138, 142, 157; *MSL* 1:45, 68, 120, 145, 6 Oct. 1815 to 3 June 1821)

Mary cannot always remain so reticent, however, and the express-repress pattern allows dissatisfaction to appear amid commiseration. "My spirits however are much better than they were—and perhaps your absence is the cause," she writes from Marlow in 1817. "Ah! my love you cannot guess how wretched it was to see your languour and encreasing illness. . . . Adieu my own one—come back as quickly as you may—with bright eyes and stout limbs" (*MSL* 1:29–30, 24 Sept.). Still sharper responses ("he really suffers a great deal—more than he ought this fine weather" [*NL* 201, 1 June 1821]) indicate the judgmental stance which no repressive instinct can stifle entirely. Whether or not Mary agreed with physicians and friends that Percy's ills were largely psychosomatic, she came to a sense of her own comparative strength.

> [With] pure air & burning sun—You would then enjoy life. For my own part I shall have tolerable health anywhere. . . . You complain of this weather—dear Love but I have seldom

known any more pleasant. (*MSL* 1:31, 26 Sept. 1817; 1:40, 7 Oct. 1817)

Perspective on male weakness brings Mary to the border of condescension, especially since Percy's ailments are compounded by his ineptitudes. (Comparable ineptitudes in *Frankenstein*, and comparable condescension from Mary, I will detail in chapter 4.) "Mr. Shelley's thoughtlessness" impels Mary in January of 1817 to write Marianne Hunt "to ask him for his dirty linen and send it to the wash for him" (*MSL* 1:17, 13 Jan. 1817). In the same month she tells Percy, "you wish to be accurate and to give me the very words of Basil M[ontagu, Shelley's attorney] but unfortunately that was the only part of your letter of which I did not understand a single word—part of it was covered with the seal & the rest nearly illegible" (*NL* 27, 17 Jan. 1817). That Percy's behavior can reach the ludicrous is affirmed by Hogg and confirmed by Mary.

> Not only did he laugh aloud, with a wild, demoniacal burst of laughter, but he slipped from his seat, and fell on his back at full length on the floor. . . . Shelley came tumbling up stairs. . . . He was . . . discussing and disputing the while, and trembling with emotion; and pouring the precious liquor [tea] into his bosom, upon his knees, and into his shoes, and spilling it on the carpet. (Hogg 1:305; 2:271, 529–30)

Ludicrousness appears in Mary's *Lodore*, where the Percy figure, Saville, "sometimes . . . was so abstracted as to do the most absent things in the world; and the quick alternations of his gaiety and seriousness were often ludicrous from their excess" (2:189). As well as she knows the ludicrous, however, Mary knows that weakness is ultimately no laughing matter. Shelley's moments of manual incompetence, which Trelawny as well as Hogg insists upon, involve more than physical clumsiness. Indifference to realities is a mode of aggression. Sailing with Shelley frightens Jane Williams so much because she realizes that the issue is not the boat's unseaworthiness; she and her children are in the hands of a man who will kill them all if given enough time. Like his expressly willful acts, Shelley's ineptitudes show him to be no respecter of persons. The self-surrendering Eros, as well as the ego-centric, contemns the mundane world. Percy loses Hogg's books (2:156), and Mary's letters (*MSL* 1:73, 27 June 1819), and Hunt's paper (*MSL* 1:106, 13 April

1820). In turbulent times at Marlow, Mary responds as the good wife should: "make your determination and I will abide by it. . . . I have said all I can say on the subject—humbly offering my reasons and leaving it to you as the manly part to decide" (*MSL* 1:36, 37, 30 Sept. 1817). Such orthodox sentiments, however, presuppose a complementarity, an agreement by "the manly part" to be decisive if the wife is deferential, which Percy cannot abide by. And Mary knows it.

> You decide nothing and tell me *nothing*. . . .
> Nothing is done you say in your letter. . . .
> Talk about going away, and, as usual, settle
> nothing. . . . Shelley is out all the morning at
> the lawyer's, but nothing is done. . . . Shelley
> is out, but nothing takes place. (*MSL* 1:37, 2
> Oct. 1817; 1:43, 16 Oct. 1817; *J* 21, 15 Oct.
> 1814; 21–22, 22 Oct. 1814; 76, 29 Jan. 1817)

Shelley's instinct for failure was at times evident to his contemporaries. "His life indeed was one hurry; he appeared to be ever impelled by a wild terror, lest he should lose, or even delay for one moment, any opportunity of placing himself in a disadvantageous position" (Hogg 2:9). Hogg does not go on to consider what Mary will dramatize in *Frankenstein*—that behavior apparently self-destructive can be ultimately self-rewarding. When, for example, Eliza Westbrook imperils Percy's marriage to Harriet, Hogg recognizes that "it was absolutely necessary to declare peremptorily, 'Either Eliza goes, or I go;' and instantly to act upon the declaration. This so necessary course the poor fellow did not take" (2:1). But Hogg assumes that Shelley wants the marriage to succeed, whereas Percy by this time is tired of Harriet. However unconsciously, he *is* following the "necessary course"—to dissolution. Mary chooses for Frankenstein's first name her husband's *nom de plume*, Victor, because she senses that the victory sought by both men can be achieved not only through inexorable will, but through a passive instinct for triumphant defeat, through the Dionysiac as well as the Platonic Eros.

BIFURCATION AND MARY SHELLEY'S FICTION

Mary Shelley's later fiction[6] targets both Erotic will and weakness, as her express-repress instinct persists in a modified form. She criticizes Percy's extremism more explicitly than during his lifetime, but she can face a particular aspect of him or of herself only by never facing all of either. In *Lodore* three characters—Lodore, Derham, and Saville—reflect aspects of Percy, but none is he. In *The Last Man* Mary projects herself into Evadne, Idris, and Perdita, but she differs from each importantly. Art and life remain discrete even as they mirror each other. Mary's later novels reflect *Frankenstein* heuristically because they present in partial, simplified form the complex configurations which obsess her masterpiece. What her later novels also show, however, is that Mary does not focus in any restrictive, vindictively petty way upon Percy. The deterioration of her marriage is the greatest sorrow of Mary Shelley's life, but we must not reduce her life and her art to it. "Half in love with easeful death" was not, after all, said by Shelley. The Romantic obsession with death and commitment to Eros were cultural phenomena that Mary Shelley recognized early in the century and confronted throughout her fiction. Percy Shelley is not her only theme because bifurcation also characterized the other men whom she knew capable of androgyny.

Lord Byron, for example, "was naturally a coward," Mary maintains, "but would do brave and even desperate things, if put to it."[7] Macho acts threaten anyone opposing the will of "a man reckless of the ill he does others, obstinate to desperation in the pursuance of his plans or his revenge" (*MSL* 1:140, 11 May 1821). As "desperate" and "desperation" indicate, however, the posturing of machismo masks its opposite, the weakness of one "naturally a coward," as Mary suggests in her wry response to Procter's worry that Byron would fight for the Greeks. "I told him that he might be at ease on that point, *Helmets so fine were never made to hack*" (*MSL* 1:265, 18 Sept. 1823). Byron appears in *The Last Man* as Raymond, who aspires to erectness but is in fact emasculate. "I appear to have strength, power, victory; standing as a dome-supporting column stands; and I am—a reed" (45). That Byron's "faults . . . [are] for the most part, weaknesses" (*J* 194, 15 May 1824) implicates his feminine side, because the passivity which could at its best allow gentle sympathy leads at its worst to lethargy and irresponsibility. Thus the man capable of androgyny can lapse all too frequently into both extremes of Eros—"now caressing and now tyrannizing . . . but in every change a despot" (*The Last Man* 33).

That Mary would associate Byron with Percy's bifurcation runs contrary to the traditional assumption that the two poets are resolutely distinct for her. Scholars have repeatedly confirmed Lovell's belief that Mary's "contrast [of the two men] is one of perfect foils" (171). In her fiction Mary does of course contrast Byronic and Shelleyan figures in terms of coloring (dark/light), voice (deep/high), and certain traits (aggressive/shy). But just as obviously, such contrasts do not account fully for the relationship between the paired characters or between their models. The debate over which character represents which poet indicates the complexity of Mary's views. Peck assigns Raymond in *The Last Man* to Byron, yet Walling locates Shelleyan elements in Raymond's political philosophy; Lovell finds Villiers in *Lodore* Byronic, whereas Norman calls him Shelleyan. Percy himself increases the confusion by reflecting both poets' circumstances in the maniac in *Julian and Maddalo*.[8] A comparable confusion is created by Lovell's turnabout; he admits that the supposedly Byronic Lodore reenacts the public school experience of Shelley. "But this substitution of Shelley for Byron is only temporary" (176). Substitution is not what is happening. Mary here and throughout her fiction is determinedly associating Byron and Shelley.

Take, for example, Falkner, whom critics link exclusively to Byron and Trelawny. Physically, Falkner exhibits two hallmarks of Shelley: "he could not stand upright" and "he was struck by premature decay" (1:141, 2:116). Sharing Shelley's philanthropic drive to mold young women, Falkner fulfills the poet's dream of raising an orphan girl according to his ideals. The comic potential in such enterprises surfaces when Falkner is linked to a figure whom Mary frequently associates with Percy. "Falkner had . . . much of the Don Quixote about him, and never heard a story of oppression without forming a scheme to relieve the victim" (1:86).[9] Finally, Mary allows Falkner what may be the most sacred experience of her life: he meets the heroine at the grave of her mother, as Mary Godwin met young Percy Shelley at the grave of Mary Wollstonecraft.

My intent is not to simply oppose earlier critics and insist that Falkner is Shelley. Unquestionably Byron and Trelawny are present too. Byronic elements blend with Shelleyan in Falkner, as they do in Lodore and Raymond and Villiers, because Mary perceives elemental similarities between the two poets. These men cannot sustain androgyny because they (and Frankenstein) share an obsession with death which impairs both the adhesion of masculine and feminine components in the psyche and the cohesion of the individual with men and women in society. What Byron shares with Shelley is what both men in turn share with Godwin, and with all too many males of the Romantic period. By recognizing the sweep of Mary's commentary upon Erotic masculinity, we can increase both our appreciation of her later fiction and our understanding of her paradigm Romantic, Victor Frankenstein.

Mary implicates all the sons of Eros in her criticism of Prometheanism by laying out a spectrum of male adequacy. With ideally androgynous men like Perkin Warbeck at one end of the spectrum, she places at the opposite end the least adequate—coarse males like King James in *Perkin Warbeck* who, "bred in civil strife among fierce Highlanders and ruthless Borderers, saw something contemptible in this [Perkin's] pity and supplication for the cottagers" (2:312). Such macho males are never characterized by the key feminine traits of sympathy, delicacy, softness; they are implacably "hard," "inflexible," "impenetrable." That such pretensions are ultimately *unmanly* is confirmed in *The Last Man* when marauding bands "talked of taking London, conquering England. . . . Such vaunts displayed their weakness, rather than their strength" (215). Machismo shrivels to impotence before a real danger like the plague.

> Our native oak, as his partisans called him [Ryland]. . . . scarcely appeared half his usual height . . . his limbs would not support him. . . . [fear] shrivelled his whole person. (175, 182)

Even an upright man can be extreme, if his desire to support the beloved derives from patriarchal egotism. Falkner's determination to save Alithea from a marriage which he abhors leads to her death and to his shame at "erecting myself into a providence" (2:51).

Men who *can* temper their maleness with feminine traits are superior to willful extremists, but even here Mary Shelley makes a distinction. Between the nadir of King James and the ideal of Perkin Warbeck are men like Lodore, who initially seems admirably androgynous, being "generous and brave as was his father, benevolent and pious as was his sister" (1:73). Lodore is actually flawed, however. "He was courageous as a lion, and, upon occasion, soft-hearted and pitiful; but once roused to anger by opposition, his eyes darted fire . . . nor could he be pacified except by the most entire submission on the part of his antagonist" (1:74). Lodore and men like him have escaped willfulness far enough to evince feminine traits ("soft-hearted"), but they constitute only an intermediate stage of development because their gender traits are not combined. "On occasion" shows that the feminine alternates with, rather than balances, the masculine. Instead of consistently softened conduct, the male whose will is challenged finds his "form swelled" (1:74) with a phallic aggressiveness which can be satisfied only by "entire submission."

Mary's spectrum is a particularly effective commentary upon willfulness because it allows for process. It can chart growth and regression, a male's move toward or from androgyny and Agape, by measuring his openness to feminine influence. Three brief examples.

With his androgynously "soft, yet bright eyes," Castruccio Castrocani in *Valperga* begins public life ideally with "an enquiring, yet a gentle mind" (1:6, 64). He matures into a young man who can avoid extremism and achieve the ideal "medium, which combines the graceful submission of youth, with that independence that is the dearest birthright of man" (1:67). War hardens him, but wounds received in a victorious fight assure him the attractive vulnerability of Mary's "delicate" poet-types.

> His cheek was pale from the consequences of his wound, and his person, having thus lost its usual decision of mien, was more interesting; but his eyes shone, and they beamed unutterable love upon her [Euthanasia]. Truly did he look a hero. (1:214)

All too soon, however, Castruccio cries, "to what extremities am I driven!" (2:226). Swinging from one extreme to the other, he regresses from the balancing of gender traits to their alternation. "When he had seen her [Euthanasia] last, he had been haughty and imperious; but now his manner was all softness, gentleness and humility" (2:283). Castruccio then regresses further. "His eyes had not lost their fire, but their softness was gone" (3:170). To indicate that he is now bereft of the feminine altogether, Mary separates Castruccio from his beloved Euthanasia and allows her to distinguish true manliness from impenetrable willfulness. "'Leave me; you are not a man; your heart is stone.' . . . she saw he was moulded of an impenetrable substance" (2:216, 3:253).

Castruccio's decline is reversed in Falkner. Initially so hardened by misfortune and guilt that he could only seek quietus in suicide, Falkner soon reveals female traits which alternate with his male drives.

> The remarkable trait of his physiognomy was its great variation—restless, and even fierce, the expression was often that of passionate and

71

> unquiet thoughts; while at other times it was
> almost bland from the apparent smoothness
> and graceful undulation of the lines. (1:25)

Although Falkner's proclivity for "going, as is usual, from one extreme to the other" (2:196) means that more anguish lies ahead, he has already demonstrated the one quality indispensable to happiness. "Falkner yielded his hitherto unbending mind to control. He was satisfied to be led, and not to command. . . . 'Henceforth I will be guided by you, my Elizabeth'" (1:45, 133). Yielding to woman means the masculine traits within the psyche acknowledge the feminine ("tenderness . . . was blended with his fiercer passions" [2:191]), so that extremism can give way to moderation. Falkner can stand trial for Alithea's death and emerge reborn. "The seeds of disease were destroyed — his person grew erect" (2:298). Upright Falkner achieves that true manliness which results from complete integration. "He was reconciled to himself and the world" (2:298).

Raymond in *The Last Man* combines the positive movement of Falkner and the final fate of Castruccio. After the last king of England has "yielded up the already broken sceptre," Raymond vows to "rear the fallen plant . . . and exalt it above all the flowers of the field" (39). Despite the phallic hubris here, Raymond can, like Falkner, submit to woman: "Take me [Perdita]—mould me to your will" (48). This receptivity to the feminine allows Raymond to surpass his rival, Ryland. "Lord Raymond rose,—his countenance bland, his voice softly melodious, his manners soothing, his grace and sweetness came like the mild breathing of a flute, after the loud, organlike voice of his adversary [Ryland]. He rose" (42). The repeated verb "rose" establishes the uprightness of manly Raymond, while "softly," "soothing," "grace and sweetness," and "mild" show his capacity for the feminine. The melodic voice here is less reassuring than it might be, however, because that "voice, usually gentle, often startled you by a sharp discordant note" (33). Raymond cannot *balance* gender traits. "The usual expression of his eyes was soft, though at times he could make them even glare with ferocity" (33). With traits alternating and polarizing, Raymond is "thus full of contradictions" (33). His readiness to be ruled by a woman seems promising, but the next hundred pages show no single, Falkner-like movement toward mature cohesiveness.

Raymond does try to accept "his domestic circle" (85), but Perdita "found it however no easy task to soften and reconcile Raymond" (90). She fails in the end. Instead of reaching the androgynous ideal, Raymond, "extreme in all things" (107), confesses the persistence of machismo. "My passions are my masters" (109). Seeking domination, Raymond finds death in war, having left the feminine behind for good.

> "Perdita," he continued, impatiently, "I know
> what you would say; I know that you love me,
> that you are good and gentle; but this is no
> woman's work—nor can a female heart guess
> at the hurricane which tears me!" (140)

Raymond's fate is Frankenstein's.

*

Mary's later fiction attacks Erotic will and weakness. Opposing will, she enters, in effect, into the Julian/Maddalo debate staged by Percy. Take Julian's and Maddalo's positions—"we might be all / We dream of" versus "men change not"—and compare them with Mary's direct address to the reader in *Perkin Warbeck*:

> Could I, or could one more fortunate, breathe
> the magic word which would reveal to all the
> power, which we all possess, to turn evil to
> good, foul to fair; then vice and pain would de-
> sert the new-born world.
>   It is not thus: the wise have taught, the good
> suffered for us; we are still the same. (3:18)

Beginning with Julian's qualified optimism, Mary sides finally with dark Maddalo. The egotism implicit in Julian-Percy's espousal of will becomes explicit in *Valperga*, when self-seeking Castruccio insists that achievement depends solely upon the will to succeed. "Let us work for ourselves alone; we may be obscure or famous, grovelling as the worm, or lofty as the kingly eagle, according as our desires sink or mount" (1:128). Mary's quite different ideal is articulated by Euthanasia.

> "What is the world, except that which we feel?
> Love, and hope, and delight, or sorrow and
> tears; these are our lives, our realities, to which
> we give the names of power, possession, mis-
> fortune, and death. You [Castruccio] smile at
> my strange words." (1:193)

Mary's repeated recourse to Percy's terms ("the will to save him is not enough without the power," "I believe him to have both the

power and the will" [*Perkin Warbeck* 1:92; *Valperga* 1:167]) highlights her disagreement with him. People and society do not, as Percy maintains, fail because we refuse to exercise the powerful will we
possess. We fail because our power to effect change is severely limited in three ways. External events are too powerful

> "I [Falkner] imagined in those days that I could
> guide events—till suddenly the reins were torn
> from my hands" (2:216)

and human faculties are too limited

> although perpetually deceived and led astray
> by our imagination, we always fancy that we
> can foresee, and in some sort command, the
> consequences of our action (*Falkner* 2:99)

to justify much hope in human activity, let alone any belief in per-
fectibility. In his naive days before plague turns the earth into a
global grave, Adrian echoes Julian-Percy's optimism: "The choice is
with us; let us will it, and our habitation becomes a paradise" (*The
Last Man* 54). Adrian's naive declaration that "the will of man is
omnipotent" (54) parodies Shelley's contention that "the power of
man is great" (*JS* 6:157). *The Last Man* teaches relentlessly that external events are as powerful as human faculties are weak. "Farewell to the giant powers of man. . . . We had called ourselves the
'paragon of animals,' and, lo! we were a 'quint-essence of dust'"
(233, 290).

   The Last Man also presents a third argument against the efficacy
of will. Beneath our conscious intentions are drives which do from
within what events do from without—shape us to their whim. Raymond fails to perfect society through "his beneficial will" (76) because internal forces prove as inexorable as external events.

> "I cannot set my heart to a particular tune, or
> run voluntary changes on my will." . . . Thus,
> while Raymond had been wrapt in visions of
> power and fame, while he looked forward to
> entire dominion over the elements and the
> mind of man, the territory of his own heart es-
> caped his notice; and from that unthought of
> source arose the mighty torrent that over-
> whelmed his will, and carried to the oblivious
> sea, fame, hope, and happiness. (47, 84)

Mary's dark view of human potency and change may seem at odds with Adrian's role in *The Last Man*. Since he leads the earth's remnant heroically and resembles Percy clearly, does he not validate Shelley's view of the efficacy of human will? Adrian, despite numerous testaments (including Mary's own), is *not* Percy, he is the Percy whom Mary wanted Shelley to be. Adrian begins like the poet, a sickly isolated figure dreaming of impossible social change. "In mental desolation, more irreparable than a fragment of a carved column in a weed-grown field . . . his voice broken—his person wasted . . . [he] sails yellow leaves and bits of bark on the stream" (49). The emasculation consequent upon emaciation is evident in Adrian's resemblance to a ruined column. The state cannot be supported by childish, or at least childlike, males who—instead of being "erect and manly . . . pillars of the state"—indulge in Shelley's life-long penchant for sailboats. Adrian is at this point no better off than the novel's macho figures—Ryland, who pretends to be an English oak but cannot support the state, and Raymond, who seems to be "a dome-supporting column" and is actually "a reed" (45).

Adrian then goes on to achieve maturity as defined by Mary Shelley: he manages a "feminine" acceptance of limitation and a purposive commitment to moderation. "From my birth I have aspired like the eagle—but, unlike the eagle, my wings have failed. . . . Congratulate me then that I have found fitting scope for my powers" (179). By leading the earth's remnant in its doomed flight, Adrian does what Mary urged and Percy rejected: he engages with the world. Mary expresses her view of Shelley's proper course of action both in *The Last Man* and in her notes to the *Complete Poems*.

> Evadne entered but coldly into his [Adrian's] systems. She thought he did well to assert his own will, but she wished that will to have been more intelligible to the multitude. (*The Last Man* 30–31)

> The surpassing excellence of *The Cenci* had made me greatly desire that Shelley should increase his popularity by adopting subjects that would more suit the popular taste than a poem conceived in the abstract and dreamy spirit of *The Witch of Atlas*. . . . Even now I believe that I was in the right. . . . But my persuasions were vain. (*CP* 388, 389; see also *CP* ix–xi, 156, 188, 314, 334, 337, 571, 640, 676.)

Adrian *heeds* Mary's advice. He forgoes the willfulness of perfectionist daydreams and righteous aloofness, and he confronts what Mary believes Percy ignored, "human passion, with its mixture of good and evil, of disappointment and disquiet" (*CP* 389). And lo! the improvement. Erect Adrian "was no longer bent to the ground, like an over-nursed flower of spring. . . . He seemed born anew" (181, 219).

In her later fiction's treatment of Erotic weakness, Mary is responding not only to Percy's daily ailments and ineptitudes, but also to the weakness portrayed in his art. Her response here is particularly important to *Frankenstein* because Mary is passing decisive judgment upon what Percy presents with an equivocation indicative of sympathy. Some Shelley works, such as *Alastor*, present the delicate, fleeing poet-figure complexly, but from 1810 to 1822 he repeatedly, as we have seen, displays toward his weak, morally problematic figures a sympathetic ambivalence which he denies to the tyrants who beset them.

At times Mary echoes in her late fiction the attraction to weak males which we saw in her private comments on delicate poet-types. Like Velluti and Percy, Horatio Saville in *Lodore* is "one of those who seem not to belong to this world, yet who adorn it most. . . . his noble purposes and studious soul, demanded a frame of iron, and he had one of the frailest mechanism" (2:20–21). Weakness is not enough to earn Mary's full respect, however. Saville resembles men apparently opposite to him, the macho types Raymond and Lodore, because none of the three can control his wife or his life. Raymond's marriage is threatened by Perdita's willfulness, but "he could not persuade himself to undertake to direct the course of events" (105). Lodore, who acts out Percy's relations with Harriet Westbrook, enjoys "moulding" women but, when his wife should be controlled, "his hand was raised—the effort made; but no change ensued" (1:162–63).

Saville manifests Shelley's ailments and ineptitudes as Mary dramatizes her sense of what would have happened if Percy had put poetry into practice and married Emilia Viviani, the Pisan woman celebrated so rapturously in *Epipsychidion*. Saville, who has Shelley's "tall . . . thin and shadowy" figure and "voice . . . broken and mournful" (2:21), fails initially, like Shelley, to emulate Adrian and become a leader. "His imagination rose high above the empty honours of the world—to be useful was a better aim; but he did not conceive that his was a mind calculated to lead others in its train" (2:221). Social disengagement parallels domestic mismanagement. Saville, who like Percy often "forgot the world around him" (2:181), is guilty of what Hogg and others lamented in Shelley—a "want of punctuality, which often caused hours to be lost, and their excursions spoiled. Nor did he ever furnish good excuses, but seemed annoyed at being questioned on the subject" (2:189). We soon learn why Saville is unreliable. "The time came when his heart was to be the dupe of his imagination" (2:174). *Lodore* is revenge. The escapist Romanticism which Mary hated in *Epipsychidion* leads weak Platonists to wed Italian harpies who dominate them. Saville is unpunctual because he must tend his wife during the fits of rage which eventually kill her.

When Mary Shelley learned in 1822 that violence and suspicion plagued the marriage of the real Emilia Viviani, she waspishly linked Pisan squalor and "Shelley's Italian platonics" (*MSL* 1:161, 7 Mar.). This apparent dismissal did not end matters. After portraying the inadequacies of Saville-Percy in 1835, Mary goes on in 1838 to relate this weakness to the type of poetry preferred by Shelley. "[*The Witch of Atlas*] is peculiarly characteristic of his tastes . . . discarding human interest and passion, to revel in the fantastic ideas that his imagination suggested" (*CP* 388). Mary in fact goes beyond the charge of escapism and, however unfairly, sees Percy's whole poetic enterprise as regressive.

> The luxury of imagination which sought nothing beyond itself (as a child burdens itself with spring flowers, thinking of no use beyond the enjoyment of gathering them), often showed itself in his verses. . . . There are few friends who remember him in sailing paper boats, and watching the navigation of his tiny craft with eagerness . . . but those who do will recollect that it was in the creations of his own fancy when that was most daring and ideal, that he sheltered himself from the storms and disappointments, the pain and sorrow, that beset his life. (*CP* x, 551)

Thus, if it is willfulness that drove Percy to his flights around Europe and his walks with Claire, it is the opposite, is weakness, that directed his flights *from* the world and Mary.

Toward Frankenstein

We have seen that Mary's ideal is an androgynous balancing of gender elements, that woman becomes the force of judgment when man deteriorates into bifurcation, and that these judgments are rendered in an express-repress mode which often requires us readers to uncover the covert and unconscious. What remains is to use Mary Shelley's later fiction to highlight the strategy by which she presents the failed androgyne in *Frankenstein*. In *Lodore* the title character is, as we have seen, the willful male who like Shelley made "freedom . . . the watchword of his heart" (1:77). But this is only the half of it. "He had a friend at school" (1:77), the feminine half of himself, who is also like Shelley.

> His slender frame, fair, effeminate countenance, and gentle habits, rendered him ridiculous to his fellows. . . . The boy [Derham] was unlike the rest; he had wild fancies and strange inexplicable ideas . . . and pored with unceasing delight over books of the abstrusest philosophy. . . . when they [the boys] jeered him, he would answer gravely with some story of a ghastly spectre. (1:77–78)

Not surprisingly, Lodore as the male half of the psyche "stood forward in . . . behalf" of the beleaguered female half (1:78), and the two become fast friends.

Just as inevitably, given the polarizing bent of the psychological type Mary Shelley is portraying, the two halves of the psyche drift apart and lose contact. "How different—and yet how similar—the destinies of both" (1:225). Both enter upon the unhappy marriage inevitable for one-sided males, and both succumb to what Mary feared for in Percy—isolation. Passive, ineffectual Derham, "incapable of sympathizing or extracting sympathy" (1:84), becomes a reclusive scholar and dies in obscurity. Lodore lives actively in the public eye for a time but he no more learns how to control his will than Derham learned to activate his. Like Percy whose dangerous temper was allied to what Mary called "irritability" (*CP* xi), Lodore becomes "a man of violent and dangerous passions, add to which, his temper was susceptible to irritability" (1:130). The result is that Lodore, threatened like Shelley with "premature age" (1:48), becomes "a recluse, having given up ambition, hope, almost life itself, inasmuch as that existence is scarcely to be termed life, which does not bring us into intimate connexion with our fellow-creatures" (1:216).

Lodore thus presents the extremes of will and weakness, of Platonic and Dionysiac Eros, as a single psyche projected into two characters. *Frankenstein* may seem similar in its presentation of Victor and the monster, but I believe Mary Shelley's masterpiece works in fact quite differently. *Frankenstein* presents the two extremes of Eros in the single psyche of Victor, and then echoes both extremes in the monster. *Frankenstein* is substantially more powerful than *Lodore* because the Platonic-Dionysiac personality in Victor and in the monster can function with an intricate intensity which its fragmented parts in Lodore and Derham can never achieve. The complexity achieved through a configuration of character analagous to the structure of Shelley's and Byron's psyches is, in turn, augmented by another strategic move of considerable importance—Mary's selection of Prometheus as the archetype of the Romantic male.

In Prometheus we can see a psyche capable of both Agape and Eros, androgyny and bifurcation. Like the acolyte of Agape, Prometheus loves his neighbor philanthropically to the point of risking Zeus' wrath in order to civilize humankind through the gift of fire. In addition to this "masculine" capacity for action, Prometheus exhibits a passive, "feminine" endurance of suffering which can be seen in light of various religious ideals, including the Christian Agape with its tradition of martyrs. (Likening her later Falkner to Prometheus (2:191), Mary defines his ethic as "'Let God's will be done!' something of Christian resignation—something (derived from his eastern life) of belief in fatality—and something of philosophic fortitude" [2:216]). On the other hand, Prometheus' active and passive propensities can be seen as the extremes of Erotic bifurcation. The acts of stealing fire from heaven and giving it to men may, for example, indicate will-to-power. By stealing fire, Prometheus appropriates a property of divinity; and by endowing humankind with civilization, he in effect usurps God's procreative power. Prometheus' suffering can, in turn, seem little more than passivity taken to the extreme of ineffectuality, since he does quite literally nothing throughout the whole of Aeschylus' play.

Mary Shelley was doubtless not conscious of all Prometheus' potential for Eros and Agape. But I believe that by terming Frankenstein in his willfulness and weakness "the Modern Prometheus" she was instinctively recognizing the negative as well as the positive potential of Prometheus. In this perception she is her mother's daughter, for Mary Wollstonecraft described the self-indulgent male in Promethean terms—"a lawless planet darting from its orbit to steal the celestial fire of reason" (41). I believe further that by associating Percy *and* Byron (*and* Godwin) with Frankenstein, Mary Shelley was indicting a whole generation and virtually a whole gender as the sons of Eros. Victor Frankenstein's relationship to Percy Shelley is thus complex: at times Victor reflects specific aspects of Shelley; at other times he expresses the Erotic drives of Promethean males *like* Shelley.

Mary Shelley thus takes an early place in what will become a long and distinguished line of nineteenth- and twentieth-century writers who examine the male psyche in its relations to women and death. Like Charlotte Brontë, Mary Shelley punishes males who fail to fulfill their androgynous potential; like Dickens, Joyce, and Faulkner, she dramatizes the male determination to effect immortality through self-generation. And like Charlotte Brontë, M. E. Braddon, and other "sensational" heirs of the gothic (including Dickens and Collins), she uses female characters to express her repressed anger at individuals and institutions, displaying in the process depths to the female psyche unacknowledged by orthodoxy. *Frankenstein* is an immense achievement both in what it reveals and in what it initiates.

Mary Shelley's masterpiece, like her private prose and her later fiction, refutes in advance the charge that Massingham will level at her a century later.

> Such sensibility [in Shelley], such exquisite
> awareness, such tenderness and power of life,
> such ideality of thought and radiant heat of
> personality—were these very difficult qualities
> for a woman to live with? (215)

As though a woman lives with qualities. But maybe Mary deserves the reproof. After all, what is Massingham doing but throwing back in her face the Shelley legend which she labored to fabricate? Yet Mary did know better, did know there were two Percys, the one who shared her dream of androgyny and Agape, and the one who succumbed to bifurcation and Eros. She could not have one without the other. She could not love them both.

3

Frankenstein: Self-Division and Projection

> I know people theorize Mick thought it would be amusing to marry his twin. But actually, he wanted to achieve the ultimate in loving himself.
>
> Bianca Jagger

> He dreams of guilt in disquiet.
>
> Simone de Beauvoir

THE WAR OF EROS AND AGAPE ENTERS *Frankenstein*[1] IN THE OPENING frame as men manifest a potential for androgyny and a penchant for bifurcation. At their best, Robert Walton and Victor Frankenstein balance gender traits admirably. Their "manly" qualities—ambition, daring, scientific intelligence, physical hardihood—are tempered by a sympathetic love of neighbor which manifests itself publicly in concern for human welfare and privately in affection for Margaret and Elizabeth. Robert and Victor also tend, however, to Erotic extremism. Masculine and feminine traits in their psyches polarize into willfulness and weakness; love for woman and concern for society are seriously undermined. After establishing bifurcation in the opening frame of *Frankenstein*, Mary Shelley goes on to show how Victor's riven psyche attempts to heal itself through the creation of the monster.

ROBERT AND MARGARET

The first androgyne was FatherSky-MotherEarth. Their sundering in mythology[2] is reflected in the opposition of Eros and Agape. "Eros is the way by which man mounts up to the Divine, not the way [of Agape] by which the divine steps down to man. . . . this upward attraction of the soul is Eros" (Nygren 178, 172). Erotic males aspire skyward in *Frankenstein*. Robert's "enthusiasm which elevates me

81

to heaven" (10) resounds in Victor's admiration for scientists who "ascend into the heavens" (42) and his exultation at having "trod heaven in my thoughts" (209). Both men reflect Percy Shelley who insists, "I could not descend to common life" (*PSL* 1:228, 10 Jan. 1812). Shelley's *Queen Mab* contrasts "native" spirituality with "earthliness," our moribund physicality. The heroine Ianthe's spirit "reassumed / Its native dignity" when "Instinct with inexpressible beauty and grace, / Each stain of earthliness / Had passed away" (1:134–37). Even when transcendence is thwarted, Shelley insists upon the Erotic equation of native and celestial. "Woe had beaten to earth a mind [Wolfstein's in *St. Irvyne*] whose native and unconfined energies aspired to heaven" (*JS* 5:144).

For Mary Shelley, the native *is* the earthly. "Human affections are the native, luxuriant growth of a heart . . . seek[ing] objects on whom to expend its yearnings" (*Perkin Warbeck* 3:351). *Frankenstein* presents nature in the form of "the mighty Jura opposing its dark side to the ambition that would quit its native country" (190). Ambitious males are forced to recognize, if not to accede to, the priority of the native. Walton in the opening frame laments that, unlike the "merchant-man now on its homeward voyage," he who has aspired beyond mundane commerce "may not see my native land, perhaps, for many years" (16). Victor soon admits "how much happier that man is who believes his native town to be the world, than he who aspires to become greater than his nature will allow" (48).

With the sky/earth opposition reflecting conflicts between masculine and feminine forces in the psyche and between men and women in society, the opening frame of *Frankenstein* sets a woman in opposition to Promethean men. Margaret Saville has been seriously undervalued by critics. She is not just "an affectionate English lady who needs to be reassured that her brother is not in too much danger" (Kiely 167); still less is she a "faceless addressee" who has "no more existence in the novel than a postal address" (Brooks 220, 219). Mary Shelley makes Robert's correspondent a woman rather than a man—a father or brother or mentor—because gender qualifies for judgment in *Frankenstein*.

This wife-mother has a name appropriate to her moral authority. "Margaret" is a jewel, a "pearl" of great price. "Saville" suggests the native and communal through the French *"sa ville."* If Mary had not wanted this French connection, she would have used the traditional English spelling, Savile. Mary gives another excellent woman, Elizabeth in *Falkner*, the married name Neville. This tie to a husband echoes Saville, since *"né ville"* (birth town) is another way of saying "native," *sa ville.* By contrast, the maiden name of Lodore's intractable wife is Santerre. She is *"sans terre"* (landless), because she lives apart from her husband and child. Marriage, from *Frankenstein* to *Falkner,* is woman's native place.[3]

Together "Margaret" and "Saville" give to this native jewel the imprimatur of Mary Shelley's own initials, M. S. Moreover, since Mary affirms her Wollstonecraft heritage by using the middle initial "W," rather than the expectable "G," she is all the more associated with Margaret whose maiden name of Walton gives her too the middle initial "W." Why does Mrs. Mary W. Shelley omit the "W." from Mrs. Margaret Saville's name? For the same reason that Mary chooses the name Walton in the first place. "Walton" as "walled-town" suggests the isolation inevitable to Prometheans like Robert and Professor "Waldman." Only by leaving Robert's bachelor realm behind—without even the trace of a middle initial—can Margaret reach *Saville,* that native community which is the union of male with female and the ideal of Agape.

That *Frankenstein* opens with a man-woman relationship shows the priority of this bond for Mary Shelley. But the fact that the man seeks to bond with another man and the woman is already married presages the fate of complementarity and androgyny in the novel. Men and women war. Margaret as the embodiment of Mary's values cannot empathize with Promethean drives. And Robert knows it.

> Do you [Margaret] understand this feeling? . . .
> I cannot describe to you my sensations. . . . It
> is impossible to communicate to you a concep-
> tion of the trembling sensation. . . . You will
> smile at my allusion. . . . Will you laugh at the
> enthusiasm I express? (9, 15, 231, 24)

Man and woman disagree in the very first sentence of *Frankenstein*: ". . . an enterprise which you have regarded with such evil forebodings" (9). By phrasing it this way, Robert says more than that Margaret has foreseen trouble: "evil forebodings" indicates that foreseeing trouble seems evil, disloyal to him. He counterattacks in two characteristically male ways. "Will you laugh at the enthusiasm I express concerning this divine wanderer? If you do, you must have certainly lost that simplicity which was once your characteristic charm" (24). This is a threat. Adopting an independent viewpoint would cost Margaret one of True Woman's premier virtues. Simplicity, tractability, is convenient for men, as Percy Shelley knew when he listed among Harriet's "greatest charms" her "simplicity," and when he implicitly qualified his praise for Mary's "originality . . . of mind" by insisting upon her "simplicity" (*PSL* 1:337, 12 Dec. 1812; 1:414, 28 Oct. 1814). Walton's other response to Margaret is a herd reflex. Defending against her skepticism his (and Shelley's) pet belief that the poles are ice-free, Robert trusts male expertise over female intuition. "With your leave, my sister, I will put some trust in preceding navigators" (10). The men of course are wrong, and the woman right. Cold increases as *sa ville* recedes. At issue are differences as basic as gender itself: the sensible versus the fanciful viewpoint, the warm versus the cold heart, ultimately the earth-abiding versus the sky-aspiring ideal.

Mary Shelley strengthens Margaret Saville's case against polar pursuits by carefully manipulating our response to Walton's crewmen. We initially accept at face value the statement that his lieutenant is "a man of wonderful courage and enterprise. . . ." But the second half of the sentence complicates this judgment: ". . . he is madly desirous of glory" (14). Next is the master of the ship who frees his fiancée to marry her lover: " 'What a noble fellow!' you will exclaim. He is so . . .(15). But again the sentence continues: ". . . but then he has passed all his life on board a vessel, and has scarcely an idea beyond the rope and the shroud."

Lest she should seem to overstate Margaret's case against aspiring men, Mary includes in the opening frame a counterinstance of exemplary male conduct. The master, having recognized the futility of his courtship, "abandoned his pursuit" (14). Futile pursuits need not end disastrously, like those of Robert and Victor and Shelley, *if* the will to master-y is tempered by the feminine traits of adaptability and sympathy. That men and women can agree about such pursuits—that an androgynous union of masculine and feminine can occur in society as well as in the psyche—is also established here. Margaret's criticism of her brother's Promethean quest puts her in agreement with their father who on his deathbed forbade such pursuits to Robert (11).

I question therefore the critical consensus that there is an admirable bond between Robert and Margaret. When Knoepflmacher calls the two "complementary" (107), he is defining what they should be, but not what they are. Robert refuses to heed Margaret. He may say and even believe that "my best years [were] spent under your gentle and feminine fosterage" (230), but he has spent most of his years trying to get out from under conventional restraints and to soar up to his Promethean heaven. Robert and Margaret, man and woman, disagree fundamentally, because the males in *Frankenstein*, like the males in Mary Shelley's life, tend to bifurcation and solipsism rather than androgyny and complementarity.

*

Robert displays both the willfulness of the ego-centric Eros and the weakness of the Dionysiac.[4] Willfulness is stressed when Mary in 1831 gives Walton the Percy-like declamation, "what can stop the . . . resolved will of man?" (231). Mary may feel a twinge of admiration at towering ambition, but she feels toward Promethean pursuits nothing like the ambivalence that Percy does when he, having associated the Arctic with the inadequacies of presocial man in *Queen Mab* (7:145–51), nonetheless sympathizes deeply with Ahasuerus "goaded by never-ending restlessness to rove the globe from pole to pole" (*CP* 818). Mary is clear: will is regressive. Robert "commence[s] this laborious voyage with the joy a child feels when he embarks in a little boat" (10). The analogy with childhood implicates not only Percy's lifelong obsession with sailing little boats but also Victor's first pursuit of the monster: "I threw the door forcibly open, as children are accustomed to do when they expect a spectre to stand in waiting for them on the other side" (56). Of course "nothing appeared" (56), because Mary wants to establish how unrelated to adult reality, how indicative of childhood fantasy, the Promethean pursuit is. Robert admits that his polar journey is not an adult decision. "This expedition has been the favourite dream of my early years. . . . [now] my thoughts were turned into the channel of their earlier bent" (11).

For both Robert and Victor, the consequence of immature willfulness is isolation. Frankenstein's inwardness impresses Walton immediately. "When he has retired into himself, he will be like a celestial spirit, that has a halo around him, within whose circle no grief or folly ventures" (23). This impregnable circle is one of the Prometheans' most damning ties with Shelley, who confesses that "the truth is, that the seclusion of my habits has confined me so much within the circle of my own thoughts" (*PSL* 1:582, 16 Dec. 1817). Because of sources in Plotinus and Ptolemy, circles in Shelley's verse are complicated images which allow at times for integration.[5] But that those circles repeatedly indicate solipsism, the withdrawal into male egotism, is unquestionable. Like the Wandering Jew who "traced a circle on the plain" ("Ghasta" 142) or the witch in "The Wandering Jew" who "traced a circle on the floor" ("The Wandering

Jew" 4:275, in *Fraser's Magazine* 3 [1831]: 676), Percy can "retire" when problems, particularly domestic problems, threaten. His self-admonition of 1815—"never suffer more than one even to approach the hallowed circle" (*J* 20, 14 Oct. 1814)—does not say what the context seems to warrant, that Claire must be kept away so Mary can remain his solemate. Indeed only one woman is acknowledged, but her place is not *within* the magic circle. "Even to approach" is all that is vouchsafed her.

Mary reads the journal entry, of course, and with her first-hand experience of Percy, she understands his tendencies to exclusion. These she highlights in *Mathilda*, where she undercuts the description of Percy-Woodville which some critics take as purely laudatory: "railed and fenced in by his own divinity, so that naught but love and admiration could *approach* him" (55; my italics).[6] Mary's express-repress reflex credits the male with divinity, but then fences him in to indicate a personality restricted and restrictive, one that cannot reach out and can never be reached, only approached, like the Hebrew God. *Falkner* is even more explicit about male unapproachability. With "suspicion, and a fierce disdain of all who injured, which seemed to his morbid feelings all who named or approached him" (1:90), Falkner resembles both Victor, who "overwhelmed by disappointments . . . retired into himself" (23), and Shelley, whom "various ills . . . caus[ed] . . . to turn his eyes inward; inclining him rather to brood over the thoughts and emotions of his own soul than to glance abroad" (*CP* 30). Mary is thus anticipating Trelawny's contention that "Shelley had in perfection the power of closing his senses of hearing and seeing, and taking refuge within his own mind" (1:81).

In *Frankenstein*, the circle motif emphasizes the exclusion of woman as a basic response of willful males, who leave the warmth of the family circle and seek the cold of an Arctic circle which is really "the circle of my own thoughts." Besides using Percy's terms against him, Mary is appropriating to womankind his ideal of "the central warmth of love." To save the freezing Victor, the crew "placed him near the chimney of the kitchen-stove" (20). The hearth, center of the domestic circle and emblem of the wife-mother, provides the warmth needed by the isolated male, as Falkner will learn years later when his "cold, clammy hand was taken in hers [Elizabeth's], so soft and warm" (2:28). How perfectly the frozen wastes represent the fatal propensities of machismo is indicated by Freud: "Ice is in fact a symbol by antithesis for an erection: i.e. something that becomes hard in the cold instead of—like a penis—

86

in heat (in excitation). The two antithetical concepts of sexuality and death are frequently linked through the idea that death makes things stiff" (*The Psychopathology of Everyday Life, SE* 6:90n).

Isolating and immature, Promethean will involves ultimately a regressive belief in the *Übermenschen*. Walton seeks a land "ruled by different laws" (10). Shelley on this question vacillates. As aristocrat he maintains that "laws were not made for men of honor" (*PSL* 1:80, 9 May 1811), though as democrat he insists that "we have one human heart— / All mortal thoughts confess a common home" (*Islam* 3361–62). Mary does not vacillate. She repudiates the very notion of super*men* ("we are all human beings, all the children of one common mother" [*Valperga* 2:156]). And she allows aspiring males no new worlds to conquer. Robert, true to his name ("bright in fame"), fantasizes about "a land never before imprinted by the foot of man" (10), but no such land exists in *Frankenstein*. The tundra has already been imprinted by Victor and the monster before Robert arrives. The hostility that Mary feels here toward male pretentiousness surfaces later in *Frankenstein* when she gives to one of William Frankenstein's "little *wives*" the name "Biron" and the initials "L. B." (62). Reducing Lord Byron to manageable size ("little") and then castrating him (Louis*a*) allows Mary to fix the overreacher in several senses.

As prototype of the failed androgyne, Walton proves weak as well as willful. After an early dream of travel got him nowhere, he aspired to poetry. "You are well acquainted with my failure" (11). In his present impotence—"now I am twenty-eight, and am in reality more illiterate than many school-boys of fifteen" (14)—Robert sounds like Shelley.

> I [Robert] have no friend.
>
> (13)
>
> I [Percy] have no friend.
>
> (*PSL* 1:466)

This friend would function similarly for each man. Robert wants someone "to approve or amend my plans. . . . to regulate my mind" (13, 14); Shelley admonishes Godwin, "my advisor, the moderator of my enthusiasm," to "direct me" (*PSL* 1:229, 16 Jan. 1812; 1:266, 8 Mar. 1812). When Robert asks Margaret "to support my spirits" (15–16), he is the conventional beset male beseeching the ministering angel, but only at one level of the psyche. Robert is ultimately not complementary with Margaret because he, like Shelley (and Frankenstein), does not finally want any woman for his other, better half. The one "whose eyes would reply to mine" is "a man. . . . You may deem me romantic, my dear sister" (13).

Robert in his weakness seeks to replace the father who has opposed, like Sir Timothy Shelley, the exploits of a Promethean son. In complaining to Margaret that communication by letter is inadequate (13), Robert is in fact rejecting as inevitably mediated his intercourse with women (particularly with one who has sided with his father) and is espousing, however unconsciously, a direct communion with men. The very motion of his journey is away from the female and toward the male, away from Margaret and on to Peter (Petersburgh) and Michael (Archangel), away from *sa ville* and on to the ultimately phallic pole.

In the process, Robert sounds decidedly "feminine" in his perturbations. "My hopes fluctuate, and my spirits are often depressed" (12). What Robert desires from a man is what the weaker vessel traditionally receives from her husband. "Wiser and more experienced than myself," this male would "confirm and support me" (23) as the oak does the ivy. The homosexual overtones here are emphasized when Robert calls Victor "a man . . . I should have been happy to have possessed" (22). Homosexuality is also a component of Victor's pursuit of the monster and of Shelley's intense relationships with various men.[7] Percy, Victor, and Robert would all be healthier, however, if homosexual union were their real goal. It would at least establish their ability to relate deeply to someone. But for Robert, Victor, and Percy, the primary significance of the male bond is narcissistic. A man can reflect each of them better than a woman can. Male love is thus one stage closer to the self-embrace which is the true goal of Prometheans and the chief reason, as we will see soon, for Frankenstein's creation of the monster.

*

Walton's split into willful and weak extremes is recapitulated in Victor Frankenstein. Despite his considerable androgynous potential, Victor resembles Percy Shelley in both his willfulness (he too goes on until stopped by premature death) and in his weakness (he too cannot accept unequivocal responsibility for the ensuing chaos). Victor is, moreover, foreshadowed by Robert in a second important way. Frankenstein too undergoes role reversal. His career, like Walton's, is marked by initial movement away from a woman, Elizabeth, and on to "a true friend" (45), the "remarkably erect" Waldman (42). In his subsequent tribulations, Victor like Robert needs to be "supported" (175). He finds a "nurse" during sickness and an "angel" during perils, but both figures are male, Henry and Alphonse (57, 178). Going to the north pole in unconscious quest of the male friend whom he has ever craved, Walton acts out what we come to see is a basic response of Victor Frankenstein. When the split between masculine and feminine halves of the psyche becomes dire enough to prevent a man from bonding with his complementary woman, he turns toward men and undergoes a role reversal which effeminates him. Educated by Walton, we are prepared for the more intricate process of Victor's psyche. The relationships

feminine .. *Robert Walton* .. *Frankenstein*
masculine .. Frankenstein .. Prof. Waldman

presage the later relations

feminine .. *Frankenstein* .. *Wolfstein* (in Shelley's .. *Walton*
masculine .. Monster .. Ginotti *St. Irvyne*) .. Monster

Victor can immediately recognize his bond with Robert ("you seek for knowledge and wisdom, as I once did" [24]), but he cannot, characteristically, evaluate the bond. We readers must. When Walton expresses the aspirations and uncertainty of all Protheans—"do I not deserve to accomplish some great purpose" (12)—Mary Shelley is asking us to question the just deserts, the moral worth, of the modern Prometheus. *We* must do it because, as she has Walton admit in 1831, "there is something at work in my soul, which I do not understand" (231).

VICTOR AND THE MONSTER

"The relation of the Monster to Frankenstein is constantly shifting and this raises an enormous critical problem because any discussion will run the risk of falsely stabilizing the connection between the two" (Seed 333). The surest proof of this "shifting" quality is the number of different critical interpretations of the monster.[8] A critic today must seek not the false stability of any totalizing explanation but the legitimate coherence of a reading consistent with itself, a reading which consciously recognizes its partial quality as it follows a single thread or threads through the whole fabric. Victor's parthenogenetic creation of the monster can be seen as, among other things, an emblem and consequence of psychic bifurcation. Will informs the procreative urge. Victor determines to surpass his father, and indeed all men, as progenitor. "No father could claim the grati-

89

tude of his child so completely as I should deserve theirs" (49). As ejaculatory Prometheus, Victor "at the summit of my desires" enjoys "the most gratifying consummation. . . . pour[ing] a torrent of light into our dark world" (47, 49). Such presumption proves costly, however. The physical weakness which increases with Victor's labors—"my person had become emaciated. . . . my voice became broken" (49, 51)—has a decidedly sexual aspect. "My candle was nearly burnt out" (52). After the creation, "I was lifeless" (57). The consequence of will is impotence.

With his Percy-like emaciation and broken voice, Victor becomes Mary's first version of the "frail" male who recurs throughout her husband's work. How differently the Shelleys view this "blighted . . . withered" figure is evident in their attitudes toward the cause of his "blasted" condition. Percy finds indomitably heroic the blasted Ahasuerus. "Even as a giant oak . . . scathed . . . A monument of fadeless ruin," Ahasuerus stands "like the scathèd pine tree's height . . . majestic even in death" (*Queen Mab* 7:259–61; "Fragment from the Wandering Jew" 2, 9). Shelley can, moreover, reward the blasted sufferer with new life.

> . . . slowly from his [Lionel's] mien there passed
> The desolation which it spoke;
> . . . as when the lightning's blast
> Has parched some heaven-delighting oak,
> The next spring shows leaves pale and rare,
> But like flowers delicate and fair . . .
> (*Rosalind and Helen* 785–90)

Though Mary admires the passive determination to resist a cruel fate, her subject in *Frankenstein* is the active will to godhead. She blasts sky-aspirers. After lightning reduces the Ahasuerus-like oak to a "blasted stump" (35), other forces of nature blast the parthenogenetic Promethean. "I [Victor] am a blasted tree. . . . blasted and miserable" (158, 187). There is no Shelleyan aura of indomitable manliness here, let alone any flowering delicate and fair.

The gender-role reversal implicit in Victor's statement that "the bolt has entered my soul" (158) and in the monster's threat that "the bolt will . . . ravish from you your happiness" (165) has in fact occurred already. During his emaciating labors on the creature, Frankenstein "became as timid as a love-sick girl" (51). He is not just castrated, he is made feminine. Or rather, effeminate. The truly feminine would be strengthened by the masculine presence, whereas bifurcation has so thoroughly isolated female from male in Victor that effeminacy is inevitable. He is love*sick*.

Parthenogenesis thus means more than creation from the self, it means creation of a self. To signal that a new creator as well as a new creature is emerging, Mary's language operates on two levels. Frankenstein in the laboratory longs for the time "when my creation should be complete" (52); later he defines the monster's awakening as the moment from which "I dated my creation" (72). Victor moves from male toward female during the creative act because the creature is absorbing his masculinity. Once alive, the creature is the expression of Victor's male self, the ego-centric Eros, as Victor is now the Dionysiac. The creature as male self is now both killer and lover. The killer expresses, as we will see in chapter 4, the antisocial aspect of Eros, which "despised man and recked so little of his personal worth that it would willingly dissolve him" (D'Arcy 39). Now we must focus on the *psychic* role of Eros and examine the amatory, as opposed to the homicidal, aspect of the monster's relationship with Victor. "Burning with love of his own body, he prays to escape from it in order to possess it; but death brings only the ironic retribution of transformation." What Kahn says here of Shakespeare's Adonis (32) is true of Erotic narcissists throughout nineteenth- and twentieth-century literature. Frankenstein desires himself because, as we shall see in detail in chapter 5, he imagines that through self-embrace and consequent self-generation he can achieve immortality.

His love object, a creature emphatically male in gender and prowess, displays physical features conventional with the ravisher. "His hair was of a lustrous black, and flowing; his teeth of a pearly whiteness" (52). The monster's first conscious act is straight out of seduction stories. He enters the sleeper's chamber, draws aside the bed curtains, and, with a smile and murmured words, reaches out his hand. Horrified into the conventional flight, the sleeper reacts revealingly: "Sometimes my pulse beat so quickly and hardly, that I felt the palpitation of every artery; at others, I nearly sank to the ground through languor and extreme weakness" (54). By attributing to a male the "palpitation" and "languor" traditional with female passion and its aftermath, Mary Shelley is suggesting a complex reversal of roles. As the monster bodies forth Victor's male self, Frankenstein becomes the effeminate beloved who like "a love-sick girl" awaits the ravishing bolt. Victor is thus strikingly similar to Freud's Dr. Schreber, whose desire to produce a new race of beings required him, so he thought, to become female ("Psychoanalytic Notes upon an Autobiographical Account of a Case of Paranoia [Dementia Para-noides]," *SE* 12:9–82). A particularly intriguing link with Shelley surfaces in Schreber's belief that he was destined to be the *"Eternal Jew."* "The Eternal Jew (in the sense described) had to be unmanned (transformed into a woman) to be able to bear children" (Chabot 15). O'Flaherty describes how in various myths the dismembered male is reassembled as female (294), and how the man transformed into woman becomes impotent (307). She even describes a male who, having bifurcated himself, attempts to make love to his female half (312). The god-aspiring aspect of self-copulation is traced by Singer from ancient Egyptian creation stories, through Christianity, and on to the Romantic period with William Blake (121–22).

My argument for role reversal in *Frankenstein* must address a basic objection to seeing Victor as the feminine, Dionysiac Eros. Why would Mary make him the effeminate half of the riven psyche when she could have dramatized self-projection more conven-tionally in terms of Pygmalion? Victor is male, so why not have him create a female? Mary patterns her narrative not upon Pygmalion but upon Percy. Shelley's narratives in both prose and verse feature obsessively the self-divided male pursuing himself. While these tales of self-division and self-pursuit make obvious the male's effeminization, they leave problematic Shelley's attitude toward it. In *St. Irvyne*, for example, Wolfstein, like Frankenstein, leaves his woman and pursues a huge male figure, "the gigantic form of Ginot-ti, who stalked onwards majestically. . . . a feeling of desperation urged Wolfstein onwards; he resolved to follow Ginotti, even to the extremity of the universe" (*JS* 5:140). As in *Frankenstein*, the ex-tremity-directed pursuit is ultimately psychic.

> He [Wolfstein] sighed deeply when he reflected on the terrible connexion, dreadful though mysterious, which subsisted between himself and Ginotti. His soul sank within him at the idea of his own littleness, when a fellow mortal might be able to gain so strong, though sight-less, an empire over him. (*JS* 5:141)

Like Frankenstein, whose recurrent professions of bafflement indi-cate limited self-knowledge, Wolfstein shows with the words "mys-terious" and "sightless" that he cannot perceive the nature of his relationship with Ginotti. We see that Ginotti as a "power I feel within myself" (*JS* 5:141) is the projected male half of Wolfstein, the now dominant force controlling the once active protagonist.

Just as Frankenstein learns that every move of his polar pursuit is scrutinized by the monster, Wolfstein knows that Ginotti "watches my every action" (*JS* 5:141). As the monster in fact orchestrates Victor's pursuit, Ginotti boasts that "every event in your life has . . . occurred under my particular machinations" (*JS* 5:170). In the process, Wolfstein like Frankenstein experiences emasculation ("his own littleness") and becomes effeminate:

> "Oh! do with me what thou wilt, strange, inex-
> plicable being!—Do with me what thou wilt!"
> exclaimed Wolfstein, as an ecstasy of frenzied
> terror overpowered his astonished senses. . . .
> In a voice which was fascination itself, the
> being [Ginotti] addressed me, saying, "Wilt
> thou come with me? wilt thou be mine?" I felt
> a decided wish never to be his. . . . My neck
> was grasped firmly. . . . "Yes, yes, I am thine."
> (*JS* 5:166, 183–84)

The emergence of the feminine in *St. Irvyne* involves more than giving to the protagonist lines conventional with women. Wolfstein's relation with Ginotti is duplicated in his sister Eloise's relationship with Ginotti (in the role of "Nempere"). Eloise too finds Ginotti-Nempere "gigantic" (*JS* 5:174). As Wolfstein succumbed to the "empire" of Ginotti "within" him, Eloise recognizes "the resist-/ less empire which he possessed within her" (*JS* 5:175). Such verbal echoes equate Eloise with the effeminate Wolfstein and thus emphasize how consistently feminine the perspective is in *St. Irvyne*. Shelley's inclination toward passivity is embodied in the very point of view adopted in his early fiction. Passive characters watch enthralled with or paralyzed by the oncoming aggressors whom they cannot escape: Wolfstein-Eloise with Ginotti-Nempere, and Verezzi-Julia with Zastrozzi-Matilda in *Zastrozzi*. However aggressive Percy is at times, his passive, feminine element is so evident that Mary knew in *Frankenstein* to make the passive figure *Victor* rather than the monster.

Shelley's empathy with the feminine in his life and art is clear enough,[9] but the meaning of role reversal in *St. Irvyne* is not. What does self-division signify here? Granted that it reflects the terrible antagonism of Agape and Eros in Shelley: to what extent does his sympathy with Wolfstein affect his judgment upon, and our response to, male self-pursuit?

Unable to answer this question with the inchoate novel of Shelley's adolescence, we can move on six years and ask it again of a poem which, though not without difficulties, defines more clearly the sexual sources of self-division and self-pursuit. *Alastor* is *Frankenstein* in miniature. Critics have often linked Victor to Shelley's self-description early in the poem ("I have made my bed / In charnels and on coffins. . . . Like an inspired and desperate alchymist / Staking his very life on some dark hope" [23–24, 31–32]), but much more is involved. Percy's Poet-protagonist, like Mary's scientist-protagonist, leaves behind a loving woman and confronts a self-projection. "Her voice was like the voice of his own soul" (153). Victor's revulsion at parthenogenesis is paralleled by the Poet's trauma at autoeroticism. Confronted with the dream woman's "parted lips . . . panting bosom," the Poet "reared his shuddering limbs and quelled / His gasping breath" (179, 182–84). The subsequent orgasm ("dissolving" [187]) is traumatic.[10] "His strong heart sunk and sickened with excess / Of love. . . . blackness veiled his dizzy eyes, and night / Involved and swallowed up the vision" (181–82, 188–89). Can this be what Holmes calls it, sexuality "celebrated and indulged" (305)? That the "sickened with excess" clause ends with "of love" does not make love an operative, redemptive force here. Too little and too late, "love" remains an afterthought which we experience as an attempt to defuse the real drama. We have this experience again when "spread his arms to meet / Her panting bosom" appears after we have already seen the protagonist's limbs "shuddering."

Autoeroticism in *Alastor* has the same consequences as parthenogenesis in *Frankenstein*, physically and psychologically. As Victor becomes physically "emaciated" and impotent (49, 51), the Poet's "limbs were lean. . . . his listless hand / Hung like dead bone within its withered skin" (248, 250–51). What apparently distinguishes the two protagonists psychologically—that the Poet seems to pursue his *female* half—is in fact their paramount similarity. Awakening after his first orgasm into a new world ("The cold white light of morning . . . / Spread round him where he stood. Whither have fled / The hues of heaven that canopied his bower / Of yesternight?" [193, 196–98]), the Poet is in fact a new being. An adult caught now in the coils of passion, he like "an eagle grasped / In folds of the green serpent, feels her breast . . . " (227–28). Especially since the Poet was earlier grasped in the arms of the dream-beloved (187), we assume that the eagle grasped by the Lamia-like serpent is feeling "her" breast, the serpent's breast. We assume, in other words, that the eagle and thus the Poet is masculine like the eagle embraced by the serpent in Shelley's source, Ovid's tale of Hermaphroditus. But the *Alastor* clause ends, " . . . feels her breast / Burn with the poison." *Her* breast is that of the eagle-Poet, who is penetrated by the now phallic beloved. The Poet, like Victor Frankenstein, has been made female by sexual experience, and sets forth in pursuit of his male half.

The outcome of the pursuit is identical in *Alastor* and *Franken-stein*. Poet, like scientist, remains locked within himself. During "daylight . . . the Poet kept mute conference / With his soul" (223–24); afterwards "A Spirit seemed / To stand beside him. . . . as if he and it / Were all that was" (479–80, 487–88). The *Alastor* landscape indicates the Poet's narcissism no less than the Arctic wastes reflect Victor's self-obsession. "Yellow flowers / For ever gaze on their own drooping eyes, / Reflected in. . . . a well. . . . Hither the Poet came. His eyes beheld / Their own wan light" (406–8, 457, 469–70). Death awaits the Poet as inevitably as it does Victor. Both men eulogize home, but neither really prefers domesticity to his fatal pursuit of self.

What all this means is clearer in *Alastor* than in *St. Irvyne*. Shelley's preface to the poem includes a sentence criticizing "the Poet's self-centred seclusion [which] was avenged by the furies of an irresistible passion pursuing him to speedy ruin" (15). I say clearer because this one sentence of criticism does not make the preface or the poem clear, as the half century of controversy over *Alastor* attests.[11] The very fact that serious readers disagree whether the critical sentence is consistent with the rest of the preface and with the poem reflects deep division within Shelley himself. Agape again wars with Eros.

In the preface, the Percy of Agape who shares Mary's belief in sympathetic communion and thus criticizes the Poet for abandoning the Arab Maid is countered by the Erotic Percy who empathizes intensely with a Poet very much like himself (emaciated, balding, vegetarian, with "lofty hopes of divine liberty" [159], questing after "knowledge and truth and virtue" [158]). The result of Shelley's self-division is that the preface is self-contradictory, its critical sentence being the one unqualifiedly negative note in an otherwise fierce paean.

> The picture is not barren of instruction to ac-
> tual men. The Poet's self-centred seclusion
> was avenged by the furies of an irresistible
> passion pursuing him to speedy ruin. But that
> Power which strikes the luminaries of the
> world with sudden darkness and extinction,
> by awakening them to too exquisite a percep-

tion of its influences, dooms to a slow and poisonous decay those meaner spirits that dare to abjure its dominion. Their destiny is more abject and inglorious as their delinquency is more contemptible and pernicious. They who, deluded by no generous error, instigated by no sacred thirst of doubtful knowledge, duped by no illustrious superstition, loving nothing on this earth, and cherishing no hopes beyond, yet keep aloof from sympathies with their kind, rejoicing neither in human joy nor mourning with human grief; these, and such as they, have their apportioned curse. . . . They are morally dead. They are neither friends, nor lovers, nor fathers, nor citizens of the world, nor benefactors of their country. Among those who attempt to exist without human sympathy, the pure and tender-hearted perish through the intensity and passion of their search after its communities, when the vacancy of their spirit suddenly makes itself felt. All else, selfish, blind, and torpid, are those unforeseeing multitudes who constitute, together with their own, the lasting misery and loneliness of the world. Those who love not their fellow-beings live unfruitful lives, and prepare for their old age a miserable grave.

'The good die first,
And those whose hearts are dry as summer dust,
Burn to the socket!'

(CP 15)

The critical Shelley of Agape insists sincerely upon "error" and "superstition," but the persistence of readers' confusion is understandable. The Erotic Shelley counters the critical nouns with laudatory adjectives, "generous" and "illustrious." Moreover, "generous" takes back the very criticism made of the Poet. "Generous" (genus, generis, race, kind, family) posits that bond with humankind which the Poet's self-centered seclusion sunders. Just ask the Arab Maid whether his error is generous.

The Erotic Shelley also counters the critical thrust of the preface by deflecting it. Most of the paragraph is directed against solipsists *un*like the poet who are too "selfish, blind, and torpid" to ever "search after . . . communities." Yet not one solipsist, let alone an "unfeeling multitude" of them, ever appears in *Alastor*. And communities appear only in the "alienated home" (76) of the Poet and in the cities abandoned by him (108–12). The poem thus denies us any experience of the two factors which justify the preface's praise for the protagonist. Since we do not experience his superiority to the multitudinous solipsists, we find inordinate the preface's extensive castigation of them. And where in the poem does the Poet actually seek after communities?

What seems slightly hysterical in the preface—Shelley's fierce castigation of the unfeeling multitude and his ardent espousal of the deep-feeling Poet—enters *Alastor* itself after the protagonist dies. Praise for him is rapturous ("ah! Thou hast fled! / The brave, the gentle, and the beautiful, / The child of grace and genius" [688–90]) and contempt for the multitude is intense ("many worms / And beasts and men live on" [691–92]). Neither emotion, however, seems warranted by our experience of a poem where the protagonist is at best flawed and the world is almost entirely absent.

Frankenstein too is about an egotist who escapes into solitude (his laboratory) in order to return to the community (as benefactor). He dies, as in *Alastor*, without achieving his goal, because both tales portray "self-centred seclusion . . . avenged by the furies of an irresistable passion." The difference between the tales is that Mary's single-minded response to male self-division provides her novel with a unity of moral and aesthetic effect which is denied to Percy's self-divided poem. Mary forgoes the convenience of castigating the multitude and portrays movingly the community absent from *Alastor*. Unlike the Percy who loves his protagonist's self-love, Mary hates the self-absorption of men who abandon adoring women. *Frankenstein* is *Alastor* rewritten by the Arab Maid.

The anger felt by Mary Shelley as Arab Maid explains why she insists upon making Frankenstein's psychic projection male, not female. Destruction is both the consequence of such projection and the function of the projected self. To make this self female would be to subscribe to a long tradition which sees woman as lethal and which represents this lethality in the figure of the femme fatale. Though Mary Shelley recognizes destructive capacities in herself and in other women (as we shall see in chapter 6), she insists that the principal source of domestic and social ruin is male. Men reject complementarity for self-projection, domesticity for self-indulgence, marriage for self-union. The monster is masculine because chaos is.

97

Alastor helps Mary see not only the troubled psyche of Percy Shelley but also his inability to face those troubles squarely. He can present the Poet as failed androgyne—a male too restless to settle down yet too weak to quest successfully—but he cannot resist an overbalancing sense of his self-portrait's superiority. He can reveal the psyche bifurcated, with the feminine preponderant, but he will not indict self-pursuit decisively. Such self-deception is highlighted in *Frankenstein* by an allusion first noted by Leonard Wolf (25). Victor describes the monster as "one who fled from me" (21).

> They flee from me, that sometime did me
> seek,
> With naked foot stalking in my chamber.

Sir Thomas Wyatt's great love poem is parodied by Victor's situation. The monster first seeks Frankenstein in his bedchamber (presumably on naked feet, since where would the creature have gotten shoes large enough?), and then flees from his bedchamber on the wedding night. Genders are ludicrously reversed as the male monster replaces Wyatt's beloveds. Parody emphasizes the amatory nature of Victor's pursuit of the male, even as it provides a standard for criticizing his inversion of conventional roles.

Mary's parody reflects Frankenstein's own grotesque parody of complementarity. Instead of uniting with Elizabeth, Victor substitutes for her. He projects his male element outward in the monster, allows the female to become dominant in himself, and spends the rest of the novel seeking to make love to his self. What Victor has done, in effect, is to create not an androgyne but a hermaphrodite. "The hermaphrodite is an earthly and physical parody of that [androgynous] state" (Hoeveler 81). Traditionally the hermaphrodite unites in one body the genitals of the two genders, which is not the case with Victor's monster. But Victor's hermaphrodite is not the monster: it is the monster and himself as unnatural male-female. The difference between this "hermaphrodite" and a traditional one, the separation of masculine and feminine into two figures, captures better than any single figure the true essence of hermaphroditism. "In the hermaphrodite the sexual separation is exaggerated . . . two separated parts, instead of their union, their fusion, in the androgyne."[12] Hoeveler shows that for Blake "the hermaphroditic self has existed [only] since the fall, since the separation of male and female" (84). As a blasphemous parody of the Incarnation (not the divine descending to redeem the flesh, but flesh aspiring to divinity), "the hermaphrodite . . . symbolizes the attempts by the anti-christ figures of Satan, Rahab, and Tirzah to form a substitute androgyne" (Hoeveler 98).

Whether or not Mary Shelley comprehended Blake, she could find blasphemous parody in a more immediate source, *Paradise Lost.* Satan couples with Sin to produce Death. Particularly since Sin is a self-projection of Satan, his self-congress consititutes in effect both Victor's dream of immortality and Milton's parody of her-maphroditism as narcissistic self-union. The Satan-Sin coupling is Eros for Milton, and is contrasted by him with what follows in *Paradise Lost*—the Agape of the Son's love for the Father and mar-riage to the Church. As reader of Milton and as orthodox Christian, Mary Shelley believes that the only way for flesh to reunite with spirit is for parents to bring forth immortal souls in their children. Victor has this opportunity with Elizabeth, but instead pursues the satanic alternative of desiring his monster-self. Hermaphroditism is the true expression of Eros, as adrogyny is of Agape.

COMPLEMENTARITY OR SELF-SUFFICIENCY

The hermaphrodite is important for our understanding of the psyche in *Frankenstein* because it implicates Percy's alternative to Mary's ideals of androgyny and complementarity. Shelley, as we have seen, rejects complementarity. The alternative which he proposes at his best is a feminist equality which partakes of Agape because it as-sures the otherness of the beloved. "The doctrine of sympathy im-plied the dissolution of sex roles . . . [and thus provided] a psycho-logical alternative to the traditional polarization of the sexes into separate spheres and complementary identities. . . . love goes wrong only when couples are joined as opposites" (Brown 3, 221). We have seen, however, that Eros leads Shelley repeatedly to deny woman's equality by occluding her otherness. Particularly with the ego-cen-tric Eros in ascendancy, Shelley sees the beloved as projection—which makes the male both lover and beloved, and thus self-sufficient.

Self-sufficient is just what the hermaphrodite aspires to be. "Rec-ogniz[ing] that it was the concept of an all-sufficient self that was the most serious threat to reintegration," Blake shows his radical antagonism to institutional Christianity by choosing the Virgin Mary as emblem for the "type of hermaphrodite who claims sexual self-sufficiency" (Hoeveler 85, 90–91). Sexual self-sufficiency is also what the Erotic Shelley aspires to. It prompts his railings against gender distinctions ("I almost wish that Southey had not made the glendoveer a male—these detestable distinctions will surely be abolished in a future state of being" [PSL 1:195, 26 Nov. 1811]). And it prompts him to create his own emblem of self-sufficiency, the "sexless bee" of The Witch of Atlas. Is this bee a hermaphrodite in Blake's pejorative sense of the term, or a version of the true asexuality which Blake espoused? Is Shelley's Witch as sexless bee distinct from the hermaphrodite which she creates, or is the hermaphrodite a projection of herself? And in either case, how does Shelley mean us to react to the hermaphrodite? Such questions about The Witch have vexed scholars for decades. Readers of Frankenstein may more profitably focus on Mary's response to the sexless bee.

Her distaste for The Witch has always seemed to me inordinate. "This poem is peculiarly characteristic of his [Percy's] tastes . . . discarding human interest and passion, to revel in the fantastic ideas that his imagination suggested" (CP 388). I now believe that what Mary actually hates is the ideal of self-sufficiency and the whole notion of self-projection which the sexless bee emblemizes. She senses in The Witch of Atlas (1820) another of Percy's responses to Frankenstein. Unlike the Shelley figure Victor Frankenstein, who creates a monstrous hermaphrodite out of fire and clay, Percy's benign Witch creates a harmless hermaphrodite out of "fire and snow" (321). The Witch asserts Shelley's purity and feminine creativity in the face of Mary's indictment of him as Promethean monster-botcher. Mary then counterattacks. Her later fiction targets self-projection, self-sufficiency, and the bee emblem in ways which illuminate retrospectively her initial indictment of hermaphroditism in Frankenstein.

Where Mary seems closest to characterizing woman as a projection of the male is where her divergence from Percy is most emphatic.

> Richard [Perkin Warbeck] had found in Lady Katherine a magic mirror, which gave him back himself arrayed with a thousand alien virtues. (Perkin Warbeck 2:236)

The key here is "alien." Lady Katherine is very different from Perkin: as a fiery Scot raised at her baronial father's court, she is anything but a mere reflection or projection of the gentle Perkin raised in Flemish poverty. Katherine in most conventional fashion can achieve the status of good wife only by being other, by remaining integral, because only then can she contribute the thousand virtues which are "alien" to her man and native to herself.

The complementary oneness which Perkin achieves with Katherine is denied to Falkner after his egotism causes Alithea's death and his subsequent "agony . . . thenceforth she was not to be the half of his existence, as he had hoped" (2:234). Wild Falkner lacks that better half which derives its force precisely from not being a self-projection, but from being located far enough outside the man to guide him morally. "The better part of yourself will, when she speaks, appear to leap out, as if, for the first time, it found its other half" (2:211). Mary can, like Percy, imagine a better self within the flawed male, but she relates that self to the beloved very differently. For Percy, the beloved is excellent in proportion as she is not other. For Mary, the individual's better half is still only half; it needs the better half of another. Only together are two better halves good enough.

However much Mary in the fiercest throes of the Shelley legend may eulogize her marriage, she knows in her heart that Percy never found her complementary. He, like his look-alike Adrian, "seemed destined not to find the half of himself, which was to complete his happiness" (*The Last Man* 65). Why? As Mary sees it, Percy never accepted her ideal of complementarity. Medwin concurs in effect when he describes Shelley in terms of the antitype ideal: "he thirst-ed after his likeness—and he found it not" (139). Adrian, who like Shelley drowns without finding his better half, speaks for Percy and Victor and all too many men, in Mary's view—"I have consorted long with grief, entered the gloomy labyrinth of madness, and emerged, but half alive" (54). When Mary Godwin eloped with young Percy Shelley, she had in mind a different type of "consort." Her growing recognition of the Promethean as a man only "half alive" may be what prompts her to have Frankenstein admit in 1831, "we are unfashioned creatures, but half made up" (232).

Mary is thus striking back at a pretense to self-sufficiency which characterizes males throughout the Romantic period. Emerson contends that "a highly endowed man with good intellect and good conscience is a Man-woman and does not so much need the comple-ment of woman to his being as another" (*Journals*, June 14, 1842). This Shelleyan view is opposed by Melville—"self-reciprocally effi-cient hermaphrodites being but a fable" (*Pierre* 259). Shelley de-lights in his fable of the "sexless bee" because his hermaphrodite means an escape from the impossible tensions of the corporeal, a benign castration. Mary hates the bee because she sees complemen-tarity as the ultimate androgyny, the complete intercourse. Again using Percy against himself, Mary takes up the bee emblem and re-verses its significance. "Bee-like" are the newly wedded Ethel and

Villiers in *Lodore* who "sipped the honey of life, and, never cloyed, fed perpetually on sweets" (2:188). Instead of the ultimately neutering dream of sexless bee, Mary very conventionally defines emotional *and* physical intercourse as the proper mode for the Promethean. "He [Castruccio] forgot ambition, and the dreams of princely magnificence. . . . and seemed to bury himself, as a bee in the fragrant circle of a rose, in the softest and most humane emotions" (*Valperga* 1:121).

II

Other

L'homme et la femme, voilà,
l'individual social.

St. Simon

He rejoices in man's lovely
peculiar power to choose life and die—
Robert Lowell

4

The Divided Self and Woman

One evening, during the access of his [Shelley's] fan-
cied disorder [elephantiasis], when many young
ladies were standing up for a country dance, he
caused wonderful consternation among those
charming creatures by walking slowly along the row
of girls and curiously surveying them, placing his
eyes close to their necks and bosoms, and feeling
their breasts and bare arms, in order to ascertain
whether any of the fair ones had taken the horrible
disease.

Jefferson Hogg

In another test, Gacy was shown a picture of a half-
clothed woman lying on a bed as a man stands near a
window, squinting at the light coming in. Eliseo said
most people describe the picture as a man rising to
go to work in the morning, but Gacy responded to it
by saying: "He might have had sex with her. He may
have killed her. But it's too late . . . " Gacy then
broke off and laughed inappropriately, Eliseo said.

UPI

With us the susceptible imagination of the mother
seems to express itself only in monsters.

Winckelmann

UNLIKE THE KARLOFF FILM OF *Frankenstein*, MARY SHELLEY'S NOVEL
disposes of the creation of the monster relatively quickly and devotes most of its attention to the social consequences of psychic
bifurcation. "[Eros] despised man and recked so little of his personal
worth that it would willingly dissolve him" (D'Arcy 39). The basic
Erotic logic—body is worthless and soul alone valuable, therefore
immortality is everything and mortals nothing—is interpreted by

Victor Frankenstein causally. Mortals must be dispensed with *in order for* him to achieve immortality. Victor envisions immortality as wholeness, as that reuniting of riven traits which can occur only after everyone is destroyed who threatens self-union by offering alternative unions. Since both women and men offer such alternatives, Frankenstein kills both. Why the paramount male, Victor's father Alphonse, dies *after* the principal female, Elizabeth, is the concluding move in Frankenstein's mad logic, and is best understood in light of his reactions to Elizabeth. His initial characterization of her dramatizes both the war of Agape with Eros and the resemblance between Frankenstein and Percy Shelley as Erotic assassins. Victor then kills Elizabeth twice—figuratively in the nightmare, literally on the wedding night.

VICTOR'S ELIZABETH

The Erotic hatred of marriage expressed in Shelley's "ineffable sickening disgust" at wedding Harriet is also at work when Victor views marriage to Elizabeth with "horror and dismay" (149). Revulsion as extreme as Victor's is not accounted for by his rationalization that he had promised to create the monstress first. What he is actually reacting against is suggested when he goes on to ask, "Could I enter into a festival with this deadly weight yet hanging round my neck?" Wolf concludes that "this allusion is not surprising. Coleridge's *Ancient Mariner* [sic] tells his story to a wedding guest who learns from it the higher dimensions of love" (222). But surely this is not how the allusion works in *Frankenstein*. Victor as potential bridegroom links himself through the allusion not to Coleridge's bridegroom or even to the wedding guest, but to the man with the deadly weight hanging round his neck, the Mariner himself. The permanence of Victor's alienation, of his irrevocably unsocial nature, is what the allusion establishes. Like the Mariner, Frankenstein can never be a bridegroom.

Victor's revulsion at marrying Elizabeth is particularly striking because his initial characterization of her seems to pay homage to True Womanhood. "Her figure . . . light and airy . . . though capable of enduring great fatigue" (30) combines the properly virginal absence of voluptuousness and the hardiness essential for dutiful labors. When these labors are required after Caroline's death, Elizabeth is ready for the wife-mother role. "Her mind had acquired new firmness and vigour. . . . she was continually endeavouring to contribute to the happiness of others, entirely forgetful of herself" (38–39). Soon Elizabeth can replace Margaret Saville as spokesperson for the "native" ideal. "Be calm, my dear Victor. . . . We surely shall be happy: quiet in our native country" (89). Elizabeth thus constitutes Victor's complement in an ideal androgyny.

> Although there was a great dissimilitude in our characters, there was an harmony in that very dissimilitude. I was more calm and philosophical than my companion; yet my temper was not so yielding. My application was of longer endurance; but it was not so severe whilst it endured. I delighted in investigating the facts relative to the actual world; she busied herself in following the aerial creations of the poets. (30)

That such an appreciation of complementarity, such a commitment to Agape, can coexist in Prometheans with a misogyny characteristic of the ego-centric Eros is manifest in Percy Shelley. His moments of courtly love and of feminist egalitarianism do not prevent recurrent revulsion at woman.

> A young lady never looks so like an angel, I [Hogg] observed to Bysshe, as when she is handing one a large cup of good strong tea. "Oh! you wretch," he exclaimed; "what a horridly sensual idea!" (2:529)

The icon of the lady at the tea urn is one of the culture's hallowed ways of reconciling spirit and flesh in woman. Half a century after Hogg's celebration of it, M. E. Braddon indicates that the icon has retained its cultural authority. "At the tea table women are most fairy-like, most feminine" (*Lady Audley's Secret* 139). To this day in Britain, the serving of tea is often preceded by the question "Who will be mother?" or "Shall I be mother?" Two apparently irreconcilable demands, that woman satisfy various appetites and that she remain pure, are met here by a sensuous bounty benignly maternal in its nurturing amplitude. Though Shelley is capable of accepting and even celebrating this compromise, he can also resist the very association of spirit and flesh, of "angel" and "sensual," as he does in his reply to Hogg here.

Other remarks by Shelley show that the Erotic dichotomy between spirit and flesh makes woman herself seem like a horridly sensual idea. Shelley applies to her his general Erotic view of humans as mere beasts ("apes asses geese") and, forgoing the "antique courtesy" of courtly love, let alone the feminist recognition of integral otherness, he reduces to animal physicality the women whom he finds inadequate spiritually. Harriet Westbrook's domineering sister Eliza is a "beastly viper. . . . a blind and loathsome worm" (*PSL* 1:520, 16 Dec. 1816; 384, 16 Mar. 1814). Elizabeth Hitchener, whom Shelley initially deified as "the sister of my soul," becomes an "ugly, hermaphroditical beast of a woman" (*PSL* 1:336, 3 Dec. 1812). Then there are the hoggish women of the journal and *Swellfoot*, and the chimera from *The Witch of Atlas*, "dog-headed, bosom-eyed, and bird-footed" (11:136). Shelley intends playfulness when he says, "I continue vegetable. Harriet means to be slightly animal until the arrival of Spring" (*PSL* 1:347, 27 Dec. 1812), but the condescension implicit here becomes explicit when he is serious. "The partner of my life should be one who can feel poetry and understand philosophy. Harriet is a noble animal, but she can do neither" (Peacock 55).

Eros also taints Victor Frankenstein's view of humankind. When he sees in the monster a "deformity of . . . aspect, more hideous than belongs to humanity" (71), we wonder about that "more." Is Victor saying that humanity even in its ordinary form is hideously deformed? Perhaps. He has, after all, built his monster out of animal as well as human parts (49, 50). And he has certainly condescended to Elizabeth as Shelley did to Harriet. In the testament to complementarity which I quoted earlier, Victor defines his forte as active "investigating," whereas Elizabeth's is only devoted "following"; her poetry is merely "aerial," whereas his science deals with "facts"; "busied herself" suggests dalliance, whereas Victor grapples with "the actual world." Worse still is the fact that misogyny does not stop at condescension. Frankenstein shares the Erotic Shelley's view of women as animals. Victor calls Elizabeth "gay and playful as a summer insect" (29). He then goes on amazingly. "I loved to tend on her, as I should on a favourite animal" (30).

Frankenstein like Shelley is reflecting the culture's self-division: with woman polarized into angel and whore, the demeaned aspect is depicted in animal imagery—pig, bitch, birdbrain. More interesting than the disease is the cure. One way to deal with the body/spirit dichotomy in woman is to accept the facts of life and follow Mary's move beyond limitation to communion. Body, however mortal, enables lovers to realize themselves through consummation and procreation. This is the way of Agape. The other way is implied in Victor's reference to Elizabeth as a "summer" bug. Woman is ephemeral, or at least can be made so. To understand Victor's double assassination of Elizabeth in his nightmare and on his wedding night, we must understand how the perception of woman as ephemeral expresses the homicidal response of Eros.

THE ASSASSINS

The first product of Percy Shelley's union with Mary Godwin is *The Assassins*. As she transcribes this narrative fragment on their elopement, Mary encounters the opposite of Percy the pacifist.

> Despising and hating the pleasures and the customs of the degenerate mass of mankind. . . . The Assassins had retired from the intercourse of mankind, over whom other motives and principles of conduct than justice and benevolence prevail. . . . The perverse, the vile, and the vicious—what are they? Shapes of some unholy vision, moulded by the spirit of Evil, which the sword of the merciful destroyer should sweep from this beautiful world. (*JS* 6:156, 163, 164)[1]

The Percy of Agape does surface in *The Assassins* and espouse "benevolence." "Love, friendship, and philanthropy, would now be the characteristic disposers of their [the Assassins'] industry" (*JS* 6:157). But even the immediate context of this sentence is Erotic. "They [the Assassins] would no longer owe their very existence to the vices, the fears, and the follies of mankind." The Percys of Agape and Eros relate here as velvet glove to iron fist.

In *The Assassins*, Percy's Erotic will expresses what is essentially the Gnostic Protestantism of the Shelley clan, combined with their inevitable aristocratic biases:[2] belief in the elect, God's righteous, the sheep and the goats.

> Not on the will of the capricious multitude, nor the constant fluctuations of the many and the weak, depends the change of empires and religions. These [the many and the weak] are the mere insensible elements from which a subtler intelligence moulds its enduring statuary. They that direct the changes of this mortal scene breathe the decrees of their dominion from a throne of darkness and of tempest. The power of man is great. (*JS* 6:157).

Replace the Puritan patriarchal God with the Romantic obfuscation of "a throne of darkness and of tempest," and business continues as usual. "The power of man is great." The elect are pure in their superiority and are thus empowered to chastize the impure and inferior. Since the Assassins "could not conceive an instance in which it would be their duty to hesitate, in causing, at whatever expense, the greatest and most unmixed delight," they believe, Shelley tells us approvingly, that "to produce immediate pain or disorder for the sake of future benefit, is consonant, indeed, with the purest religion and philosophy, but never fails to excite invincible repugnance in the feelings of the many" (*JS* 6:163).

My associating Shelley and Victor as assassins may seem unfair, because there is a basic difference between the violence in *The Assassins* and in *Frankenstein*. Percy's Assassins slaughter the many but cherish the elect: why would Mary have Frankenstein ignore the many and slaughter the family? She is dramatizing Percy's life, not his novel. Mary as domestic feminist portrays her husband as domestic assassin. She presents family violence in *Frankenstein* because she sees in Percy what other contemporaries do—a readiness to apply Eros' contempt for humanity to the humans around the hearth.

> He [Shelley] would sit at table reading some
> book, often reading aloud, seemingly uncon-
> scious of the hospitable rites in which others
> were engaged, his bread bullets meanwhile
> being discharged in every direction.

These bullets are among the most telling features of Hogg's biography (2:322). The bread of life becomes a missile of aggression.

> [Walking down the street] he occasionally
> rolled up little pellets of bread, and, in a sly,
> mysterious manner, shot them with his
> thumb, hitting the persons—whom he met in
> his walks—on the face, commonly on the
> nose, at which he grew to be very dextrous.
> (2:320)

Humor is an element which Percy would no doubt insist upon here, as it is when he concludes that the misogynist at table with him and Hogg "ought to have been thrown out of the window" (1:303) or when he descants "with grim delight" upon his relish for panada. "I am going to lap up the blood of the slain! To sup up the gore of murdered kings" (Hogg 2:321, 322). But the domestic violence evident here cannot always be kept comic or kept hidden, as Percy's nightmares and visions attest, and as Claire Clairmont knew.

Caricature for poor dear S. He looked very
sweet & smiling. A little child playing Jesus
Christ . . . about the room. . . . Then grasping
a small knife & looking mild Shelley says I will
quietly murder that little child.[3]

A child is the first victim of Frankenstein's monstrous will. Victor's scientific experiments, which make possible this horror and
his family's eventual decimation, reenact Shelley's own youthful
experiments, which threatened the household generally (carrying a
firestove through Field Place, setting fire to the butler) and children in particular (placing siblings hand in hand to be electrified,
attempting to electrify the scout's son). The word "mould" recurs
in *The Assassins* because "to mould a really noble soul into all
that can make it[s] nobleness useful and lovely" (*PSL* 1:163, 28
Oct. 1811) challenges Shelley irresistibly. It also challenges Frankenstein. He molds from clay a being more suitable to his purposes
than mortal Elizabeth can ever be. Behind this male desire to mold
is a will to power which Mary Shelley exposes throughout her fiction. After Falkner has adopted the orphaned Elizabeth in order to
"mould her heart to affection, teach her to lean on him only"
(1:51), Mrs. Raby tells Elizabeth unsentimentally, "he adopted you,
because it best pleased him to do so" (2:166).

As a young woman who eagerly consigned herself to Percy for
cultivation, Mary knows the pleasures and benefits of his brilliant
mind. But she also feels hostility, as her choice of a Promethean
protagonist indicates. By having Victor share Prometheus' traditional inability to create a *female* creature,[4] Mary establishes the
independence of her gender and herself from that relentless molding
which orthodoxy sanctioned in husbands. That a second Prometheus tradition is also carried on by Victor—the botching of even a
male creature—shows Mary's insistence upon the weakness of
willfulness. Her masterpiece itself, begun with Percy's encouragement and handed over for his correction, insists subversively upon
its own autonomy, as she establishes when she supplements Percy's
1818 preface with her own introduction in 1831. "I certainly did not
owe the suggestion of one incident, nor scarcely of one train of feeling, to my husband" (*F* 229). This contention has been disputed as to
factual accuracy[5] but Mary's larger rhetorical point is incontestable.
Frankenstein is her homage to the intractability of matter, to the
limits of male powers of cultivation, to herself as the product not of
Percy Bysshe Shelley but of the most intellectually brilliant union
of the generation. *Frankenstein* insists that the humble but crucial

molding which counts most, the cultivation of a human relationship, can only be deformed if subjected to the random violence
of will.

The Nightmare

When the domestic assassin's will to mold is frustrated by the
intractability of matter—especially by woman's possession of a
body as well as a spirit—he follows the dictates of Eros and exterminates what has failed to match his idea. Body and sexuality, death
and female roles whirl together in Victor's famous nightmare.

> I thought I saw Elizabeth, in the bloom of
> health, walking in the streets of Ingolstadt. De-
> lighted and surprised, I embraced her; but as I
> imprinted the first kiss on her lips, they be-
> came livid with the hue of death; her features
> appeared to change, and I thought that I held
> the corpse of my dead mother in my arms; a
> shroud enveloped her form, and I saw the
> grave-worms crawling in the folds of the flan-
> nel. I started from my sleep with horror . . . I
> beheld the wretch—the miserable monster
> whom I had created. (53)

First, compare this with Neville's nightmare about *his* Elizabeth in
Falkner.

> "You haunted my dreams, accompanied by
> every image of horror—sometimes you were
> bleeding, ghastly, dying—sometimes you took
> my poor mother's form . . . snatched cold and
> pale from the waves." (2:224)

Neville's psychological state is simple enough. He loved his mother,
and forces intervened to kill her; he now loves Elizabeth, and intervening forces threaten her too. Since the threat is totally external, it
in no way reflects deep-seated antagonisms within Neville. *Falkner*
can therefore dramatize the eventual triumph of love over misfortune and unite hero and heroine in bliss eternal.

Frankenstein is another story. Victor's nightmare projects the
deep-seated difficulties that *Falkner* eschews. The male desire to get
beyond woman is satisfied by her death in this nightmare, which
relates both to Shelley's art and to his life. Compare Victor's kiss in
the nightmare and Laon's kiss in *Islam*, when woman is dispatched
and Laon is freed to get on to the male whom he actually needs.

A woman's [Cythna's] shape, now lank and
cold and blue,
    The dwelling of the many-coloured worm,
Hung there [from a tree]; the white and
hollow cheek I [drew]
    To my dry lips . . .
. . . .
When from that stony gloom a voice [the
Hermit] arose,
    Solemn and sweet . . .
. . . .
He struck my chains, and gently spoke and
smiled.
                            (1333–36, 1356–57, 1360)

Causation differs radically in the *Islam* and *Frankenstein* scenes.
Events in *Islam* are connected only chronologically, so that Laon is
preserved from responsibility. Cythna dies *and* the Hermit appears:
Laon merely witnesses the sequence. In fact, rather than acknowledge that Cythna is victimized by Laon's drive toward the Hermit,
that she dies because Laon needs an older male, Shelley in a characteristic turnabout makes *Laon* the victim. Cythna's death denies to
the desiccated protagonist the sustaining moisture that he needs
desperately. Laon is forced to seek the male.

Frankenstein, on the other hand, insists upon male responsibility. Unlike Laon, who kisses an already dead woman, Victor kills
Elizabeth with his kiss. A wish-fulfillment ending like the one in
Islam is then denied him. The monster appears to Victor as suddenly as the Hermit does to Laon, but Mary Shelley's protagonist
flees from rather than bonds with the new male force, presaging the
final isolation of womanless men. Mary is striking back at males
who try to dispense with wife-mother. One such male is Percy
Shelley—with his famous vision (on the very night of the ghost story project's inception) of a woman whose nipples were replaced by
eyes and with his subsequent depiction (possibly in reaction against
Frankenstein) of the bosom-eyed monstress of *The Witch of Atlas*.
In both cases mother-wife is superseded. The nurturing function of
the mother and the tactile attractiveness of the wife are each precluded by those eyes. Since Percy was staring at Mary at the time of
the vision, she cannot escape implication in the negation of roles
sacred to her.

Other links between Victor's nightmare and Percy's life illuminate Frankenstein's drive to escape wife-mother. That Percy and

Mary pledge and possibly consummate their love on the grave of Mary Wollstonecraft is well known, but the full significance of the act is not. Both women in Old St. Pancras Church Yard are "Mary Wollstonecraft Godwin." Making love to the daughter involves Percy with the mother; uniting with the living woman bonds him with the dead. The same blurrings of mother with daughter and of death with sex occur in Victor's nightmare, where a kiss kills the beloved who becomes the mother's corpse. Both these blurrings in *Frankenstein* are best understood in light of Percy Shelley's vexed relations with women.

Like the two Mary Wollstonecraft Godwins in Old St. Pancras, mother and daughter at Field Place have the same name. Percy's inevitable, if unconscious, anxiety at this blurring of his beloved Elizabeth Shelleys[6] is exacerbated when sexual rivalry shatters the conventional distinction between mother and daughter. Mrs. Shelley's attempt to marry Elizabeth to Edward Graham is seen by Percy (however erroneously) as the elder woman's scheme to cover up her adultery with Graham at the expense of the younger woman. Daughter thus becomes mother's rival and is contaminated by adult femininity—in Shelley's mind, as in Frankenstein's nightmare.

Victor's Elizabeth is bound to him so affectionately as sister that some tension between her and his adoring mother is virtually inevitable, but rivalry is particularly intense in this case because sister-daughter is also fiancée. That the daughter-fiancée causes the mother's death is obvious enough. What I want to stress is how Mary Shelley goes out of her way to emphasize the homicidal, as opposed to the accidental, nature of the act. Elizabeth infects Caroline not with influenza or smallpox or some other traditional disease, but with the malady of Percy's own sister Elizabeth—scarlet fever. The sexual connotations of a scarlet fever are crucial. Mary could so easily have had the good mother die in the conventional, and expectable, role of nurse. Instead Caroline, uncharacteristically and unconventionally, leaves the nursing to others and dies apparently gratuitously. This "gratuitous" dying "without benefiting anyone else" is criticized by Ellis (132), but the very pointlessness of the death is Mary's point. Denied any other rationale for the mother's death, we must see its psychological significance. The daughter as future wife destroys her older rival in order to possess their beloved Victor exclusively. His response to this predatory sexuality is reflected in his nightmare diction: "in the streets," Elizabeth is angel turned whore.

The blurring of mother and daughter roles in Victor's novel and in Shelley's life means that the women have failed to live up to male ideals. Shelley and Victor respond alike. They assassinate. When young Elizabeth Shelley fails to respond to Hogg as Percy wishes, he decides that "she is now *not* what she was, she is not the singular angelic being whom you adored & I loved; I mourn her as *no more*, I consider the sister whose happiness is mine as dead" (*PSL* 1:93, 21 May 1811). Eros is equally operative when Victor wishes Elizabeth to death in the nightmare. And like Shelley, who says "as well might you [Hogg] court the worms which the soulless body of a beloved being generates" (*PSL* 1:95, 2 June 1811), Victor generates grave-worms in the corpse of his ephemeral beloved, the summer insect.

Both domestic assassins are equally hard on failed mothers. Harriet's refusal to nurse Ianthe enrages Percy because it is more than "unnatural," it is part of a pattern of maternal failure which includes his mother's supposed adultery, her repeated inability to sympathize with him,[7] and her inevitable place in oedipal configurations with Sir Timothy. Maternal failure recurs in Shelley's art, where puissant mothers neglect needy sons. "Where wert thou, mighty Mother, when he [Keats-Shelley] lay, / When thy Son lay, pierced by the shaft? . . . Wake, melancholy Mother, wake and weep! . . . now, thy youngest, dearest one, has perished" (*Adonais* 10–11, 20, 46). Harriet's maternal failure combines with her intellectual (and possibly sexual) limitations to evoke from Percy a description of their union which sums up the Erotic view of sexual relationships. "I felt as if a dead & living body had been linked together in loathsome & horrible communion" (*PSL* 1:402, 3 Oct. 1814). This is Victor's very situation as his nightmare kiss links him to the dead Elizabeth-Caroline.

Victor, like Shelley, feels himself failed by women on every side. Elizabeth has both killed his mother and presumed to replace her. Caroline has abetted in this displacement by dying; she has displaced Victor by introducing the interloper Elizabeth (whom he calls his mother's "favourite" [37] at the very moment Caroline contracts her lethal fever); and she has joined him incestuously to a sister whose role as mother-surrogate means that Caroline has wed her son to herself. Like Shelley, Victor responds to such failures of the ideal by assassination. His nightmare kiss dispatches Elizabeth to Caroline's grave, where both women can be finished off by the phallic worms. The monster then appears as the alternative, the male whom Victor-Laon-Shelley prefers to failed females.

Like mother and daughter, sex and death blur in the Promethean mind. Percy calls marriage to Harriet "a knell" (Hogg 2:554); Victor sees union with Elizabeth as fatal. "I was like the Arabian who had been buried with the dead, and found a passage to life aided only by one glimmering, and seemingly ineffectual, light" (48). Ostensibly Victor is using the story from *The Arabian Nights* to emphasize his intellectual enlightenment during the monster-making process. Unconsciously he is suggesting why he began that process. The "dead" with whom the Arabian Sinbad is buried is *his wife*. Since the surviving mate is doomed to entombment with the dead spouse, marriage becomes literally the "loathsome & horrible communion" of "a dead & living body . . . linked together." Sinbad thus confirms what Victor and Shelley (and their culture) have feared about marriage all along. Woman is fatal. Sinbad's intelligence enables him to escape from his dead wife, and Victor determines to use his own intellect to give life to a creature too huge and too male to prove ephemeral.

Elizabeth seems particularly lethal to Victor because she is more than vulnerable to death, she is redolent of it. Again Victor resembles Percy Shelley, whose sense of woman as sexual destroyer is unusually strong. In *Zastrozzi* Matilda dreams that "Verezzi, consenting to their union, presented her his hand; that at her touch the flesh crumbled from it, and, a shrieking spectre, he fled from her view" (*JS* 5:71). Later in Shelley's "The Sunset" (1816), "the youth and the lady mingled lay / In love and sleep—but when the morning came / The lady found her lover dead and cold" (24–26). And in the late "Ginevra" (1821), "We toll a corpse out of the marriage-bed" (79). Elizabeth's killing of Caroline is especially threatening to Victor because he sees his own conjugal emotions resembling his mother's fatal attraction to the daughter-fiancée. Caroline died, he says, because she desired Elizabeth's "society" so much that she "entered her chamber" precipitately (37). Desiring Elizabeth's society conjugally will require Victor to enter her chamber in two senses—crossing the bridal threshold and penetrating the bride physically. The woman who killed his mother to possess him could kill him by possessing him.

Woman means death to Victor for the same reason that she does to Shelley—because she represents flesh itself. When Shelley says that "the love of the sexes, however pure, still retains some taint of earthly grossness" (Hogg 1:117), FatherSky is indicting MotherEarth. Shelley's moments of delight in sensuality do not prevent him, as we have seen, from rejecting the earthly as matter-*mater*, as body-woman. Victor feels the same Erotic revulsion. To create the monster he must associate with that ultimate in earthly grossness, mother earth herself. He takes parts for the monster from slaughter houses as well as from charnel houses because body is all animal and moribund to him. Toiling "among the unhallowed damps of the grave" (49), consorting with "the lifeless clay" (49), Victor is, like Shelley, a living being linked in "loathsome & horrible communion" with a dead one. No wonder Frankenstein dreams of sex with a corpse.

THE WEDDING NIGHT

The ultimate conjunction of sex and death in *Frankenstein* occurs when Elizabeth is actually murdered on her wedding night. Killing Elizabeth involves both the willfulness of the ego-centric Eros and the weakness of the Dionysiac, because the murder is a form of rape which reveals both machismo and dysfunction in Victor. The sexual aspect of the murder is obvious enough—the beautiful woman throttled by the huge male on her bridal bed. That Victor has already been characterized as a rapist is also clear. Like other Promethean scientists who "penetrate into the recesses of nature, and shew how she works in her hiding places" (42), Victor "pursued nature to her hiding places" (49). Mary emphasizes this predatory aspect of Victor by having him describe himself in 1831 as "always having been embued with a fervent longing to penetrate the secrets of nature" (238). But why she associates science with rape, what motive she posits for the violation, is less obvious.

Woman—mother nature and mother-wife—is viewed by both scientist and rapist as a use object rather than as a precious other. Both men want to get something from her rather than to be something with her. In Frankenstein's particular case, sexual intercourse is impossible because he feels Erotic nausea at life and body, but woman remains indispensable because he still feels desire. What he desires from Elizabeth is freedom. Only her death, he unconsciously imagines, will free him to transcend mortal unions and reach immortality through Erotic self-union. Elizabeth in effect dies so that Victor will not have to. Rape-murder as the ultimate use of woman defines the Erotic alternative to Agape's ideal of androgynous marriage. Besides the willfulness obvious here, there is weakness, since rape attests to the cowardliness and the ultimate dysfunction of the bifurcated assassin. Before examining Mary Shelley's presentation of will and weakness on the wedding night, we must recognize that Percy Shelley is implicated as strongly here as he was in the earlier stages of Victor's relations with women.

117

The intensity of Mary Shelley's involvement with Elizabeth on the wedding night (Mary and Elizabeth are kinswomen in the Bible) is indicated by the biographical elements she includes in the scene. Victor's anxiety—"this night is dreadful, very dreadful" (192)—echoes Shelley's description of his anxiety during the elopement: "How dreadful did this time appear" (*J* 3, 28 July 1814). Just as Victor is divided between concern for his woman and concern with their pursuer, Percy "was divided between anxiety for her [Mary's] health and terror lest our pursuers should arrive" (*J* 3). The arrival of Elizabeth's pursuer and the ensuing strangulation have been linked by critics to a comparable scene with Mary and Percy at Lerici: "He saw the figure of himself strangling me, that had made him rush into my room, yet fearful of frightening me he dared not approch [sic] the bed" (*MSL* 1:180, 15 Aug. 1822). The link with *Frankenstein* takes us beyond event to motivation. Just as Victor wants to both protect and destroy Elizabeth, the words "that had made him rush" can mean that Percy enters Mary's room either to protect her or to enact his dream of strangling her. As Victor keeps Elizabeth ignorant of the monster both to avoid alarming her and to preclude self-defense by her, "fear of frightening me" can mean that Percy wants to avoid either alarming Mary or awakening her into self-defense.

Bizarrely revealing as the Lerici episode is—Shelley acting out four years after *Frankenstein* events in the novel which reflected his murderous will before 1818—it is no odder than another of his caprices, which contributed directly to the novel's wedding-night scene. Shelley makes elopements into threesomes. The morning after the wedding night with Harriet, Hogg appears and Shelley exults, "we will never part again! You must have a bed in the house!" (Hogg 1:437). When Hogg desires *Harriet's* bed and is dismissed from the house, Eliza Westbrook reconstitutes the threesome. Her dismissal opens the way for Elizabeth Hitchener. And of course Percy does not allow himself even one night alone with Mary on their elopement, but includes Claire from the very beginning. Shelley either fears complete conjugal intimacy or finds no one woman sufficient to his emotional needs, or both. Reversing the old adage and making three company adds a touch of the ludicrous to his destructive relations with women. Self-deception is so frequent with Shelley—his raptures of love and his protestations of guiltlessness—that *Frankenstein* includes in the wedding-night threesome of Victor, Elizabeth, and the monster a groom whose self-deceptions approach the ludicrous. Since this scene completes the polarization of masculine and feminine elements in Victor's psyche even as it assures that psyche's isolation from woman as other, I will analyze it in some detail, first the devices which reveal extreme willfulness beneath Victor's sympathetic surface and then the parody which reveals the sexual inadequacy—the ultimate effeminacy—of the bridegroom as failed androgyne.

Victor's questions—"Why am I here to relate the destruction. . . . Could I behold this and live?" (193)—encourage us to question many of his acts, to see the will beneath the sympathy. Why, for example, does Victor not thwart the monster beforehand, either by destroying it outright or by understanding its threat? Destroying the monster is definitely possible. "I would have seized him; but he eluded me" (166). Victor then asks our question: "Why had I not followed him, and closed with him in mortal strife?" (166). Our suspicion that "I suffered him to depart" (166) because Victor did not really want him stopped is strengthened after the murder when the creature "eluded me" (194). The repetition of "eluded me" emphasizes how little has changed in the elusive relation of creator and creature. The monster escapes both times because he effects what Victor wants each time. This is also why Victor fails to understand the monster's threat. " 'I will be with you on your wedding night!' Such was my sentence" (185). The sentence against Victor as bridegroom is pronounced by Victor as monster. The actual meaning of the threat becomes clear to Frankenstein too late (193), just as Elizabeth is embraced by him on the marriage bed too late (193). "I will kill thee, / And love thee after," says Othello, speaking for the sons of Eros (5.2.18–19). Only after the fact can Frankenstein do what he should have done earlier, because only now is the failure assured which is Victor-y.

The monster's threat indicates how Mary Shelley uses formal elements to reveal Victor's murderous will on the wedding night. As the threat is open to two interpretations, and as Victor is operating on both conscious and unconscious levels, she provides a second, subversive layer to language also. "[I resolved] not to join her until I had obtained some knowledge as to the situation of my enemy. She . . ." (192). By "enemy" Victor consciously means the monster, of course. But "my enemy. She" suggests that the real enemy is Elizabeth. A similar use of language has occurred a few lines earlier: "I resolved . . . not [to] relax the impending conflict until my own life, or that of my adversary, were extinguished. Elizabeth . . . " (192). The words "my adversary were extinguished. Elizabeth" say more than Victor consciously intends. "Extinguished Elizabeth" is what will allow him to relax. That "my adversary" can be "Elizabeth" is emphasized by Victor's first calling their honeymoon house a "retreat" (191)[8] and then vowing to inspect "every corner that might afford a retreat to my adversary" (193). In this battle of the sexes, Victor "reflected how dreadful the combat . . . would be to my wife" (192). He means literally that Elizabeth would be frightened by his battling a monster, but unconsciously he knows how much more dreadful will be her own battle with the monster. That battle ends with Elizabeth's "dreadful" scream (193).

Characterization is made two-leveled by Mary's associating Victor's wedding-night actions with scenes and stereotypes that he is unaware of. Elizabeth's murder completes, for example, his two earlier nightmare scenes. As "the dim and yellow light of the moon" came in through the "shutters" of Victor's bedroom and illuminated the monster after the nightmare (53), so on the wedding night the "shutters" admit "the pale yellow light of the moon" and again reveal the monster (194). Both scenes present the creature's "grin" (53, 194); the first time he reached out his hand, now he points a finger (53, 194). The two scenes are linked because the second involves more than Victor admits, more than the creature's hate and revenge. The second scene is linked causally to, is required by the first. The consummation sought by the male and female halves of Victor's psyche cannot occur when the creature first enters the creator's bedchamber because marriage to Elizabeth has yet to be removed as an alternative to solipsistic union.

To indicate how impossible this alternative is for Victor psychologically, Mary Shelley links the wedding night scene to a second nightmare. On the boat from Ireland, Victor dreams of "the fiend's grasp in my neck"; on the wedding night, "the . . . mark of the fiend's grasp was on her neck" (181, 193). Victor in his nightmare moment *is* Elizabeth in her nightmarish death, because destroying the complement destroys the self. The monster's embrace with Elizabeth on the bridal bier thus images not the eventual union of Victor's willful and effeminate extremes but the suicidal nature of such an attempt. Self-love is self-destruction.

With a protagonist who pretends to ultimate masculinity and yet cannot appreciate his bride, Mary Shelley goes beyond revealing murderous will and parodies the weakness of such willfulness. Using stereotypes comically is not unusual for her. She repeatedly calls Percy "Don Quixote" when his manly indignation and idealistic endeavors lead to naught (see chapter 2, note 9). Percy is also implicated when Mary parodies a second male type. Compare Per-

120

cy's courtly croon to Jane Williams, "Awake! arise! and come away" ("To Jane: The Invitation" 48 [1822]) and Mary's 1831 revision which satirizes the creature by having him intone words appropriate to a courtly lover with his lady fair but absurd for a monster with a servant: "Awake, fairest [Justine], thy lover is near . . . my beloved, awake!" (251). On the wedding night Mary introduces a third male stereotype that fiercely undercuts Victor himself. The anxious bridegroom.[9] That there is a ludicrous side to Victor Frankenstein has only recently been noted by scholars. Small calls Victor's reaction to the monster's creation "almost ludicrous" and his expedient of a bogus confession "absurd" (160, 174). Seed finds Victor "a particularly unimpressive Faust. . . . he comes across as a very unimpressive figure" (330, 335). Recognizing that Frankenstein "is not very good at his trade," Strevick shows effectively that "Frankenstein, in short, is a failure, not in a grand and tragic manner but in a manner closer to low comedy, bumbling, inattentive, inept, and ineffectual" (224, 225). Strevick goes on to ask why Victor is presented this way. "Nothing in the logic of Mary Shelley's narrative could have compelled her to imagine ritual humiliations for Victor Frankenstein . . . [to make him a] comic failure" (232). The logic of Mary's practice derives in part from the nature of Percy's life.

The comic stereotype of the anxious bridegroom may seem inappropriate to Victor, since he ostensibly fears not his adequacy with the bride, but his combat with the monster. At a deeper level, however, Victor does dread intercourse with Elizabeth. He sees the night expressly in terms of manliness: "thoughts of mischance" are "unmanly" (190). Especially with Elizabeth "fearless," he is "half ashamed" of his fears (191). And afraid he is. "Dreading . . . a thousand fears . . . anxious . . . watchful . . . terrified . . . agitation . . . agitates . . . fear" reverberate throughout the three pages. "My right hand grasped a pistol which was hidden in my bosom; every sound terrified me" (192). Victor's gesture of phallic uncertainty here and his unwitting association with the female ("bosom") are as ludicrous as his misconception of the whole situation. "I resolved that I would sell my life dearly" (192). Since we know that Victor's life is *not* in danger, his bravado here makes him seem less like a heroic bridegroom than like a pander selling "dearly" the love of his life. "'Oh! peace, peace, my love,' replied I. 'This night and all will be safe'" (192) sounds like the bridegroom's loving assurance to his anxious bride that the difficulties of the first night will give way to the pleasures of a lifetime. But the decency of such an admonition contrasts with Victor's unconscious meaning—that he will be safe after tonight because Elizabeth will threaten him no more. Especially since his words "peace, peace" recall Elizabeth's earlier pledge of true devotion, "I would sacrifice my life to your peace" (89), we have little doubt of Mary Shelley's feelings here.

Victor's wedding night victory is pyrrhic. The blurring of sex and death which occurred in the first nightmare (and in Percy's grave-yard lovemaking with "Mary Wollstonecraft Godwin") finds its ultimate expression in Elizabeth's "bridal bier" (193). (This phrase is one of Shelley's additions to the MS.) This is a victory for Victor insofar as it ends the anguishing struggle to separate mother-sister-wife. All Frankenstein women are now dead, so there can be no separate female roles and no positive potential for sexuality. Elizabeth lying on the bridal bier "lifeless and inanimate" (193) has literally become "the lifeless clay . . . the inanimate body" which served the Promethean scientist. MotherEarth is vanquished by FatherSky. As Victor embraces her we see yet another version of "a dead & living body . . . linked together in loathsome & horrible communion."

Frankenstein's victory over moribund flesh is pyrrhic because the distinction between the dead and the quick proves harder to establish than he imagined. Two quotations from Shelley point up the difficulty.

> a dead & living body . . . linked together . . .
> "She can't bear solitude, nor I society—the quick coupled with the dead."

In the first case, Percy is alive and Harriet is dead; in the second (Trelawny 1:105), Percy is dead and Mary alive.[10] This turnabout reflects a fact of *Frankenstein* and a truth about Eros: banishing the woman to figurative or literal death leaves the man finally moribund and useless too. "The children of the earth who begged to be relieved of their bodies as a way of escaping from sex ironically become images for the imprisonment of human consciousness in mere physicality." This tradition, which Kahn (30) traces from Ovid to Shakespeare, can be extended to Mary Shelley and her gothic heirs. Will is weakness. Victor, still "emaciated" as bridegroom (187), responds revealingly to Elizabeth's wedding-night scream: "My arms dropped" (193). Impotence characterizes Victor because the process of his effeminization is now complete. His male energy is fully projected outward in destroying Elizabeth, the rival for his own affections. Effeminacy is confirmed by Frankenstein's last act in the scene. "I fainted" (193).

When Victor revives, his effeminate orientation directs him toward men. Not only does he follow the monster, who has "plunged into the lake" (194), but the bridegroom who rowed Elizabeth across the water earlier in the day now hires "men to row" him back (195). Victor tries at first to join this male retinue as one of the guys ("I . . . took an oar myself" [195]), but he cannot pull his own weight. "Incapable of any exertion," he "threw down the oar" (195). The discarded oar, like the ineffectual pistol, indicates that manly action is out of Frankenstein's hands. "Leaning my head upon my hands" (195), he is reduced to a self-embrace which does not, cannot include the heart.

5

The Divided Self and Man

It was Grandfather's and when Father gave it to me
he said, Quentin, I give you the mausoleum of all
hope and desire. . . . I give it to you not that you may
remember time, but that you may forget it now and
then for a moment and not spend all your breath trying to conquer it.

Quentin Compson

A son can never, in the fullest sense, become a father. Some amount of amateur effort is possible. A
son may after honest endeavor produce what some
people might call, technically, children. But he remains a son. In the fullest sense.

Donald Barthelme

ELIZABETH'S DEATH DOES NOT FREE VICTOR TO PURSUE THE MONSTER.
At the end of his voyage back across the lake is father. Alphonse's
subsequent death raises basic questions about Victor's psychological development and *Frankenstein*'s formal structure. If the Erotic
son is driven to kill all rivals to self-union, is Alphonse's death part
of this process? What threat does he pose to Victor, and why is Alphonse the last of the Frankenstein fatalities? Victor, like so many
sons, dreams of siring himself, but the hope of escaping to immortality by incorporating father and eliminating mother generates
doubt and guilt, particularly because the son knows of an alternative. Rather than assassinate the father, the son can follow him in
a traditional cycle which will lead eventually to death but will allow
for love and purpose and continuity.

In dramatizing the son's options, Mary Shelley confronts us with
an issue first raised in her husband's review of *Frankenstein* and
reiterated by readers for generations. How could she have done it?
How could a young woman with little experience of the world see so
deeply into the male psyche? Answering this question must precede
analysis of father-son relations in the novel.

Defining the role of father for Mary Shelley has been both fostered and impeded by recent criticism. Feminism with its recognition of the importance of *mother* has prevented any overrating of father. In the context of Kleinian arguments by Chodorow and Dinnerstein that Freud's neglect of the pre-oedipal years has caused serious undervaluing of the maternal role in child development, literary critics such as Gilbert and Gubar, Jacobus, Poovey, and Todd have established the importance of Mary Wollstonecraft for Mary Shelley. Feminist readings can, however, go too far in the opposite direction. Mother can achieve such prominence that father is cast into shadow. Poovey's chapters are the best overall appraisal of Mary Shelley's novelistic career that I know, but I cannot agree that "in Mary Shelley's own youth and in *Falkner* (and, in a slightly different sense, in *Frankenstein*) the motherless daughter's relationship with the father carries the burden of needs originally and ideally satisfied by the mother; in a sense, the relationship with each father is only an imaginative substitute for the absent relationship with the mother" (168). Mary Shelley, in fact, insisted upon the superiority of a father's tuition for daughters, devoted much of her fiction to father-directed emotions and events, confessed privately to untoward affection for Godwin, and expressed this affection in a novel so shocking that her father suppressed it.

A second approach to Mary Shelley, that of the psychoanalytic critics of *Frankenstein*, gives immediate prominence to father, since the oedipal model presupposes generational conflict. Preeminence, however, is again accorded to mother. The primary object of Frankenstein's affection is presumed to be his mother, Caroline, and the primary object of his scientific labors is presumed to be the discovery of a principle of life which would bring her back from the dead. Despite unquestionably valuable insights by Hirsch, Kaplan and Kloss, Knoepflmacher, Rubenstein, and others, the oedipal model has tended to occlude deeper levels of the psyche where Mary Shelley moves beyond mother love. Here Freud's "negative" Oedipus is a more useful paradigm, because here the son desires to murder *mother* in order to get to *father*.[1]

Father looms so large for both Mary and Percy Shelley that no one critical approach can account for him fully. At their most idealistic—and thus most traditional—the Shelleys encourage a critical methodology which integrates the traditional disciplines of biographical and close textual analyses. By utilizing this approach with Mary's later fiction and with Percy's *The Revolt of Islam*, I can not only indicate the prominence of father for the Shelleys, but also establish the ideal against which their more subversive and important art was created. Reading this indirect, overdetermined art in light of the negative Oedipus will help answer questions about *Frankenstein, Prometheus Unbound,* and *The Cenci,* and will, I hope, add to our understanding of the vexed role of father in the Romantic period and in the subsequent generations whose children we are.

THE PROMISE OF PARADIGMS

In a biographical nexus as amazing as the persons involved, Percy's intricate conflicts with father are illuminated by Mary's incestuous attractions to father. Her admiration for Mary Wollstonecraft, unquestionable though it is, cannot match the intensity of what she called "my excessive and romantic attachment to my Father" (*MSL* 2:88, 17 Nov. 1834). Mary, like her Mathilda, "clung to the memory of my parents; my mother I should never see, she was dead; but the idea of [my] unhappy, wandering father was the idol of my imagination" (11). The primacy of father is confirmed by Mathilda's venerable steward: "You are like her [mother] although there is more of my lord in you" (24). In her last novels, Mary continues to insist how much fathers love daughters. *Perkin Warbeck* presents De Faro who "could not prevail on himself to leave his lovely, unprotected girl behind" (2:178); *Falkner* attests that "no father ever worshipped a child so fervently" as Falkner does Elizabeth (1:300). Mary never gets over Godwin's coldness. She is forty-one years old when she says, "My Father, from age and domestic circumstances, could not *'me faire valoir'*" (*J* 205, 21 Oct. 1838). Even here in middle age, Mary can bring herself to this terrible admission only by insulating the reality in French phrasing (when English would suffice), in italics (which she does not always apply to foreign expressions), and in quotation marks (which are unnecessary), and by atoning for the aggression by capitalizing "Father" (which she by no means always does).

Percy too makes father paramount. The intensity of his feelings— which finds negative expression in *The Mask of Anarchy*'s rage at "GOD, AND KING, AND LAW" and poor Sir Timothy—expresses itself positively in Shelley's lifelong search for lawgivers. After Dr. Lind, who taught science, occult lore, and the right to be different, comes Hogg. "I [Percy] took you for one who was to give laws to us poor beings who grovel beneath" (*PSL* 1:171, 10 Nov. 1811). Then Shelley finds Godwin. The older man's enormous authority comes in part from his confirming what the young philosopher needs to believe— that reason can control passion and assure perfection. But Godwin

126

also answers the needs of a rebellious son. Fuller has it backwards when she says that "from the time he [Shelley] read this [*Political Justice*], he regarded the circumstances of his birth as shaming, and only possible to live down by the dedication of his mind and position to the elevation of those less endowed" (45). Percy's rebelliousness predates his reading of *Political Justice* because his anger was father-directed before it was political. Godwin serves less to generate rebellion than to canonize it. He lessens the guilt while encouraging the crime. (I am speaking here of how Godwin's philosophy operated upon Percy psychologically. Godwin's actual advice was that the young heir reconcile himself with his wealthy father. If Godwin was dispassionately concerned with patching up the hallowed relation of parent and child, he was also passionately aware how much Percy's financial gifts to him depended upon the son's access to the father's purse.) Godwin allows the son both to have *him* as new father and to have a non-psychological and thus largely guiltless rationale for rejecting the old father.

Mary can see so accurately into Percy because she shares with him more than an obsession with father: daughter and son here share the same object of desire, William Godwin!

*

Percy and Mary each project their desires for father onto the screen of art. Seeing how desire is ideally satisfied there will help us to understand why such satisfaction proves impossible in the Shelleys' marriage and how their dissatisfactions are figured forth in *Frankenstein*.

> "If I have rashly violated that venerable form, at once majestic and defenceless, may I be forgiven?" ("The Coliseum," *JS* 6:305)

> Byron thinks that Laocöon's anguish is absorbed in that of his children. . . . Not so. Intense physical suffering . . . seems the predominant and overwhelming emotion. . . . [The elder son's] eyes are fixedly bent on Laocöon—his whole soul is with—is a part of that of his father. His arm extended towards him, not for protection, but from a wish as if instinctively to afford it, absolutely speaks. . . . In the younger child, surprise, pain, and grief seem to contend for mastery. He is not yet arrived at an age when his mind has sufficient self-possession, or fixedness of reason, to analyze the calamity that is overwhelming himself and all

127

that is dear to him. ("Notes on Sculptures," *JS*
6:310)

The "Coliseum" passage presents filial aggression. "Violated"
seems inappropriate since the young man has only *spoken* harshly,
but the application of phallic terminology to verbal action indicates
how sexual the son's aggressions are. Their causes and consequences are reflected in "majestic and defenceless." The paternal
majesty that makes the son worshipful can also oppress him; the
parental defenselessness that allows him to repay oppression fosters
guilt, because the now strong son should protect the once protective
father. "May I be forgiven?" asks the guilty son. "If you can forget,
doubt not that we forgive" (*JS* 6:305). A conditional has answered
the son's conditional because forgiveness depends upon self-for-
giveness. This proves particularly difficult because of the "we."
From two sides guilt strikes the young man who has injured both
the "venerable" father and the answering daughter. The whole
scene—aged wise man, adoring daughter, intruding youth—dramatizes Percy's current situation with Mary's adored father, to whom
he had recently addressed deservedly harsh words. This tense relationship is all the more agonizing for Percy because it reenacts his
situation at Field Place, where a beloved woman, Mrs. Shelley, was
caught between an offended father and an offending son. Percy in
"The Coliseum" cannot bear either to lose his surrogate father or to
have Godwin repeat Sir Timothy's abusiveness.

In the Laocöon passage Shelley is not admitting to filial aggression. Here the issues are rejection, affection, and rivalry. Disagreeing with Byron about the object of paternal concern, Shelley sees
embattled Laocöon as Sir Timothy—an old man who rejects his progeny and is absorbed in his own pain. Rejection seems particularly
undeserved to the elder son because he is not responsible for the
pain. On the contrary, he "instinctively" seeks to protect a father
defenseless like the old man in "The Coliseum." Such affection is
all the more worthy of paternal regard because the younger son cannot match it. Percy, who demonstrated dangerously aggressive feelings toward the brother John born late in his reign at Field Place
(Hogg 1:10–11) and who could not help considering that brother a
rival for Sir Timothy's title and estates in 1819, describes in the
Laocöon group a sibling inferior precisely because he does not match
the elder brother and does resemble the father. The elder son has
"sufficient self-possession" to gaze "fixedly," whereas the younger

boy lacks "fixedness" and displays the opposite of self-possession, a self-absorption similar to Laocöon's. Caught in an alienation like the elder son's, how can Shelley achieve solidarity with the father?

The answer is dramatized in *The Revolt of Islam* and *Prince Athanase*. "In the deep / The shape of an old man did then appear, / Stately and beautiful; that dreadful sleep / His heavenly smiles dispersed, and I could wake and weep" (*Islam* 1347–50). Union with the father can occur, as we saw in chapter 4, only after woman is removed. Kissing the hanged Cythna's "hollow cheek" (1335) cannot relieve Laon's physical and spiritual desiccation, but the Hermit as good father is androgynous enough to be female as well as male. His "solemn" voice is "sweet" (1357); his "giant" arms nurse Laon tenderly (1364). First the physical desiccation is relieved ("my scorched limbs he wound / In linen moist and balmy" [1365–66]), then the spiritual. "That aged man, so grand and mild, / Tended me, even as some sick mother seems / To hang in hope over a dying child" (1401–3). Since the Hermit is equally effectual in the manly arts—he controls the intellectual discussion as decisively as he "ruled the helm" of the ship (1380)—he could prove overbearing. In fact, Laon initially feared "it was a fiend" (1383). But the Hermit does not play the heavy father. Like his model, Dr. Lind, who defended Percy against Sir Timothy, the Hermit can cut the old ones down to size with "A glance as keen as is the lightning's stroke / When it doth rive the knots of some ancestral oak" (1466–67).

Up to this point Shelley has been following the precedent of Wordsworth's *Excursion*. Youth in need of wisdom finds all-wise aged man. Shelley now goes beyond Wordsworth toward Freud. *The Excursion*, as Shelley (in effect, if not consciously) sees it, fails to recognize that discipleship is only half the battle. No matter how devoted a pupil the son is, he can never achieve full manhood and thus can never get beyond the aggression of "The Coliseum" fragment and the alienation of the Laocöon note. Laon—whose name as a contraction of Laocöon encapsulates the whole father-son situation—must transcend oedipal emotions and achieve adulthood without triumphing over the father so violently as to generate guilt. This process Shelley portrays subtly.

Canto 4 has already indicated a limitation in father. The "tower of stone" where the Hermit takes Laon "was a crumbling heap" (1415–16). The cause of the Hermit's limited potency is soon defined.

> custom maketh blind and obdurate
> The loftiest hearts;—he had beheld the woe
> In which mankind was bound, but deemed
> that fate
> Which made them abject, would preserve
> them so;
> And in such faith, some steadfast joy to
> know,
> He sought this cell.
>
> (1486–91)

Although he emerges from reclusion during the revolution and does inspire the people, the Hermit has no delusions about his efficacy. "But I, alas! am both unknown and old, / . . . I am cold / In seeming" (1558, 1560–61). What effect he does have he owes to Laon.

> "For I have been thy passive instrument"—
> (As thus the old man spake, his
> countenance
> Gleamed on me like a spirit's)—"thou has lent
> To me, to all, the power to advance
> Towards this unforeseen deliverance . . ."
>
> (1549–53)

The Excursion offered the son no way out because it confined him to a single-staged relationship with an elder who dispensed wisdom in propositional statements ("the good die first" [300]) and in exemplary tales ("The Ruined Cottage"). Thus the best the younger man could do was to acknowledge and embrace the elder's wisdom.

From such permanent dependence Shelley finds an escape by insisting that the father-son relationship be two-staged. Although his Hermit does address Laon's problems, Shelley presents no propositional statements and no exemplary tales. In fact he allows the Hermit no dialogue at all at this point. The elder's role is largely maternal: he creates a nurturing ambience in which the young man's psyche heals itself. Then stage two can begin. The son takes over the role of Wordsworth's seer and provides the elder with ideas and the "power" to effect them. Likening Laon's tongue to "a lance" (1566), the Hermit confirms the son's phallic manhood by crediting him with that transition from language to action which the father could never make.

Son also surpasses sire in *Prince Athanase*, where Dr. Lind again appears as the Shelley figure's "one beloved friend" (125), is again androgynous ("gentle and majestical" [160]), again plays the "mas-

130

ter" to Percy's "pupil" (174), and once again partakes willingly in the reversal of the Wordsworth situation.

> The youth, as shadows on a grassy hill
> Outrun the winds that chase them, soon outran
> His teacher, and did teach with native skill
> Strange truths and new to that experienced man;
> Still they were friends . . .
>
> (176–80)

This last line is crucial for *Islam* as well as for *Prince Athanase.* In surpassing the father, the son must not generate a guilt that would blight his flowering manhood. "Strengthened in heart, yet sad, that aged man / I left" (*Islam* 1693–94). Syntax here shapes meaning. "Strengthened . . . that aged man" is not what the lines actually say, but it is what we initially read. Compare the lines with the syntactically more orthodox "strengthened in heart, yet sad, I left that aged man." Why does Shelley allow us to make a mistake and attribute to the Hermit what is happening to Laon? By having the strengthened male seem to be father and actually be son, Shelley bonds the two in the very act of distinguishing them. We can mistake the elder for the younger because they are really one. "That aged man I left" reinforces this. By inverting the syntax, Shelley can go beyond establishing the fact of parting and suggest its consequences. "That aged man I left" can be read as "I left that aged man" and "I, that aged man, left": Laon leaves the Hermit and leaves *as* the Hermit. "That aged man I" weds father and son. With the "I" placed on the next line we never lose sight of the "sad" reality that father and son are indeed separate and separating. But the separation is spared any rupturing violence because the men's psychic integration is confirmed by syntax even as time's passing is insisted upon by diction.

Integration with the father allows Laon to go on and integrate with mankind. "Their friend, their chief, their father" (1833) defines his relation to the momentarily united inhabitants of Islam. When hostilities resume, "in joy I found, / Beside me then, firm as a giant pine / Among the mountain-vapours driven around, / The old man whom I loved" (2416–19). The Hermit's progress from ruined tower to towering pine does not indicate any maturation on his part. The growth is Laon's. Whereas the word "violated" in "The Coliseum" revealed the son's desire to aggress phallicly upon father-as-female,

131

the association of phallic pine with father in *Islam* establishes that Laon is now confident enough of his own powers to recognize the manhood of his father and of every other male. A benign coda is now possible. The Hermit's glorious death in battle can complete the generational transfer, because father and son have achieved the only equality possible to creatures bound upon the wheel of time. Each is assured the dignity of his place in the generational cycle.

Victor Frankenstein has the opportunity to join this generational cycle with Alphonse. His refusal reflects to some extent Percy's refusal of comparable relationships with Sir Timothy and other father figures. Both Mary's response to Percy here and her presentation of father-son disasters in *Frankenstein* derive from her own ideals of father-child relations.

*

Mary's father problem, her "excessive and romantic attachment" to Godwin, finds in her late fiction a resolution as idealized and conventional as Percy's in *Islam*.

> On a bed of [forest] leaves lay an old man [a hermit]: his grey hairs were thinly strewn on his venerable temples, his beard white, flowing and soft, fell to his girdle; he smiled even in his sleep a gentle smile of benevolence. I knelt down beside him; methought it was my excellent father. (*Valperga* 3:92–93)

All her life Mary as well as Percy is the child in the fairy tale who wanders through the psychic forest seeking father. He materializes in *Valperga*, as he did in *Islam*, to fulfill through art the fantasy denied in life. Like Percy's Hermit, Mary's is all-sufficient because androgynous. "Soft . . . gentle . . . benevolence" signal his feminine capacity to nurture, while masculine authority is assured by his role as spiritual guide. "Venerable" characterizes this "excellent father" as it did Percy's surrogate father in "The Coliseum"; a smile associated with sleep establishes the benignity of both *Valperga*'s hermit and *Islam*'s. The conjunction here of "temples" and "knelt" reflects the willingness of both Shelleys to revere properly androgynous paternity.

The quest for father recurs in virtually all of Mary's novels. Besides *Mathilda*, where the mother's death frees daughter and father for untoward desires, and *Frankenstein*, where the mother's death spawns the surrogates and passions discussed in chapter 4, there is *Falkner*, where the mother's death impels Elizabeth toward a foster father; *Lodore*, where the mother's abandonment of her daughter assures Ethel's dependence upon "the only parent she had ever known" (2:80); *Perkin Warbeck*, where motherless Monina returns to her manly father after intervals of (platonic) devotion to Perkin; and *Valperga*, where Euthanasia considers her bond with father "the dearest tie she had to earth" (1:167) and where orphaned Beatrice venerates both "my good father, the bishop" and "my excellent father" the hermit (3:70, 93). That nineteenth-century fiction abounds in motherless heroines indicates the appeal of this situation to the culture; how much more strongly does it affect Mary Godwin, whose situation it actually is. Exploring the nature of father-daughter bonds, Mary defines various forces at work, ranging from physical, psychological, and intellectual support to maternal care and conjugal attraction.

A father in Mary's fiction can provide what the *Islam* Hermit gave immediately to Laon, physical support. As Percy's Hermit carried the sick son in his giant arms from the boat to safety, De Faro in *Perkin Warbeck* carries his injured daughter in equally adequate arms *to* a boat and safety. Her childlike sense of security resembles Laon's: "She was in the extremity of illness, even of danger and lay, like a child, in the arms of the dark, tall weather-beaten mariner, who . . . stood as a rock that has braved a thousand storms, his muscles seemed iron" (2:264). Psychological support follows, as in *Islam*. Father-as-lawgiver allows dutiful daughter the security of obedience while he lives and a confidence in right conduct after he dies. "His slightest word was ever a law with me," says Ethel in *Lodore*, "and now that he is gone, I would observe his injunctions more religiously than ever" (2:78).

For heroines more intellectual than Ethel, moral guidance is augmented by intellectual support. "The desire of pleasing her father made her [Euthanasia] indefatigable in her [scholastic] exertions" (*Valperga* 1:28). Despite her reverence for Mary Wollstonecraft as a theorist of pedagogy, Mary Shelley insists that "there is a peculiarity in the education of a daughter, brought up by a father only, which tends to develop early a thousand of those portions of mind, which are folded up, and often destroyed, under mere feminine tuition" (*Lodore* 1:29). More is involved for the heroine here than simply the pleasure of learning.

> It devolved upon Fanny [in *Lodore*] to attend to, to wait upon, her father. She was his pupil—he her care. The relation of parent and child subsisted between them, on a different

> footing than in ordinary cases. Fanny nursed
> her father, watched over his health and
> humours, with the tenderness and indulgence
> of a mother . . . (1:223)

Another daughter becomes the mother of her father-child when Elizabeth in *Falkner* "watched him [Falkner] as a mother may a child" (2:146). And reenacting with her blind father the role of Milton's daughters which will inspire Dorothea Brooke a half-century later, Euthanasia "was as faithful to his wants as his own orbs had been" (*Valperga* 1:167). Unlike George Eliot who emphasizes the misguided and self-destructive aspects of Dorothea's devotion to Casaubon, Mary Shelley reveals the erotic underside to devotion like Euthanasia's. The daughter is replacing not the male's mother but his wife, so that emotions more than daughterly are in the air.

"She idolized her father . . . her idolized father . . . her father whom she idolized" seem particularly obsessive because three different heroines are involved: Ethel in *Lodore* (1:37), Elizabeth in *Falkner* (1:125), Clara in *The Last Man* (280). The obsession is Mary Godwin's. She insists, however, that incestuous feelings are reciprocal. Whereas it is the daughter in *Falkner* who "felt herself bound . . . by stronger than filial ties" (1:110), the father is the one who knows "more than a father's fondness" in *Lodore* (1:42).[2] Such fondness makes him the aggressor, "penetrating the depths of her soul" with his "dark, expressive eyes" (1:62), while it is the "rapturous" daughter in *Falkner* whose "thrilling adoration . . . dreamt not of the necessity of a check, and luxuriated in its boundless excess" (1:67). When Elizabeth exclaims, "God preserve you, my more than father" (*Falkner* 1:120), Mary Godwin is speaking.

Feelings more than daughterly are frequent in nineteenth-century fiction, but incest is not. The traditional way to channel untoward emotion is followed by Mary Shelley in her fiction after *Mathilda*. Suitors replace sires. In a century when bridegrooms were admonished endlessly to carry on the paternal guidance of the weaker vessel, Neville is told by Falkner, "You must compensate to my dear child for my loss—you must be father as well as husband" (2:309). Neville can replace Falkner so smoothly because he is the same character. Similar physically (dark, olive, craggy) and psychologically (prone to macho rage but open to feminine influence), both men live under the same cloud, "the mysterious wretchedness that darkened the lives of the only two beings, the inner emotions of whose souls had been opened to her" (1:156). Although Elizabeth encourages Neville in the quest for his mother's killer which eventually brings Falkner to trial, Elizabeth's endeavors are therapeutic, not punitive. Only after Falkner has publicly confessed his part in Alithea's death can he be forgiven by Neville and reconciled to him. Only *then* can the triangle of Elizabeth-Neville-Falkner be guaranteed permanence. The conventional marriage which resolves the love plot thus provides an unconventional wish fulfillment. *Falkner* ends not with the wedding of Elizabeth and Neville but with the cemented bond between Neville and Falkner, because only the union of suitor and father assures that the daughter can at last consummate the passion which has driven Mary's heroines. And herself.

The union of Elizabeth and Neville reflects a shared vision which illuminates wonderfully the father-directed emotions of Mary and Percy. "How strange the chance that led the daughter of the destroyer to share the feelings of the unhappy victim's son" (2:124). Ultimately what Elizabeth shares with Neville are not only his feelings about Alithea but his desire for union with Falkner. Like Percy and Mary with Godwin, Neville and Elizabeth both seek father, and the same father.

*

Why does Mary not find with Percy the resolution of complexes and the completeness of union which Elizabeth achieves with Neville? Mary certainly tries to put *Falkner* into practice—to move from father to suitor by recreating the elder man in the younger. "Until I met Shelley I [could?] justly say that he [Godwin] was my God" (quoted by Nitchie [89] from an unpublished letter in the Abinger collection). Mary abandons herself to Percy with the most orthodox completeness. "Perhaps she [I] will one day have a father till then be every thing to me love" (*MSL* 1:4–5, 28 Oct. 1814). Mary of course remains deeply concerned with Godwin, but she makes Percy her god—investing "every thing" in him and expecting as much in return. If she has gotten beyond father ties and united permanently with Percy, why can Percy not get beyond father problems and unite exclusively with her? *Islam* seems to second Mary's espousal of the "normal" teleology of relationships. After the Hermit's death, Cythna—who, it turns out, is not actually dead—reenters the plot and is united with Laon in ecstatic congress.

Why art and life do not reflect each other for Percy will become clearer if we turn back to *Islam* and see that beneath its apparently idealistic surface are subversive forces at work. Why does Shelley put himself in the awkward position of having to resurrect Cythna? Why hang her in the first place? If Laon needs to be alone with the

Hermit to achieve solidarity, Cyntha's capture and abduction at this point in the plot are convenient enough. The very unnecessariness of Cythna's hanging indicates how necessary it must be to Shelley. Especially since her corpse is presented so gruesomely, the assassination of woman—as opposed to her absence—seems a precondition of male solidarity for Shelley.

Islam reverses *Falkner* by paralleling it too exactly. Percy as well as Mary is seeking father *as end.* The ostensibly similar teleologies—daughter going beyond father to suitor, and son going beyond father to beloved—involve, in fact, quite different processes. While the woman has only to change the object of her affection, the man must change the gender of his. That a male is the object of Percy's desires as well as of Mary's desires is indicated not only in the Hermit scenes of *Islam*, but in much of Shelley's life. If we compare the duration and intensity of Shelley's bonds with men and women, we may well agree with various scholars that the paramount figures of his emotional life are Hogg, Trelawny, Byron, and Williams. Men are also the paramount object when the prevailing emotion is rage. Inadequate fathers—Sir Timothy, Godwin, Wordsworth, Rousseau—obsess the poet-son to the end, to *The Triumph of Life.* Either way, rage or affection, the lesson is the same. Either solidarity is achieved and woman is superfluous, or solidarity is denied and the son's continued search for father keeps woman secondary.

Islam proves subversive in a different way if we view it in light of the Erotic desire for self-union. Is even a father-son bond possible for Prometheans? Male solidarity obviously constitutes a threatening alternative to self-union because the father becomes a rival who must be extirpated. But solidarity is even more threatening than that. It *fosters* death. Initially the son's escape from mother and body may be directed toward father and mind, but soon he recognizes that father is not only as mortal as mother and thus as incapable of assuring the son's immortality, father is more mortal. Uniting with him involves death as a precondition, rather than simply as a consequence. Equality *means* mortality, since the son can ascend to the father's place upon the wheel of time only if he acknowledges the elder man's humanity and thus accepts the inevitability of his own descent to death. Father is the ultimate threat to self-union because he provides a model so attractive that the son may accept mortality to achieve it.

There is something else about father, however, something promising for Eros. Father *in death* seems to offer an escape from mortality that mother, dead or alive, cannot. So important to Prometheans is this aspect of father-son relations that it informs the major literary productions of both Mary and Percy Shelley.

VICTOR AND ALPHONSE

I want to begin my discussion of Victor and Alphonse in what may seem an unlikely place—the Arab Maid of *Alastor*. Mary in the opening frame of *Frankenstein* established her position on father-son conflicts, as we saw, by having Margaret Saville agree with Mr. Walton about Robert's foolhardiness. Since no one in the body of *Frankenstein* succeeds Margaret as arbiter, Mary proceeds more indirectly. In *Alastor*, the Arab Maid did what Mary considers natural and what she herself did for Percy—steal away from the father and tend upon the beloved. Woman's reward in *Alastor* is abandonment. "Self-centred seclusion" makes the male too obsessed with his antitype to bond with his complement. *Frankenstein* recapitulates the Arab Maid scenario, twice. "The Arabian," Safie, leaves her father and travels to her beloved Felix. Her reward is felicity. Elizabeth travels from her father to the home of the male destined to be her complement. Her reward is assassination. This contrast between Felix's and Frankenstein's treatment of woman functions as Margaret Saville did in the opening frame—to signal that something is seriously wrong with the Promethean's relationship with father.

Felix, despite many hardships, feels no apparent antagonism toward a father excellent like the best old men in Mary's and Percy's art. Like the blind seer in "The Coliseum," M. De Lacey responds positively to the wanderer who comes seeking knowledge and love; like the hermits in *Islam* and *Valperga*, he is served devotedly by an excellent daughter. With this ideal father, Felix achieves the solidarity which allows him, like Neville, to go on to complementary union with the beloved. Why cannot Victor do the same with Alphonse and Elizabeth?

Critics in recent years have found oedipal tensions in the Victor-Alphonse relationship. They note that the son is hurt by his father's belittling Agrippa; that Victor consequently fears to share with Alphonse his new readings in alchemy and his later experiments in monster-making; that Victor feels exiled from the family when he is sent to Ingolstadt; that he associates Alphonse with the monster after Henry's murder; that he feels bound to his parents "by a silken cord" and includes "seemed" in his description of their love for him.[3] These and other pieces of evidence fit so readily into psychoanalytic patterns that we can forget we are dealing with a character, not a patient. Especially since the text is a *narrator's* account, we must ascertain the *author's* intent. "When I would account to myself for the birth of that passion . . . I find . . . " (32). Victor is accounting to himself. What "I find" is self-justification. Events which some psychoanalytic readers have taken as factual evidence may be convenient pretexts, as Kaplan and Kloss demonstrate with Victor's initial horror at the creature.

> Why should Frankenstein react in this astounding way? . . . because the creature is ugly in appearance! At least this is the only explanation Frankenstein gives us. . . . But what an achievement is here. Ugly or not, it moves, breathes, lives! . . . With the description he gives, he might just as easily and more realistically, have marveled that the resemblance to man was so close. . . . if we are to understand him, and the novel as well, we must presume that this terror, having its origin in other causes, is transferred to a convenient pretext. (122, 123)

Convenient pretexts are Victor's stock-in-trade. Particularly in passages defining the reasons for his behavior, Frankenstein's reactions often seem inordinate, the effects disproportionate to the causes. As we seek underlying motives, we must look carefully at Victor's placement of the blame on Alphonse, and also at Levine's less extreme judgment that "fathers and sons are almost equally responsible and irresponsible" (a 21). We must, in other words, remain alive to distinctions between narrator and author, between Victor's assertion and our experience of it.

Take, for example, Alphonse's remark about Agrippa:

> My father looked carelessly at the title-page of my book, and said "Ah! Cornelius Agrippa! My dear Victor, do not waste your time upon this; it is sad trash." If, instead of this remark, my father had taken the pains to explain to me, that the principles of Agrippa had been entirely exploded, and that a modern system of science had been introduced . . . I should certainly have thrown Agrippa aside . . . (32–33)

Victor is correct: Alphonse should explain, not simply dismiss. But just as unquestionably, the *magnitude* of Alphonse's failure is relevant too. Is our experience really that "a rationalist, like Godwin, the elder Frankenstein rather cruelly chastens his son's youthful imagination" (Knoepflmacher 104)? Alphonse's "my dear" is neither rationalistic nor cruel, as Godwin's chastenings of Mary show. She could easily have made Alphonse's dismissal of Agrippa seem cruel enough to warrant Victor's reaction. Instead what we experience is a minor mistake. What parent has not missed by at least this much the proper tone in a random moment? (And random the moment is: on vacation, on a rainy day indoors, with a child who has never before evinced an interest in science.)

That Victor is finding convenient pretexts is signaled in his admission that "if, instead of this remark, my father had taken the pains to explain . . . I . . . should probably have applied myself to the more rational theory of chemistry which has resulted from modern discoveries. It is even possible, that the train of my ideas would never have received the fatal impulse that led to my ruin" (33). Is it really? "Probably" and "possible" foster suspicions in us which are confirmed when Alphonse *does* explain about modern science.

> The catastrophe of this tree [hit by lightning] excited my extreme astonishment; and I eagerly inquired of my father the nature and origin of the thunder and lightning. He replied, "Electricity;" describing at the same time the various effects of that power. He constructed a small electrical machine, and exhibited a few experiments; he made also a kite, with a wire and string, which drew down that fluid from the clouds. This last stroke completed the overthrow of Cornelius Agrippa. (35)

Is our experience of this passage actually that "the 1818 version of the novel is even harsher on the old man. . . . Alphonse is also blamed for leading his son to science when he conducts a Franklin-like experiment" (Knoepflmacher 104–5)? Alphonse can't win for trying. Here he does all that Victor faulted him for omitting before: he is patient; he explains; he even demonstrates. How does Mary treat him harshly here? Or rather, what does it mean that "the 1818 version of the novel" treats him harshly? Is the treatment attributable to the author or to the narrator? That *Victor* is trying to implicate Alphonse in his youthful swerve toward destructive studies is clear. But we must distinguish between Victor's attempt and Mary's, between Victor's attempt and our response.

After the Franklin-like experiment, Victor "by some fatality . . . did not feel inclined to commence the study of any modern system" (35). In its vagueness, "some fatality" carries on from "probably" and "possible," but it goes beyond these words as the clearest signal yet that the prime force operating upon Victor is not Alphonse, but something internal. The 1818 edition introduces at this point a lecture course which "some accident" prevents Victor from attending "until the course was nearly finished. The lecture . . . was entirely incomprehensible to me" (36). Accidents are so often convenient pretexts for Victor that we are not inclined to see external forces operating strongly here, and this interpretation is confirmed by the 1831 edition. The lecture course is deleted, Alphonse is replaced as Victor's electricity mentor by "a man of great research" (238)—and still the boy does not go on to study modern science.

> By some fatality the overthrow of these men [Agrippa, Albertus Magnus, Paracelsus] disinclined me to pursue my accustomed [scientific] studies. It seemed to me as if nothing would or could be known. All that had so long engaged my attention suddenly grew despicable. By one of those caprices of the mind. . . . In this mood of mind I betook myself to the mathematics. . . . Thus strangely are our souls constructed. . . . Destiny was too potent, and her immutable laws had decreed . . . (239)

By repeating the word "fatally," which begs the question it seems to answer, Mary directs us away from Alphonse and toward Victor. "It seemed to me . . . suddenly . . . caprices of the mind . . . mood of mind . . . strangely . . . Destiny . . . laws had decreed." What is happening inside Victor he does not understand and does not want to understand. Mary, I believe, tries to avoid in 1831 exactly what Dussinger faults her for—"indecisiveness" (42) about Alphonse's role in 1818. Having initially established that Victor's "family was not scientifical" (34), Mary needed the boy familiarized with modern science and she chose Alphonse as the handiest teacher—forgetting that he was not scientifical. Later, in the Thomas copy, she caught her mistake and reminded herself in the margin, "you said your family was not scientific." In 1831 she corrects the mistake by keeping Alphonse consistently non-scientific and inventing clumsily the man of great research who teaches Victor what she wants him to know. Mary never, I feel, intended a rivalry between Alphonse and Victor as scientists, never intended the father to have any large role in the son's disastrous move toward monster-making.

Father and son do not seem almost equally responsible and irresponsible. Instead the son absolves himself of irresponsibility by making the father responsible.

To appreciate Victor's motivation here, we must, I feel, heed a distinction present in Freud and important in recent psychoanalytic work—a distinction between the Oedipus as a fantasy projected by the son upon the innocent father and the Oedipus as a son's correct perception about the father. Psychoanalytic critics have tended to assume the latter as the Frankenstein situation, whereas I am proposing the former. Take, for example, Victor's blaming Alphonse for his going to Ingolstadt.

> When I had attained the age of seventeen, my parents resolved that I should become a student at the university of Ingolstadt. I had hitherto attended the schools of Geneva; but my father thought it necessary, for the completion of my education, that I should be made acquainted with other customs than those of my native country. My departure was therefore fixed at an early date. (37)

"I" *attain* seventeen, but the family does the rest. "My parents resolved . . . my father thought . . . My departure was therefore fixed." The son is already feeling himself driven from home and mother by his rival the father (and may also be feeling, as the plural "parents" indicates, that mother is siding with father) when suddenly Caroline dies. What ensues is analyzed well by Dussinger. Victor blames his mother's death upon his father's banishing of him; then Alphonse's continued insistence upon Victor's departure makes the son see things the opposite way—that the father blames *him* for Caroline's death and is punishing him with banishment. "The narrator, it would be possible to say, wants to lessen his guilt involved in his secret rebellion against the enervating domestic order by attributing the decision to leave home to his father" (Dussinger 43). Victor's word "early" supports Dussinger by indicating not only that the date is soon, but that the son feels it is too soon, feels he is being forced to leave early. We should not take it this way, however. That sons become "acquainted with other customs than those of . . . [their] native country" is a traditional goal of fathers. Particularly in Mary's fiction, sons repeatedly practice the wisdom preached in *Lodore*: "At seventeen years many their fortunes seek" (3:158). At seventeen Lodore goes off to Oxford (1:82); Lionel, admonished by Adrian in *The Last Man* to "begin life . . . you are seventeen," sets off for "the necessary apprenticeship" in a foreign land (24–25). And barely a month before her seventeenth birthday, Mary Godwin elopes with Percy Shelley.

The contrast between Victor's reluctance and Castruccio's eagerness—"he entered his seventeenth year . . . his fervent desire [was] to quit what he thought a lifeless solitude" (*Valperga* 1:37)—shows how closely Victor resembles Shelley. Shelley, who at various times suspected Sir Timothy of seeking to exile him to a madhouse and to the Peninsular Wars, sees the inevitable need to go away to school as a father-generated plan of banishment. *He* responds by setting a washroom fire which could have consumed Field Place.

The parallels with Percy's life and the analogues in Mary's fiction confirm our sense in *Frankenstein* that Alphonse is not malevolent, especially since he sympathetically postpones Victor's departure after Caroline's death. Victor downplays the sympathy by mitigating Alphonse's agency. "I obtained from my father a respite of some weeks" (38). The emphasis is upon "I." That what "I" do is *obtain* a "respite" stresses the son's subservience and his struggle to wrest a concession from father. The real heavy father in *Frankenstein* is M. Clerval, who for a long time forbids his talented son to attend Ingolstadt. Why would Mary portray Henry's father this way except to highlight Victor's father? Instead of the psychological pattern which *Frankenstein* implies—that Alphonse's traditional goal and sympathetic postponement of it screen his "real," oedipal design—we experience the well-intentioned plan of a father properly ambitious for his gifted son.

A last complaint of Victor's is added by Mary in 1831:

> Much as they [Victor's parents] were attached
> to each other, they *seemed* to draw inexhausti-
> ble stores of affection from a very mine of love
> to bestow them upon me. . . . while during
> every hour of my infant life I received a lesson
> of patience, of charity, and of self-control, I was
> so guided by *a silken cord*, that all seemed but
> one train of enjoyment to me. (234; my italics)

As with Alphonse's dismissal of Agrippa, my point here is not to deny the presence of tension, but to define its magnitude. "Seemed" and "cord" indicate Victor's sense of insecurity and constraint. But since any child doubts parental love occasionally, and since every child is bound to parental will indubitably, the question is whether "seemed" and "cord" justify a sense of estrangement as enormous as Victor's becomes. Is Mary not insisting upon the facts of life—that even this virtually ideal home cannot be perfect, that tension will exist in any human relationship? Confronted with a matter of degree, we feel that the ravages which Victor perpetrates upon home are heinously disproportionate to his sufferings there.

Where does Victor get an "oedipal" sense of father-son relations nearly a century before Freud? The obvious answer—that sons have ever felt abused by fathers—is bolstered by a more historiographical source. Gothic fiction, as Wilt argues, makes paternal abuse a major theme. "The son must die so that the old man may live" (29). This paradigm which recurs from *The Castle of Otranto* through *Dracula* is prominent in Godwin's *Caleb Williams* and *St. Leon*. In *Frankenstein*, however, the son's oppression by the father informs not the plot of the novel but the mind of the protagonist. Victor interprets life as though it were a gothic novel. Mary Shelley drama-tizes not the oedipal paranoia of the gothic tradition but the dangers of such paranoia, the dangers of approaching complex realities with the self-justifying convenience of a paradigm. *Frankenstein* is, in this sense, anti-gothic. It is orthodoxy's counterattack against the dark tradition which had exposed the self-deceived convenience of *its* sentimental paradigms. In another sense, however, Mary's very skepticism about gothic paranoia is very gothic. Lewis, Maturin, Hogg, Beddoes, as well as Brown, Poe, Hawthorne, and Melville, all share her distrust of the son's self-justifying rage, even as they, like her, make oedipal emotions central to their art. Mary Shelley's crit-ical examination of all paradigms, oedipal and sentimental, is what drives her and her readers beyond Victor's self-justifying explana-tion to the darker teleology of him and Percy.

*

What is the nature of the antagonism toward Alphonse which Victor expresses in oedipal terms? Psychoanalytic critics have right-ly seen Victor's philanthropic rationale for monster-making as a convenient pretext. The claim that he is creating life in order to save mankind from death screens Frankenstein's deeper desire to resusci-tate his dead mother. Readers can, however, recognize this second level and still sense another, even deeper motive, since Victor's de-votion to woman is not all it might be. He kills women. As a wish fulfillment, Victor's dream is manifestly *not* oedipal: the nightmare kiss functions not to awaken the mother from death, as in Sleeping Beauty, but to reduce Elizabeth to Caroline's moribund state. Victor is then free to move beyond woman to father. In Freudian terms,

Victor's feelings are not oedipal (kill the father to possess the mother) but negative oedipal (kill the mother to possess the father).[4]

Why father? The answer, as we have seen, cannot lie in any illusion of paternal immortality. In fact, one reason why Percy rages against old men is that he too is aging, and prematurely. When he says, "I have lived to be older than my father" (*MSL* 1:189, 27 Aug. 1822), he is reflecting not only upon his superior wisdom but upon his greying hair and wasted body. Confronted with the danger of becoming *like* his father, Shelley determines to *become* his father.

This determination is proclaimed, quite amazingly, on the title pages of his first two books of verse. *Original Poetry* is authored by Victor (and Cazire); *Posthumous Fragments of Margaret Nicholson* is "edited" by John Fitzvictor. Victor and Fitzvictor. What Shelley desires ultimately is not what *Islam* idealized, not that place upon the wheel of time which allows to both son and father the dignity of all roles from birth to death. Victor and Fitzvictor, father and son: Shelley desires to become his own father because as Victor-Fitzvictor he can sire himself.

How this promises immortality is dramatized in *Prometheus Unbound*. Demogorgon is eternal. Like Percy, he is older than his father; but unlike Percy, he is not threatened by age. The son who kills the father lives forever. The Demogorgon who descends as killer-son with Jupiter in act 3 emerges by himself as Eternity in act 4. He is no longer "son" because he no longer has a father. Even as fantasy, however, Demogorgon seems unsatisfying: since Shelley is not eternal, how can he take Demogorgon for a model? The answer to this question lies in Shelley's understanding of his myth; his association of Demogorgon with Eternity comes not from Peacock or Milton but from Boccaccio. In *The Genealogy of the Pagan Gods*, Demogorgon is the principle of force who cohabits with the Witch of Eternity. Shelley takes this union of male and female and combines the two principles into one character. Demogorgon becomes hermaphroditic by ingesting the female principle of eternity. Percy can do likewise. By containing both masculine and feminine, as self and antitype, he becomes self-sufficient.

Like the snake swallowing its tail, the male can provide both the phallus and its receptacle. Siring oneself assures immortality by closing the generative cycle and thus precluding death. Victor-Fitzvictor. For this most perversely solipsistic version of his antitype idea, Shelley finds sanctioning precedents in both Romantic satanism and orthodox Christianity. One of the things which attracts the Romantics to Milton's Satan is his daring claim to self-generation. This parodies the Christian notion that "the Father pours himself out into the Son; the Son, knowing himself separate, makes the astonishing choice to curve that stream of being back toward the progenitor" (Wilt 14). Victor's discovery of the secret of life *abolishes* Alphonse by supplanting the biological process which made the father a father. Rather than curve the stream of being back to Alphonse, Frankenstein as the only begetter of a new system of begetting curves it into himself. Eros again repudiates the Incarnation. Frankenstein seeks victory by blasphemously, hermaphroditically becoming the alpha and omega.

Although Frankenstein's desire to become Fitz-Victor is achieved partially by giving birth to himself as monster, he remains a son so long as he, like Demogorgon, has a father. Alphonse must die. Mary's *Frankenstein* and Percy's life and art thus feature early in the nineteenth century a motif central to literature and literary biography for the next hundred and fifty years—sons desiring to extirpate fathers and to sire themselves. Both the desire and its consequences are summed up in Freud's words to Dostoevsky: "You wanted to kill your father in order to be your father yourself. Now you *are* your father, but a dead father." Recent critics have found this motif in novelists as diverse as Melville ("behind these [Pierre's] stratagems lies the desire to be one's own father") and Joyce ("Stephen is the son-type in the process of fathering himself"). In Dickens, Thackeray, and Faulkner, this process is made still more intricate by the son's attempt to recreate himself through language. Pip, "the metaphorical writer-as-son[,] also attempts to give birth to himself in writing, to beget or engender himself without the help of fathers"; Esmond, "the fatherless son[,] is allowed, in a sense, to be father himself through the first-person narrative"; and Quentin can become in effect the sire of Jason, Sr., if he can articulate the Compson history and thus "seize his father's authority by gaining temporal priority."[5] Mary Shelley agrees emphatically with all these writers about "the lunacy of attempting . . . to engender the self," but the most relevant context for her masterpiece remains Percy Shelley. He provides Mary with an immediate example of the "poetic will," the reaction against father and the concern with self-generation which has characterized the last two hundred years and which has been called by Harold Bloom "an argument against time, revengefully seeking to substitute 'It is' for 'It was.' Yet this argument always splits in two, because the poetic will needs to make another outrageous substitution, of 'I am' for 'It is.' Both parts of the argument are quests for priority."[6]

In the analysis which follows I will often discuss Victor in terms of works written by Shelley *after* 1818. Two considerations warrant this. As Percy's "handwriting was very early formed and never altered," so the artistic products of that hand show remarkable consistency. The dismissal of the living Godwin as dead in the 1820 "Letter to Maria Gisborne" repeats the 1815 dismissal of Wordsworth. More important, the psychological moves I will define in *Prometheus Unbound* and *The Cenci*—expressing the need to assassinate and to deny responsibility for the act—repeat at the highest levels of art what Shelley had been doing at least since he introduced plagiarism into *Original Poetry* and then blamed Elizabeth Shelley for it. Victor in 1818 can anticipate Shelley's moves in 1819 because Mary has learned through grim experience her husband's instinctual responses. In that intricate literary interaction between *Frankenstein* and *Prometheus Unbound* and *The Cenci*, it is as though Percy learns from Mary what he had taught her. Or rather, he reaffirms in 1819 what she had urged him in 1818 to repudiate.

For Victor as for Shelley, father looms large. In fact, too large. Patricide can find expression only through the effeminate, Dionysiac form of Eros, because father-killing is too awful for the active, ego-centric Eros to contemplate. "Woman's way," killing by indirection, is the only way to go here. Shelley shows the way. Fundamental to the basic myth of Prometheus is father-killing. Jupiter destroyed his sire, Saturn, and was in turn threatened by his own offspring. Attractive as this situation is to the Erotic Shelley, it does not lead to the absolute annihilation he requires. "The *Prometheus Unbound* of Aeschylus supposed the reconciliation of Jupiter with his victim. . . . I was averse from a catastrophe so feeble as that of reconciling the Champion with the Oppressor of mankind" (*CP* 205). Reconciliation is the theme of *Islam* and *Prince Athanase*, but this is not always Shelley's response. While *Islam* reveals the ideal acceptance of paternal manhood which Agape encourages, other poems express the Erotic son's attack upon the manhood of sires who have failed to measure up. Shelley finds it difficult to discover limitations in an authority figure and still acknowledge that man's masculinity. Wordsworth is a "moral eunuch" in *Peter Bell The Third*, an "unsexual man" (314, 551). Shelley cannot face directly the sexuality of that ultimate elder, Sir Timothy, so he strikes back by claiming superior maturity. "I have lived to be older than my father, I am ninety years of age. . . . the life of a man of talent who should die in his *thirtieth year*, is, with regard to his own feelings, longer than that of a miserable priest-ridden slave" (*MSL* 1:189, 27

Aug. 1822; Medwin 434). Although Shelley credits himself here with that experiential wisdom which Laon and Prince Athanase accede to, his life cannot achieve what his art enacts—the friendship between younger and older male which assures their equality and manhood. Unable to be reconciled to Wordsworth or Godwin or Sir Timothy, Percy Shelley never resolves his obsession with fathers. Instead he does with them what he does with wife-mothers who fail. He assassinates.

> Deserting these [truth and liberty], thou
> leavest me to grieve,
> Thus having been, that thou shouldst cease to
> be.
>
> ("To Wordsworth" 13–14)

Needless to say, Wordsworth is very much alive in 1815. But not to Shelley. Unlike *Islam*, where the limitations of the elder male can be acknowledged and accepted, "To Wordsworth" tolerates no deviation from the ideal. Once Wordsworth acts as he should not, he, like Elizabeth Shelley, is *"no more."* The same happens to Godwin. With a switch of verb tense and a switch to neuter gender, Shelley can switch off a man whose life has failed to measure up.

> [In London] . . . You [the Gisbornes] will see
> That which was Godwin . . .
> . . . .
> You will see Coleridge—he who sits obscure.
>
> ("Letter to Maria Gisborne" 196–97, 202)

And Sir Timothy? Again Shelley finds it hardest to deal with his real father, but again he manages to make his point. The need to defeat rather than to bond with father shapes both of Shelley's greatest long works.

Unlike *Islam* which idealized the reconciliation advocated by Agape, *Prometheus Unbound* effects the extermination required by Eros. Shelley transforms father from loving Hermit to quintessential evil. The son's response to him is not the guilt-producing one of patricide, but the noble one of assassin.[7] What might seem self-indulgent becomes obligatory: the world must be redeemed from evil.

This change cannot preclude guilt entirely, so Shelley further justifies assassination by aligning himself with two of the canonical traditions of his time. As Romantic, he models his rejection of reconciliation upon the heroic defiance of Satan in *Paradise Lost*. Satan is, however, hardly a model to all readers (or to Shelley as erstwhile Christian), so the poet acknowledges the "ambition, envy, revenge" (*CP* 205) of Milton's character and makes Jesus Christ another of his own party. "Christ the benevolent champion, falsely identified with the Son of God, must destroy the notion of the Father in the mind of Man in order to vindicate his own humanity and goodness" (Marshall 45). Since guilt still remains a possibility so long as killing remains the theme, Shelley makes the ultimate gesture and declares Prometheus perfect—"the type of the highest perfection of moral and intellectual nature, impelled by the purest and the truest motives to the best and noblest ends" (*CP* 205).

An apparently insuperable dilemma now confronts Shelley: either someone perfect cannot kill, or a killer cannot be perfect. The way out of this dilemma is explained by Mary herself. "According to the mythological story . . . the offspring of Thetis . . . was destined to be greater than his father. . . . Shelley adapted the catastrophe of this story to his peculiar views. The son greater than his father . . . was to dethrone Evil" (*CP* 272). In Shelley's "peculiar" view, the "son" is *two* men, who reflect his contradictory responses to father. Prometheus is the Percy of Agape who, as son, is oppressed by fathers yet remains as perfect in love as they are sunk in evil. Then, since the "son" in the Greek myth is not Prometheus, the actual offspring of Thetis can express the homicidal rage of Eros. Demogorgon does what Percy-Prometheus cannot and what Percy-Assassin must. Demogorgon does the dirty work and keeps Prometheus' hands clean.

Deflection of guilt occurs in a different way in *The Cenci.* Father is again made so monstrously evil that no substantial sympathy can devolve to him, and the agent of assassination is again removed sufficiently from Shelley (Beatrice is female and modeled from life)[8] to prevent his direct implication. To make all the more certain that guilt cannot surface, Shelley resorts to another characteristic expedient—indignation. He criticizes the woman who does his bidding, as he blamed his sister Elizabeth for his own plagiarism in *Original Poetry.*

> Undoubtedly, no person can be truly dishonoured by the act of another; and the fit return to make to the most enormous injuries is kindness and forebearance, and a resolution to convert the injurer from his dark passions by peace and love. Revenge, retaliation, atonement, are pernicious mistakes. If Beatrice had

thought in this manner she would have been
wiser and better. (*CP* 276)

The long controversy over *The Cenci* resembles the *Alastor* debate:
in both cases, prefatory statements seem at odds with the works
themselves.[9] My point is not to contest the moral stance taken in
the *Cenci* preface ("turn the other cheek" is impeccably Christian),
or to belabor the fact that Shelley did not always turn the cheek
when his was the one struck (as in the Rhine boat incident of 1814,
the Rome Post Office fight of 1819, and the Pisa fracas of 1822).
My point is the priggish inflexibility of the preface's attitude toward Beatrice. A man who assures a woman that rape does not really touch her essence and that she must submit to whatever deg-
radations lie ahead—this man should employ warier rhetoric. The
lack of syntactic complication in "if Beatrice had thought in this
[my] manner, she would have been wiser and better" contrasts
with the manifold complications of Beatrice's actual situation. She
cannot escape the house; no one would shelter her anyway; and
her father will unquestionably carry out his threat to rape her
again and again. Shelley's sentence, however, is not badly written.
Its syntactic stiffness and righteous tone are the inevitable consequences of its therapeutic—as opposed to rhetorical—purpose. Its
function is not only, or at least not primarily, to persuade us that
Beatrice acted wrongly, but to convince Shelley that he feels properly. The Shelley of Agape guiltily uses the preface to insist upon
the proper attitude toward patricide, after his unconscious Eros has
already used the play to satisfy homicidal desires. Readers of the
play empathize consistently with Beatrice because the Erotic Shelley enjoys her patricide. She is, after all, destroying Sir Timothy,
and Godwin, and Wordsworth, and . . .

Alphonse evokes comparable conflicts in Victor. The son feels
too much of Agape's love and sympathy to allow Eros any direct
expression of hostility. The most that the Erotic Victor can do
overtly is to hurt Alphonse indirectly by omission. The son stays
away from home protractedly and fails to write to his father regularly. During Victor's long silence at the time of the monster's creation, "I [Victor] knew well . . . what would be my father's feelings" because

> I well remembered the words of my father: "I
> know that while you are pleased with your-
> self, you will think of us with affection, and
> we shall hear regularly from you. You must

pardon me, if I regard any interruption in your
correspondence as a proof that your other duties are equally neglected." (50)

That Victor's rationale at the time—"I could not tear my thoughts
from my employment"—is a convenient pretext is admitted by
him later. "I then thought that my father would be unjust if he as-
cribed my neglect to vice, or faultiness on my part; but I am now
convinced that he was justified" (50–51).

Father and family continue to suffer as Victor continues his silence. That the Frankensteins feel "uneasy that they hear from you
so seldom" (55) is Henry's message upon arriving in Ingolstadt.
When Victor recovers from his illness, Henry asks,

> "I may speak to you on one subject, may I
> not?"
>   I trembled . . .
>   ". . . your father and cousin would be very
> happy if they received a letter from you in
> your own handwriting. They hardly know
> how ill you have been, and are uneasy at your
> long silence."
>   "Is that all?" (58)

Ostensibly "Is that all?" reflects Victor's relief that Henry has not
brought up the more dire "subject" of the monster. But Mary Shelley could have expressed that fear less damningly. "Is that all?"
confirms our sense of how little the Erotic Victor regards the sufferings of Alphonse and others.

Elizabeth then seconds Henry. Her 1818 exhortations—"Your
father attempts to conceal his fears. . . . write yourself, and make
your father and all of us happy" (59, 62)—are amplified in 1831 in
order to emphasize Alphonse's need and thus Victor's cruelty.
"One word from you, dear Victor, is necessary to calm our ap-
prehensions. . . . confirm this intelligence [of improved health]
soon in your own handwriting. . . . I entreat you, write!" (242,
243). Victor's response is again self-divided.

> "I will write instantly, and relieve them from
> the anxiety they must feel." I wrote, and this
> exertion greatly fatigued me. (62)

What fatigues the Erotic Victor is having to assuage guilt by sustaining the orthodox responses of Agape. "Must" is the key. Victor
at best sounds condescending when he imagines how the poor fam-

ily *must* be hanging on his every word. But suffer they must. Frankenstein will take out upon them the hostility that he cannot help feeling.

"Must" assumes particular weight because hostility to Alphonse drives Victor beyond omission to commission. He first proceeds indirectly.

> "Hideous monster! Let me [William] go. My papa is a Syndic—he is M. Frankenstein. . . . "
> "Frankenstein! you belong then to my enemy . . . you shall be my first victim." (139)

William is doomed only when he is identified as a son; murder was not inevitable, or apparently even intended, before that. Victor's first strike at Alphonse is thus through his beloved son (who in his own right warrants punishment as a sibling rival for the father's affection, and for the mother's love too, since William is in possession of Caroline's portrait. Emblematic of Victor's sense of domestic exclusion is the fact that when word of William's death calls him back to Geneva, "the gates of the town were already shut" [70].) The traditional association of "little brother" and penis emphasizes the castrating intent of striking at the father through his offspring. As an indirect move, it saves Victor from having to lay a guilt-fostering hand upon the father. Since the act *is* indirect, however, since little William is only a stand-in for Alphonse, a second attack must be launched against the now vulnerable sire.

Guilt and awe generated by Agape continue to require that Eros proceed indirectly, so Victor resorts to both of the tactics practiced by Shelley in his long poems. As Shelley displaced his dark deeds upon another (Demogorgon, Beatrice Cenci, and Elizabeth Shelley), Victor has created the monster to enact his murderous will against his family. His hands remain legally as clean as Prometheus'. In fact the monster does not even dirty *his* hands with Alphonse's blood. The creature could have swum across the lake and throttled the unsuspecting sire before Victor reached Geneva to warn him, but this would have brought patricide too close to home. The most fiendish thing about the sequence of events generated by Frankenstein's Erotic unconscious is that it results, in effect, in Alphonse's suicide. By succumbing to grief, the old man dies of natural causes, and lets Victor off Shelley-free. The son does remain conscience-ridden, however. "An apoplectic fit was brought on" (196). *By whom*, the sentence cannot admit. The question of responsibility, of agency, need not even have come up, had not guilt prompted Victor to self-indictingly forgo the active construction ("he died of an apoplectic fit") which would have acquitted him entirely.

Victor further deflects guilt through indignation. Like Shelley in the *Cenci* preface, he vilifies his surrogate. In face-to-face encounters, he accuses the monster of having "diabolically murdered" innocent "victims" (94); in a retrospective move like that of Shelley's preface he concludes that the creature "shewed unparalleled malignity and selfishness" (215). Since this is society's reaction (everyone abhors the monster), and since this would surely be Alphonse's reaction (you have slaughtered my children), Victor's indignation testifies to his orthodoxy, as Shelley's indignation did in the *Cenci* preface.

Even if Victor's need for clean hands precludes the monster's throttling Alphonse, grief over little William and Justine (and Caroline), *could* have caused him to die conventionally from sorrow before Elizabeth's murder. The unconvincing thing about fictional deaths from sorrow is precisely that they can occur whenever the novelist requires. Why does Mary Shelley require so many corpses, and why is Alphonse's death the last?

William Justine Henry Elizabeth Alphonse

The deaths proceed in order of increasing importance of the relationships for Victor: a tie with a child, then with a peer, then with the closest male peer, then with the still closer female peer, and finally the ultimate bond with father.[10] With each increase of intimacy, there is a greater threat to the self-union which promises immortality. And, as we have seen, father is the supreme threat, because solidarity with him is an alternate ideal. " 'And whose death,' cried I, 'is to finish the tragedy? Ah! my father, do not remain in this wretched country'" (180). Victor's covert message—"to finish . . . my father"—answers the question it poses. Victor at some deep level knows the teleology that he will not acknowledge. Mary stresses Alphonse's climactic placement in the family fatalities by having Victor say in 1831, "I turned to contemplate the deep and voiceless grief of my Elizabeth. This also was my doing! And my father's woe" (246). Victor knows. After Elizabeth's "voiceless" death by strangulation comes the father's death from "woe."

But there is more. As the last fatality, Alphonse fits not only into a scale of increasing intimacy but also into a reversal of alphabetical order.

W - J - H - E - A

Whether Mary consciously intended this reversal—for an author attentive to names to do it accidentally seems unlikely to me—the fact of reverse alphabetization reflects her reaction to self-union. The reversal establishes Victor's motion to father as regressive. "Regressive" can mean two things. Insofar as Victor-Shelley is capable of the intimacy and solidarity of Agape, regressive has the positive associations of the term in Freud's clinical papers (particularly "Remembering, Repeating, and Working-Through")[11] and in more recent discussions of transference (particularly by Lacan and Kohut). The analysand cannot simply be *told* what is the matter with him; he must work back to the original trauma and either re-experience it or experience a comparable moment through the transference. If this were what Victor was attempting, if he were returning to his childhood relationship with Alphonse in order to understand and relive it, then "regression" would mean that the son was making that peace with the parent which is essential if psychological and social maturity is to match biological development. Particularly if we see the father in light of *Totem and Taboo* and Lacan, phallus as law is what the son should be oriented to. Victor's pursuit of the monster could then signal a therapeutically male orientation. But since Victor pursues the monster with unnatural attraction and homicidal rage, and since his own father is ultimately absent because Victor has killed him, "regressive" has the negative connotations of ordinary parlance.

W - J - H - E - A. After "A" there is nothing else. It is the beginning as end, Alpha as Omega of I AM. Suppose Mary had named Victor's father Bartholomew or Benedict or Bardolph. Suppose, in other words, that after mother (*Caroline*) and father (*Bardolph*) there remained *A*. Son would have some role beyond, before family. But father is the end of the line. Beyond mother there is Alphonse, but beyond Alphonse—Alpha—there is only silence. In his desire to become Victor-Fitzvictor, in his determination to predate his predecessor and sire himself, Frankenstein has regressed from society to preexistence, to the letterless wordless tundra of the pole's self-centered seclusion.

III

Complication and Conclusion

There are many people who give the impression "of being pursued by a malignant fate" or possessed by some "daemonic power," but analysis reveals that "their fate" is for the most part arranged by themselves.

Freud

. . . with great talents one has great surprises.

Henry James

6

The Women of
Frankenstein

There's a power in this world you never dreamed of,
I told him.

John Hawkes

The world has been to me a harsh step-mother.

Mary Shelley

There is no monster who does not tend to duplicate
himself or to "marry" another monster, no double
who does not yield a monstrous aspect upon close
scrutiny.

René Girard

GRANTED THAT *Frankenstein* IS, LIKE MANY NINETEENTH-CENTURY
texts, concerned with origins, why have I focused so exclusively
upon *male* anxiety? Cannot Victor reflect Mary's relations with parents literary and biological as well as Percy's? Barbara Johnson answers in the affirmative by noting that Mary Shelley italicizes both
the sentence in her *Frankenstein* preface *"[I] thought of a story"* and
the wedding night threat to Victor:

> Both are eliminations of the mother, since the
> story that Mary writes is a tale of motherless
> birth, and the wedding night marks the death
> of Frankenstein's bride. . . . what is at stake
> behind what is currently [and in Mary's pref-
> ace] being banalized under the name of female
> fear of success is nothing less than the fear of
> somehow effecting the death of one's own par-
> ents. . . . In order to prove herself worthy of her
> parentage, Mary, paradoxically enough, must
> thus usurp the parental role and succeed in giv-
> ing birth to *herself* on paper. Her declaration of

157

existence as a writer must therefore figuratively repeat the matricide that her physical
birth all too literally entailed. (9, 8)

However mother-oriented Mary and *Frankenstein* are, I believe they
are more father-oriented. The exemplary household of the De Laceys features a father and no mother. The De Laceys lament financial
privation and geographical isolation, but they never once mention,
let alone eulogize, Mme. De Lacey. Father and daughter can and do
carry on. I believe that Mary Shelley's concern with origins is best
understood by keeping the focus on Godwin and distinguishing her
father-orientation from Percy-Victor's. Mary does not desire to
become her own father. As a dutiful daughter of the most orthodox
stripe, she intends to *please* father, to show Godwin that she is a
worthy stand-in for the son he wanted.

The very desire to please, of course, propels an accompanying
rage. This rage focuses primarily upon Godwin, as the death of
William Frankenstein will show. But father also becomes the
occasion, as well as the focus, of rage when his possessive daughter
annihilates rivals for his affection. Understanding Mary's father-oriented anger in *Frankenstein* is difficult because guilt causes her to
employ screens and indirection extensively. We must do the hard
work of uncovering her anger, for if *Frankenstein* were only what I
have described so far, if polarization of masculine and feminine elements plagued male psyches exclusively, then the novel would be
limited by female chauvinism. Women characters would be so thoroughly idealized (which is how most critics see them) that Mary
Shelley would have succumbed to her own brand of the perfectionism which she faulted in Prometheans. Just the opposite is the
case. Mary and her women are not only flawed, as all human beings
are; they are flawed *like* Prometheans. As novelist Mary faults Victor for calling Elizabeth "animal," yet as wife she calls herself "the
Dormouse" who longs for "our little mousehole to retire to" (*MSL*
1:14, 5 Dec. 1816). Mary faults Victor and Walton for defining happiness in sky-aspiring terms, yet she defines herself as "fortunate in
having fearlessly placed my destiny in the hands of . . . a bright
planetary spirit . . . [who] raised me to the height of happiness"
(*MSL* 1:186, 27 Aug. 1822).

That Mary Shelley shares traits with the Prometheans is nearly as
important as her critique of Prometheanism. She is exasperated
with Percy not only because she has idealized a severely limited
man, but because she shares in his limitations. She knows that both
genders can be judged by an ideal of androgyny and a standard of

Agape only if she establishes that neither gender inherits the ideal genetically and that both are prey to its antithesis, Eros. *Frankenstein* therefore examines True Woman as it does Promethean man—in terms of androgyny and bifurcation. Mary Shelley does not, however, deal with women quite as we have seen her deal with men. Her presentation is self-expressive as well as self-revealing. She does more than reveal will and weakness in woman; she expresses through them her own Erotic drives. She self-indulgently liberates herself into the pleasures of willfulness, and she self-defensively absolves herself from the charge of weakness. She victimizes through art those whom she cannot touch in life, and she demonstrates that woman is the victim, not of a femininity prone to effeminacy, but of external forces beyond her control.

As an expression of woman's dissatisfactions and a means of receiving satisfaction, *Frankenstein* takes part, if always uneasily, in the revolt against authority which shakes the Romantic period and reverberates throughout Victoria's reign. Mary Shelley and her women relate particularly to the intense efforts of Charlotte Brontë, M. E. Braddon, and the sensational sixties, where domestic angels as criminal characters, as notorious authors, and as voracious readers signal trouble in the house.[1] The express-repress instinct which hides its own subversions unites *Frankenstein* to its comparably self-divided Victorian successors. "Paradoxically, it is often the very blatancy of sexual stereotypes in these novels that alerts us to the complex, psychologically and socially accurate material that the novel is trying both to suppress and to explore" (Barickman, MacDonald, and Stark 18–19). Particularly with a novelist so young and so early, our response should be not criticism for what Mary Shelley hid, but wonder at what she dared.

Female Androgyny

At her best Mary, like Percy, achieves an impressive balance of gender traits. After establishing "gentleness" as "always her distinguishing characteristic," Lord Melbourne insists that "with this softness there was neither irresolution nor feebleness; but the sternest resolution, the most steadfast purpose, would be carried out" (109). Besides the "feminine" tendency to cherish home, husband, and baby, to incline toward passivity, and to seek "support," Mary Shelley with her much-heralded "masculine mind" is capable of the mastery of recondite languages and the sustaining of scholarly labor which woman was traditionally considered incapable of. Her feminine and masculine aspects appear in the two heroines of *Lodore*.

"Nothing could be in stronger contrast than these two girls;—the fairy form, the romantic and yielding sweetness of Ethel, whose clinging affections formed her whole world,—with the studious and abstracted disciple [Fanny] of ancient learning" (1:226–27). Mary Shelley is particularly insistent upon the possibility and value of a "masculine" mind in woman. "Within [Fanny] . . . was discernible an embryo of power, and a grandeur of soul, not to be mistaken" (1:226). An intellectual woman can manage both to forgo dependence upon men and to achieve superior relations with women.

> Such a woman as Fanny was more made to be loved by her own sex than by the opposite one. Superiority of intellect, joined to acquisitions beyond those usual even to men; and both announced with frankness, though without pretension, forms a kind of anomaly little in accord with masculine taste. Fanny could not be the rival of women, and, therefore, all her merits were appreciated by them. They love to look up to a superior being, to rest on a firmer support than their own minds can afford; and they are glad to find such in one of their own sex, and thus destitute of those dangers which usually attend any services conferred by men. (3:10–11)

The excellences of Fanny and Ethel, of the aggressive and the passive, balance harmoniously in Mary's best women, as they do in Percy's Cythna who is "strong and mild" (*Islam* 951) and in his Beatrice Cenci "in whom energy and gentleness dwell together" (*CP* 278). For Mary, "the most perfect woman it was ever my fortune to meet" is her daughter-in-law, Lady Jane Shelley, who unites active and passive traits, like Mary's best heroines. Lady Jane has "vivacity and a winning softness" (*MSL* 2:334, 24 Sept. 1849), as Katherine in *Perkin Warbeck* has "vivacity, and yet softness" (2:64) and Elizabeth in *Falkner* is "admired [for] the enthusiasm and yet the softness, the sensibility and firmness" of her personality (2:285).

Firmness is crucial. Woman cannot fulfill her role as moral guide if her passive inclination to accommodation is not complemented by an active instinct for resistance. When a rescuer attempting to help Lucy escape the plague in *The Last Man* wants "to get rid of her mother . . . Lucy was firm here" (254).[2] Idris can be equally firm when mother is victimizer rather than victim. "Firm and resolute," Idris "appeared to be the only being who could resist her mother. . . . there was a fearlessness and frankness about her" (65, 51). Mary Shelley is careful not to let a heroine's capacity for masculine decisiveness get out of hand and, as the nineteenth century would say, unsex her. Idris with her "extreme mildness" (51) manages to refuse her mother's last demand "mildly" (267). Mary's most ideally androgynous characters thus tend to reflect what is both a basic assumption of the nineteenth century and a pattern traditional with one type of mythic androgyne. The feminine remains predominant in heroines, as the masculine did in males like Perkin Warbeck. Idris "although firm and resolute on any point that touched her heart . . . was yielding to those she loved" (65).

Women in Mary Shelley's fiction do not, however, achieve the androgynous ideal simply by virtue of their sex. Mary knows painfully that polarization threatens woman too. "My temper," she confesses, "[is] at the same time quick & brooding" (*MSL* 2:161, 16 Aug. 1842).[3] That her feminine and masculine traits are divided between *two* heroines in *Lodore* points to the difficulty of achieving and sustaining androgynous integration. Ethel's need for support is extreme enough to indicate a basic limitation in True Woman and in Mary herself. "[Unable] to rely on and act for herself. . . . Ethel was taught to know herself dependent; the support of another was to be as necessary to her daily food" (1:40). The other extreme is a "masculine" hardness of heart which can derive either from too intellectual an orientation or from too icy a reaction to thwarted love. Bookish Fanny is prey to the first type of hardness, but Mary Shelley self-protectively whisks her offstage before it can set in. The second type of hardness Mary reveals self-expressively, when Euthanasia reacts to Castruccio's perfidy with an "altered mien . . . coldness . . . had changed her heart from a fountain of burning love to an icy spring (*Valperga* 2:231). Mary's later heroines and Mary herself provide the best introduction to the bifurcation of *Frankenstein*'s women.

WILL AND WOMAN

In women less perfect than Lady Jane, vivacity can lead to relentlessness of will.

> The very natural vivacity of her [Katherine's] nature made her disdain not to have her will, when once it was awakened. . . . the smallest opposition appeared rebellion to her [Cornelia's] majesty of will. . . . the concentrated self-will . . . [of Perdita] was destined to destroy

even the very idol [Raymond]. (*Perkin Warbeck*
3:204; *Ladore* 2:53; *The Last Man* 83)[4]

The same process which brought men like Falkner from an initial
penchant for willfulness to a final balance of gender traits can redeem Mary's willful women too. As Lionel "was softened and humanized" in *The Last Man* (22), Beatrice "was softened and humanized" in *Valperga* (3:63). With Beatrice, however, the change is only
momentary. Permanent improvement is an arduous process for
willful women, as *The Last Man* demonstrates. The old queen's
"passion for command" and "love of rule" (22) are described with
male imagery and are doomed to failure. "Her double shot [of crit-
icism] proved too heavy, and fell short of the mark" (20). The ex-
queen is unsexed. "Her body was evidently considered by her as a
mere machine. . . . There is something fearful in one who can thus
conquer the animal part of our nature" (52). The heartlessness inevitable in one "entirely made of mind" (52) prompts her, like the
Erotic Victor and Shelley, to simply dispatch whoever fails to meet
her standards. "It was useless," she writes to Adrian and Idris, "to
address again the injured parent, whose only expectation of tranquility must be derived from oblivion of their existence" (63–64).
Like Sir Timothy and Godwin dealing with their errant children,
she "positively declined any communication with them" (64).

However much the ex-queen is like Godwin, Sir Timothy, Percy,
Victor, and all willful men, she is *not* male, and that proves advan-
tageous in Mary's fiction. Redemptive suffering can reach the mother through her children. Idris's death forces the willful queen to recognize the superiority of her daughter's femininity. "Had I during
her life once consulted her gentle wishes, and curbed my rugged
nature to do her pleasure, I should not feel thus" (262). Recognition
leads the queen out of machisma. "The *hard, inflexible*, persecuting
woman, turned with a *mild* expression of face, and said [to
Lionel] . . . 'take me, and govern me as you will'" (263; my italics).
Androgyny is not reached overnight, of course, but soon "proud of
heart as she was, she bathed her pillow with nightly tears" (267).
Eventually the old queen can unite with her ideally feminine son
and effect a social-political androgyny that reflects her new balance
of psychic traits.

> He [Adrian], the servant of love, and prince of
> tender courtesy, opened it [his heart] wide for
> her admittance. . . . Her understanding, cour-
> age, and presence of mind, became powerful

auxiliaries to him in the difficult task of ruling
the tumultuous crowd. (280–81)

The old queen thus moves from "love of power" (13) to power
as love, but other female characters in Mary Shelley prove that this
move from Eros to Agape is no more inevitable for women than it
was for Raymond or Castruccio. Mary at her most optimistic may
contrast love and willfulness—"how much of self-will . . . must
we not sacrifice, when we devote ourselves to the pleasures and
services of others" (*Perkin Warbeck* 2:221)—but she insists in her
darker moments that woman's love can also be a mode of will.
With "the power . . . to rule him [Lodore] absolutely," Countess
Lyzinski "wound him to her will" (1:142, 136). What is conventional with countesses of melodrama becomes serious when
Mary's narrators exclaim, "Oh, who would rule by power, when so
much more absolute a tyranny is established through love" (*Falkner* 2:262), and "This . . . is power! Not to be strong of limb,
hard of heart, ferocious, and daring; but kind, compassionate and
soft" (*The Last Man* 19). The conventional language of romance
sounds no less sinister when woman's love is thwarted. Perdita's
"power . . . had greatly decayed. He [Raymond] was no longer her
slave—no longer her lover" (*The Last Man* 91). The word "power"
whirls through the section of *Valperga* where Beatrice in the
thralls of passion tries to master fickle Castruccio.

> I am more powerful in my weakness . . . there
> is a cloud over you which words of power can
> dispel . . . child of a sleeping power . . . I feel
> no power . . . Have you never owned a
> power? . . . You own this power? . . . What do
> you tell me of power? . . . Command me and
> my powers . . . far less power over
> them . . . would you exert your own
> power? . . . to gain a moment's power over
> Castruccio . . . I have already tempted the
> powers above me . . . that innate
> power . . . the heavenly powers deign not to in-
> terfere . . . powers . . . power . . . power . . . him
> who before defied my powers . . . mistress of
> the powers of air. (3:125, 126, 129, 130, 131
> [three times], 133, 134 [twice], 135, 136 [twice],
> 137, 139 [three times], 151, 153.)

Beatrice's attempt to handle a willful male by emulating his willfulness is foolish and foredoomed; Euthanasia's separation from Cas-

truccio is the only way. But Mary Shelley knows the frustrations and fury of a woman scorned. Willful Beatrice expresses Mary's desire to match power with power, to repay hurt with hurt.

Mary Shelley's own willfulness surfaces throughout her life. Thornton Hunt attests to "the decision of purpose which ultimately gained her the playful title of 'Wilful [sic] Woman'" (189). Agreeing with Hunt without agreeing to the "playful," Trelawny implicates Mary in his own willfulness, as he implicated Percy in his mulishness. "We are both somewhat self-willed and cross-grained, and choose to love in our own fashions" (Dowden 2:472).[5] Mary agrees. In "The Choice" she applies to herself the word "impenetrable" (36) which characterized males bereft of feminine softness. She is equally honest about her will to power. "When he [Percy Florence] has a *desire* for a thing . . . then he wd. go thro' fire and water—in this he is like me" (*MSL* 2:89, 17 Nov. 1834). Her desire to be intellectually one of the boys surfaces when she fears that she has slipped into effeminacy. "The paragraph from my letter which Hunt has done me the honour to quote [in *The Examiner*]—cuts a very foolish figure—it is so femininely expressed that all men of letters will on reading it acquit me of having a *masculine* understanding" (*MSL* 1:41, 7 Oct. 1817).[6] More disturbing are moments when Mary reveals a Promethean will to mold. "I neither like life—nor the mechanism of society—nor the modes in which human beings present themselves—but I cannot mould them to my will, and in making up my mind merely to take them as they are, enthusiasm fades" (*MSL* 2:18, 27 July 1829). And at least once when she signals that will is illusory, Mary seems nonetheless overborne by a Percy-like intoxication with the force of force: "When our purposes are inflexible, how do insurmountable obstacles break before our strong will, so that often it seems that . . . with perseverance we might attain the sum of our desires" (*Perkin Warbeck* 3:329).

The violence inevitable with male force surfaces in Mary when she shares Percy's Erotic loathing for "the nauseous draught of life" (*MSL* 2:87, 30 Oct. 1834). The desire "to absolutely annihilate" human beings appears as early as the elopement, where Mary encounters the coarse barge crew and passengers, "such uncleanly animals. . . . these loathsome 'Creepers'" (*J* 12, 28 Aug. 1814). Was the seed for *Frankenstein* sown this early? ". . . uncleanly animals, to which [not whom] we might have addressed the Boatman's speech to Pope—'Twere easier for God to make entirely new men than attempt to purify such monsters as these.'" Certainly Mary, like Percy and Victor, slips readily enough into viewing people as animals. She calls a Strasbourg student, Hoff, "a kind of shapeless animal"; she sees the Pisans "crawling and crab-like through their sopping streets"; she says of the Irish radical George Cannon, "it is disgusting to hear such a beast speak of philosophy" (*J* 13n, 1 Sept. 1814; 141, 12 Nov. 1820; 37, 7 Feb. 1815). That Erotic nausea can reach a murderous extreme in Mary Shelley and can even be directed against family members is what implicates her most tellingly in Promethean will to power. Expectably, Mary's attack-retreat syndrome precludes gross onslaught upon the enemy, just as Victor-Prometheus avoided frontal attacks upon Alphonse-Jupiter. How "woman's way" allows Mary to express her will indirectly in *Frankenstein* can be suggested briefly through one biographical (and admittedly conjectural) incident.

In the summer of 1822 Mary hates Lerici partly because her uncanny prescience finds it redolent of death.

> I could not endure that he [Percy] should go—I called him back two or three times, & told him that if I did not see him soon I would go to Pisa with the child—I cried bitterly when he went away. . . . my ill spirits encreased; in my letters to him I entreated him to return—"the feeling that some misfortune would happen," I said, "haunted me": I feared for the child, for the idea of danger connected with him never struck me. (*MSL* 1:181, 15 Aug. 1822)

Especially since she has always feared the water, and since Shelley (even with the more experienced Williams) is pathologically prone to accident in sailboats, how can Mary "never" have "connected with" Percy her "idea of danger?" She had already described his drowning in prescient detail in *Mathilda*. At Lerici Mary is, I believe, transferring to the younger Percy her intuition about the elder, in the same way that Victor transferred to himself the monster's threat against Elizabeth. By not admitting that the danger is to Percy Bysshe, Mary need not prevent it; or rather, she can express her worry in such a "womanish" way (threatening to leave, crying bitterly) that he will inevitably ignore it. By 1822 the Shelleys' marriage has broken down quite completely. Percy has already dreamed of strangling Mary. She, devastated after her near-fatal miscarriage, wants out. She can never leave Percy, so he must go.

*

The murderous will which nears the surface of Mary Shelley's life in 1822 appears more indirectly in *Frankenstein*. To understand the diverse intricacy of her drives, we must get beyond the traditional view of the novel's women. Johnson, despite moments of insight and sympathy, speaks for many critics when she says, "it is thus indeed perhaps the very hiddenness of the question of femininity in *Frankenstein* that somehow proclaims the painful message not of female monstrousness but of female contradictions. For it is the fact of self-contradiction that is so vigorously repressed in women" (9). Yet what has Johnson herself done but repress the self-contradictory aspects of women in *Frankenstein*? "All the interesting, complex characters in the book are male. . . . the females, on the other hand, are beautiful, gentle, selfless, boring nurturers and victims who never experience inner conflict or true desire" (7). How likely does this seem, when, as Johnson herself notes, Mary Shelley was caught

> between the courageous, passionate, intelligent, and suicidal mother Mary knew only through her writings and the vulgar, repressive "pustule of vanity" [Mrs. Clairmont] whose dislike she resented and returned. . . . Mary must have known at first hand a whole gamut of feminine contradictions, impasses, and options. (9)

Mary, who knows firsthand the emotions evoked by a stepmother, a female peer introduced into her beloved father's home, and a half brother named William, writes a novel whose heroine encounters a stepmother, a female peer introduced into her beloved stepfather's home, and a stepbrother named William. How could *Frankenstein* not express Mary's contradictions, impasses, and options? Yet Johnson says no. "How indeed would it have been possible for Mary to represent feminine contradiction *from the point of view of its repression* otherwise than precisely in the *gap* between angels of domesticity and an uncompleted monstress, between the murdered Elizabeth and the dismembered Eve?" (9). Mary does it the way any self-conflicted but resolute writer does—by countering surface with depth. Angel traits which the Mary of Agape reveres sincerely are subverted by the same dark drives of Eros which warp Frankenstein's and Percy's sincere dreams of philanthropy and domesticity.

Readers have long recognized the monster as an extension of Mary Shelley's dark side, her "conscious or unconscious awareness of the monster woman implicit in the angel woman" (Gilbert and

Gubar 240). Mary in fact expresses her awareness of the monster woman *through* the angel woman. What Nina Auerbach finds characteristic of Victorian literature and art surfaces throughout Mary Shelley's writings. " 'So like, and yet so unlike' are the female angel and the demon. It requires only the fire of an altered palette to bring out the contours of the one latent in the face of the other" (107). The homicidal capacities of hearthside heroines which flourish in the Victorian period (Florence Dombey and Romola wish their fathers dead, Lady Audley and Lydia Gwilt put felonious wishes into practice) appear less flagrantly but no less intensely in Mary Shelley. In *Valperga*, Mary inconceivably names the heroine "Euthanasia"; in *The Last Man*, she exterminates humankind by a plague continually called "she"; in *Proserpine*, she threatens all living things through the goddess Ceres' vow to strike the earth "barren" (act 2). When Bowerbank contends that "we look in vain for this tone of fierce outrage against social injustice in the females of *Frankenstein*" (423), she is overlooking Elizabeth's 1818 tirade against the judicial system. "Oh! how I hate its shews and mockeries! when one creature is murdered, another is immediately deprived of life. . . . you [Justine] may glory in escaping from so miserable a den" (83). Moreover, Mary like Victor-Percy does not restrict to society her feelings of outrage. Family too evokes the homicidal Eros. As Percy creates Demogorgon and Beatrice Cenci as surrogate assassins, Mary has her kinswoman Elizabeth.

Mary and Elizabeth cause their mothers' deaths, but more is involved here than an expression of authorial guilt. The particular nature of the Mary/Elizabeth kinship is suggested by the heroine's last name. Why "Lavenza"? Mary begins learning Italian in October of 1814; she is reading Ariosto and Tasso in 1815, and studies them with Polidori in the *Frankenstein* summer of 1816. One of the Italian words for vengeance/revenge is "vendicanza." Do here what Shelley did with Laocöon-Laon: take letters from the beginning and the end of the word. Then prefix the feminine article "La". And "La-ven-za" is the female avenger, a form of influ-enza which strikes down people whom Mary Shelley cannot receive satisfaction from in life. Attack-retreat. Mary's Erotic will is extreme enough to demand the assassination of a wicked stepmother, an inadequate father, and intruding peers, but like Percy she feels too strongly the guilt and awe of Agape to proceed directly. Indirection, woman's way, is the only way.

Mrs. Clairmont is in Mary Godwin's view the wicked stepmother come to life. By changing the plot of *Frankenstein* in 1831 so that

167

Elizabeth kills *two* mothers, her own as well as Caroline, Mary emphasizes that forces more sinister than accident are at work in the mother-daughter relationship. My earlier discussion of Caroline's death focused upon Elizabeth as a daughter who felt the "scarlet" fevers of passionate rivalry with mother and passionate attraction to brother. Now I want to stress that Caroline is more than mother. "Decide," Sr. Lavenza writes to Alphonse in the 1818 edition, "whether you would prefer educating your niece yourself to her being brought up by a stepmother" (29). Through the apparently melodramatic introduction of the wicked stepmother, Mary projects her own hostilities into the narrative. Elizabeth does not, despite her father's "whether," have any real choice. Either her father's second wife or her aunt will be a stepmother.

"The world has been to me a harsh step-mother," Mary has Evadne say in *The Last Man* (80). The motherless author with an unsympathetic stepmother chooses for her motherless heroine's apparently ideal stepmother in *Frankenstein* the name C-a-r-o-l-i-n-e, which is a virtual anagram of C-l-a-i-r-m-o-n-t. (Anagrams recur at another intensely autobiographical moment in Mary's fiction: representing Percy's Harriet and Emilia as the woman loved by the Shelley figure Saville in *Lodore*, Mary names them C-o-r-n-e-l-i-a and C-l-o-r-i-n-d-a.) In *Frankenstein* there is apparently no such thing as a *good* stepmother. Beneath the unimpeachable surfaces of the name "Caroline" and the character Caroline abide the other name and the other reality. Mary self-protectively endows Caroline with all the traits of ideal motherhood and uses the anagram to further mask her real intention. She can then attack.

Attacking does not cease with Mrs. Clairmont's fictional extirpation because the stepmother's cruelty is not simply gratuitous. Rivalry, mortal rivalry for Godwin, is what pits Mrs. Clairmont against Mary. The daughter cannot be satisfied by the stepmother's death, because other rivals also threaten Mary's "excessive . . . romantic attachment" to her father. Sibling rivalry is acted out in *Frankenstein* as Elizabeth plays important covert roles in the fates of little William and of Justine.

William's fate is two-fold: terrible death and bliss eternal. Elizabeth is implicated in both. She insists three times upon what we know is impossible—that *she* murdered the little boy (67, 68, 74). Her ostensible meaning, that she gave to William the locket which attracted the killer, does not warrant the intensity and protractedness of her self-castigations. We feel her protesting too much, as Victor did when he rationalized about not marrying her. Elizabeth's insistence upon herself as the murderer links her with the monster and highlights other links. Like the monster whose eyes are "dun white" (52), Elizabeth after the murder has "lustreless" eyes (73). Like the monster, she is associated with the moon (84). And, most important, Victor's epithet for her, "insect," recurs when he calls the creature "vile insect" (94).

Why link Elizabeth with the monster? Mary Shelley has scores to settle with males named William. In her half brother William she sees both the son craved by Godwin (teenage Mary wrote the speeches that young Master Godwin declaimed before company) and the proof of her father's intimacy with hated Mrs. Clairmont. Although the attack-retreat syndrome requires Mary to protect Elizabeth from direct implication in murder by giving her maternal love for little William, Elizabeth is also, as I will show soon, given a daughterly affection for Alphonse as intense as Mary's for Godwin. Elizabeth would not keep saying that she has killed a rival sibling unless she, or rather her author, wished on some level to do so.

The other William is Godwin himself. As Mary's primary target, he determines little William's two-fold fate because he evokes contradictory responses in Mary. Her affection is expressed through Elizabeth's devotion to Alphonse, so her antagonism toward Godwin must find some other outlet. Mary begins with the murder victim's name. Few readers in 1818 would know that "William" was Mary's half brother and her son and her own prenatal nickname;[7] but every reader of *Frankenstein* in 1818 could associate "William" with Godwin after reading the dedication: "To WILLIAM GODWIN . . . These Volumes Are respectfully inscribed By The Author." Godwin's lifelong coldness, plus his recent abusiveness, makes antagonism and retaliation almost inevitable from a daughter already prey to incestuous guilt. Mary, having cut Byron down to size by reducing him to a child and then castrating him, now reduces Godwin to a comparably manageable size and then throttles "little William."

The text encourages this reading in several ways. Mary stresses young William's size—"he is very tall of his age" (62)—because William is meant for bigger things. He must stand in for the adult Godwin, who also "has already had one or two [not so] little *wives*" (62). More important, the death scene of little William as described by the monster evokes a response more complex than one might expect.

> As soon as he beheld my form, [says the mon-
> ster] he placed his hands before his eyes, and
> uttered a shrill scream: I drew his hand forcibly
> from his face, and said, "Child, what is the
> meaning of this? I do not intend to hurt you;
> listen to me." He struggled violently; "Let me
> go," he cried; "monster! ugly wretch! you wish
> to eat me, and tear me to pieces—You are an
> ogre—Let me go, or I will tell my papa." "Boy,
> you will never see your father again; you must
> come with me." "Hideous monster! let me go;
> My papa is a Syndic—he is M. Frankenstein—
> he would punish you. You dare not keep me."
> (139)

Granted that the situation is frightening, the boy does not respond as he would if Mary Shelley were seeking merely to evoke the sympathy conventional with two familiar types, the victimized child and the Wordsworthian seer blest. William lacks the passive sweetness of the first type. And unlike the innocent perceiver of inner truths, he sees in terms of surfaces, stereotypes, and class.

Shouting "ugly wretch" and "hideous monster," William seems as incapable of seeing beyond the creature's surface as is the rest of the superficial world. Even at so frightening a moment, the child would be most touchingly victimized and most thoroughly Wordsworthian if he, like old M. De Lacey, responded to the inner goodness which the creature expresses in the words "I do not intend to hurt you; listen to me." William seems all the more myopic because he sees stereotypes. "You wish to eat me, and tear me to pieces . . . ogre." And class pride is unmistakable when William shouts, "My papa is a Syndic. . . . You dare not keep me."

By having the child be the one who covers his eyes with his hands and the monster the one who tries to uncover them, Mary dramatizes the creature's long struggle for a fair seeing. His failure is reflected in "hands . . . hand." That the creature pries away only one hand—leaving (in effect) one of William's eyes covered—suggests that perception is impeded by internal, psychological forces which cannot be countered by external actions like monster's here. William's one-track mind is produced by inner forces beyond the creature's control. "What is the meaning of this?" should be the child's line, but it is the monster's because roles in the scene are reversed. The child victimizes the creature by doing violence to his

170

good intentions. "The child . . . loaded me with epithets which carried despair to my heart" (139).

Why would Mary Shelley make William so arrogant and shrill, so nasty, if she wanted to evoke from us the compassion accorded murdered innocents? Why, moreover, would she go out of her way to link William to Victor? "William had run away to hide himself. . . . had lost himself, and was exposed to all the damps and dews of night" (67). The "damps" of "midnight" (49) surrounded the monster-making Victor when he too had gone away to hide himself from the community and to lose himself in silence and secrecy. Hide-and-seek describes well Victor's time away from home. In turn, William's game of hide-and-seek need not be described in terms evocative of Victor's exploits ("to hide himself" is not the idiom proper to the game) unless Mary Shelley intends more than child's play. Will little Will grow up to be another Frankenstein? Certainly "damps" links the younger boy's acts before the monster's arrival and Victor's labors before that monster's birth; then the boy rejects the creature with the same unfeeling contempt which Victor evinces after his birth. Mary wants to prevent us from reacting too severely to the creature because he is expressing her own murderous response to an often myopic and unattractive William Godwin.

She then complicates matters by adding a second stage to little William's fate. As she first cut Byron down to size and then endowed him with what she thought he needed, a mate in a chaste union, so she can, after thoroughly disciplining Godwin, allow him what she hopes he needs. Herself. "He now sleeps with his angel mother" (69). The earlier horrific union of woman and death in Victor's nightmare is redeemed now by True Woman. But the price is violation of the ultimate taboo. What seems to safely distance Mary's act from any suggestion of incest—"William" is reduced to a dead child and she herself is transformed into an angel mother—shows, on the contrary, the full range of Mary's incestuous inclinations. William—father, son, and brother—can now join her in a consummation that is in every sense out of this world.

Justine allows Mary to express her antagonism toward peer-aged rivals for Godwin's affection. Young women invade his home as Justine does the home of Elizabeth's beloved Alphonse. Like Justine, both Claire and Fanny could be looked down upon in terms of class. The Clairmonts, to put it kindly, came from nowhere; and Fanny, as Mary said unkindly, was a slave (*J* 30, 17 Dec. 1814). On the other

hand, Mary felt sincere affection for both young women. The result-
ing tension is why Elizabeth's courtroom defense of Justine involves
the very nature of advocacy. To express oneself intensely is to risk
bringing forth *all* that is intensely felt—Eros as well as Agape. Elizabeth at the trial is expressing Mary's conscious and unconscious
feelings. The play upon friend-fiend which recurs throughout
Frankenstein reflects these feelings: friendly emotions are linked to
fiendish ones which surface amid even the sincerest praise. I will
begin with a scene which has never received close critical analysis.

Elizabeth with apparently impeccable Romantic orthodoxy discusses with Alphonse the future of Ernest.

> I . . . proposed that he should be a farmer;
> which you know, Cousin, is a favorite scheme
> of mine. A farmer's is a very healthy happy life;
> and the least hurtful, or rather the most bene-
> ficial profession of any. My uncle had an idea of
> his being educated as an advocate. . . . But, be-
> sides that he is not at all fitted for such an oc-
> cupation, it is certainly more creditable to
> cultivate the earth for the sustenance of man,
> than to be the confidant and sometimes the ac-
> complice, of his vices; which is the profession
> of a lawyer. I said, that the employments of a
> prosperous farmer, if they were not a more
> honourable, they were at least a happier spe-
> cies of occupation than that of a judge, whose
> misfortune it was always to meddle with the
> dark side of human nature. My uncle smiled,
> and said, that I ought to be an advocate myself,
> which put an end to the conversation on that
> subject. (59–60)

Does the conversation end because female seriousness is stifled by
male glibness, or does Alphonse point instinctively to a flaw in Elizabeth's argument? She can distinguish so conveniently between
farmers and lawyers only by assuming that "the dark side of human
nature" is something external and thus avoidable. She is making a
distinction between employments similar to that traditionally
made between gender roles. True woman escapes the tainting inevitable to man, who dirties himself in the dark world outside the
home. Yet Elizabeth herself admits what Alphonse finally points
out, that she too is an advocate. "A favorite scheme of mine" is one
held intensely and protractedly. Since we all have favorite schemes,

Mary Shelley insists that we are all advocates of what we need. Everyone is in touch with life's dark side because it is inside everyone, farmers as well as lawyers, men and women. That Elizabeth knows this at some deep level is suggested by her slip, "the least hurtful, or rather the most beneficial profession." What she says first is what she means; all ways of life are hurtful, tainted. It is only a matter of degree.

Elizabeth's advocate speech functions like the phrase "vile insect" and the name "Lavenza" to encourage us to look beneath the heroine's conventional surface and see the complexity of her actions. Mary Shelley establishes before Justine's trial the universality of passion's drives because she wants to make us aware of the dark side of all people, even Elizabeth the courtroom advocate. In the process, however, we must remain open to other, less deeply psychological aspects of Elizabeth's situation. She has no training in law and no experience in court; she has not even had time to prepare a speech, since she speaks out only when Justine's character witnesses fail to come forward. Sincerity is no more an issue with Elizabeth than it was with Victor or Shelley; the Elizabeth of Agape feels true affection for Justine, whatever the Erotic Elizabeth may feel. Above all we must recognize that even a perfect speech would not have saved the servant. The Genevese are so incensed that Justine *and* Elizabeth will inevitably be overwhelmed by mindless rage.

This very fact, however, is what signals the subversive nature of the mistakes in Elizabeth's speech. Mary Shelley need not include any mistakes. Since even perfect oratory would not have forestalled the verdict demanded by the Genevese and required by the plot, something other than the plot must have caused the mistakes. Readers who find Elizabeth's inexperience a sufficient cause will not buy my more psychological explanation. But mistakes from inexperience are trickier than they look, in art as in life. The heroines of melodrama are traditionally capable of wonders. Over and over again women with no legal training rise up in tense situations and declaim like Cicero. Elizabeth fails to speak perfectly because *Frankenstein* is no melodrama. Below the surface is transpiring another drama, which warps Elizabeth's speech. Her lack of preparation—in law, on this particular day—functions not to cause the mistakes in her speech but to facilitate them. Subversive emotions surface because Elizabeth has neither the experience nor the time to control them. Screens which conceal such emotions day by day prove insufficient at this dire moment, especially since the situation is so tempting. Once fate has put the antagonist's head upon the block, antagonism takes over.

Elizabeth's scarlet fever, which kills Caroline, strikes Justine too (61). The servant recovers, however, and encounters Elizabeth again in court.

> "I am," said she, "the cousin of the unhappy child who was murdered, or rather his sister, for I was educated by and have lived with his parents ever since and even long before his birth. It may therefore be judged indecent in me to come forward on this occasion; but when I see a fellow-creature about to perish through the cowardice of her pretended friends, I wish to be allowed to speak, that I may say what I know of her character. I am well acquainted with the accused. I have lived in the same house with her, at one time for five, at another for nearly two years. During all that period she appeared to me the most amiable and benevolent of human creatures. She nursed Madame Frankenstein, my aunt, in her last illness with the greatest affection and care; and afterwards attended her own mother during a tedious illness, in a manner that excited the admiration of all who knew her. After which she again lived in my uncle's house, where she was beloved by all the family. She was warmly attached to the child who is now dead, and acted towards him like a most affectionate mother. For my part, I do not hesitate to say, that, notwithstanding all the evidence produced against her, I believe and rely on her perfect innocence. She had no temptation for such an action: as to the bauble on which the chief proof rests, if she had earnestly desired it, I should have willingly given it to her; so much do I esteem and value her." (79—80)[8]

The key to Elizabeth's deep feelings toward Justine is the apposition in "she nursed Madame Frankenstein, my aunt, in her last illness with the greatest affection and care." Why stop the flow of the sentence with "my aunt" to establish a fact which is self-evident after "cousin" in the first line of her speech? *"My"* aunt stakes out precious territory. However much Caroline is a hated rival to Elizabeth

the sister-fiancée, she is a beloved mother to Elizabeth the motherless daughter. Elizabeth will admit to Justine's affection for Caroline only after confirming her own superior tie to the mother figure. Elizabeth has already established herself as virtually a daughter
to Caroline by the correction interposed in her first sentence. "I
am . . . the cousin of the unhappy child . . . or rather his sister."
Now Caroline, who is "my" to Elizabeth, is only "Madame" to Justine. That the servant's roots are elsewhere is then confirmed by the
reference to "her own mother." And when the servant returns to the
Frankensteins, she comes to "my" uncle's house. Even Elizabeth's
insistence that Justine "was beloved by all the family" establishes
that the servant is not part of "the" family. "All" includes Elizabeth
and excludes Justine.

In stressing the servant's status as outsider, Elizabeth goes beyond establishing her own claim to Caroline; she also dismisses Justine as a rival for Alphonse's "house" and heart. We are prepared for
rivalry here because Elizabeth's acknowledgment of Justine as surrogate wife-mother ("acted . . . like a most affectionate mother")
occurs in light of the intense ties which Elizabeth herself has already established with Alphonse. Calling William "my darling in-
fant" and "my little William" (67, 76), she joins herself to Alphonse
as parent and thus as spouse. Alphonse reciprocates. Writing to Victor, he refers to "my niece, and your two brothers" (67) rather than
"my niece and two sons" or "your cousin and two brothers." The
older male thus establishes as *mine* the woman whom *you* younger
males expect to possess someday. How Alphonse thrives under Elizabeth's care after Caroline's death and Victor's departure is proclaimed by Elizabeth herself. "Your father's health is now so vig-
orous, that he appears ten years younger since last winter" (59). Is so
drastic a rejuvenescence necessary if Mary Shelley means only that
Alphonse has recovered from depression?

Elizabeth's possessiveness toward Alphonse is emphasized in
1831. "I am rewarded for any exertions," she writes to Victor, "by
seeing none but happy, kind faces around me. Since you left
us . . ." (243). As Victor's unconscious antagonism toward Elizabeth was expressed in "my enemy. Elizabeth," her equally repressed antagonism toward him also overrides punctuation. "Happy faces since you left" is what we experience. That Victor too
senses Elizabeth's unconscious pleasure at his parting is confirmed
in 1831. Having experienced a bittersweet moment in 1818 when
Elizabeth "wept . . . as she bade me farewell, and entreated me to
return happy and tranquil" (151), Victor now faces an Elizabeth si-

lent and dry-eyed. "She longed to bid me hasten my return—a thousand conflicting emotions rendered her mute" (253). One of Elizabeth's emotions is of course her conscious desire not to increase Victor's sorrow at parting. But his words show him seeing more in her silence. "A thousand" allows for so many "conflicting" emotions that Victor can include and thus tacitly acknowledge the negative ones which pain him; yet "a thousand" is sufficiently hyperbolic and vague that he need not increase his pain by isolating the negative emotions so sharply that he must confront and understand them. "She longed to bid me hasten my return" thus functions less as an objective statement of fact than as wish fulfillment in the face of more complex, less flattering possibilities. Especially in light of additional words which Mary gives to Elizabeth in 1831—"little alteration, except the growth of *our* dear children, has taken place *since you left us*" (243; my italics)—we see how the son who has already felt exiled by his father can implicate Elizabeth in this exiling. He sees her intent upon replacing Caroline by excluding all rivals for Alphonse's affections, himself as well as Justine. Caroline, after all, had married a father figure in Alphonse: why should not her replacement do the same?

Elizabeth's courtroom praise of Justine backfires damningly. "Notwithstanding all the evidence produced against her, I believe and rely upon her perfect innocence." If literature were mathematics, if words existed only on the propositional and not also on the experiential level, this sentence would say that Justine is excellent. But we respond more complexly, because Elizabeth's testamental "I believe" occurs only after she has reminded us of all the reasons for disbelief, of "all the evidence" against Justine. "I believe" simply cannot function mathematically to negate our experience of "all the evidence." Equally inflammatory are "she was warmly attached to the child who is now dead" and "the unhappy child who was murdered." Elizabeth could just as easily and more economically have said "she was warmly attached to William" and "I am the cousin of the deceased." Elizabeth's words "murdered" and "now dead" fan the outrage which the Genevese can vent in only one direction, at Justine. "Attached" is doubly lethal in this context. By linking the young woman to the dead boy and by stressing her responsibility to him, "attached" does just what the defense must avoid doing—attach Justine to the killing. At the very least she seems derelict in a sacred duty.

She seems all the more venal when Elizabeth discusses motive. "If she had earnestly desired it [the miniature], I would willingly have given it to her; so much do I esteem and value her." The very mention of desire reifies that desire, as though (however illogical this seems, it is a truism among trial lawyers) one can only speak about that which has some reality. In addition, the syntax of the sentence focuses attention upon the advocate, not the defendant. "I" is the subject of both main clauses because Elizabeth's good nature is what is really established. A trusting lady betrayed by an ungrateful servant is exactly what the class-oriented Genevese take her for.

> Excellent Elizabeth! A murmur of approbation was heard; but it was excited by her generous interference, and not in favour of poor Justine, on whom the public indignation was turned with renewed violence, charging her with the blackest ingratitude. (80)

The ambiguity of Mary Shelley's syntax here suggests the willful nature of Elizabeth's apparently heroic advocacy. "A murmur of approbation . . . was excited by her generous interference, and not in favour of poor Justine". The imperfect parallelism of "by" and "in favour of" causes the latter construction to seem linked syntactically with both "approbation" and "interference," generating two contradictory readings. The jury's approbation of Elizabeth is emphasized by the syntax's requiring us to add a phrase to the end of the sentence: "approbation . . . not in favour of poor Justine, but in favour of good Elizabeth." The subversiveness of Elizabeth's interference, however, is hinted at by the syntax's prompting us to read the end of the sentence differently. We focus not upon "approbation" but upon "interference," and we read "interference, and not in favour of poor Justine, but against her."

The subversive undercurrent to Elizabeth's speech has its counterpart in Victor's own defense of Justine. "I replied earnestly, 'You are all mistaken; I know the murderer. Justine, poor, good Justine, is innocent'" (75). As "earnest" advocate, Victor seems to espouse Justine wholeheartedly. But he, like Elizabeth, is actually ambivalent. "The murderer. Justine" functions like "my enemy. Elizabeth" to make us experience an equation which denies the distinction that he is supposedly making. Moreover, Victor omits the one thing which is even more damaging than what Elizabeth should omit: he omits the reason why Justine is innocent. As Elizabeth is dispatching a wife-mother rival, Victor is applying his Erotic will to a mother substitute who is expressly said to resemble Caroline (61). Antagonism very like the one I am locating in Victor and Elizabeth is described by Gallop in Freud's Dora. "She [the nurse] is so much a part of the family that the child's fantasies (the unconscious) do not distinguish 'mother or nurse'. . . . she must be expelled from the family" (145, 147). In *Frankenstein,* Promethean man *and* true woman both feel willful antagonism and vent it in similarly lethal ways.

Even Justine is not without a suggestion of passionate will. "If . . . she had *earnestly* desired it. . . ." That Justine too may have earnest desires which preclude her being the paragon praised by Elizabeth and Victor is indicated in several ways. Immediately before William's murder we learn that Justine's (admittedly unstable) mother "accused her of having caused the deaths of her brothers and sister" (61). We cannot help recognizing that Justine does have a bad track record when Elizabeth enumerates the dead whom the servant has nursed— Caroline, Mme. Moritz, William. We also learn that incestuous drives may be operating in Justine who "had always been the favourite of her father . . . through a strange perversity, her mother could not endure her" (60). And the key word "earnestly" recurs in the context of William's death. "She had been looking for the child, and demanded earnestly, if any thing had been heard concerning him" (78). We no more suspect Justine of consciously wanting to kill the boy than we suspect Elizabeth of consciously wanting to convict the servant. But we do see that even so innocent a victim-woman as Justine is not exempted from suggestions of unconscious Eros. Instead, Justine's link with Elizabeth is confirmed by the advocate herself. "I rely on her innocence as certainly as I do upon my own" (76). No one is innocent, not in the sense proclaimed by True Womanhood's advocates at their most orthodox. Since Elizabeth has already been associated with the monster, both women are implicated in Eros when Justine says of her browbeating by the priest, "I almost began to think that I was the monster that he said I was" (82). Who is not a monster? Who lacks will?

WEAKNESS AND WOMAN

The Mary who watched from the corner scarcely daring to breathe as Coleridge intoned *The Ancient Mariner* in her youth confesses years later her inability to "[put] myself forward. *I cannot* do that; it is against my nature" (*J* 206, 21 Oct. 1838). What sounds like the opposite of the Promethean drive for victory—"I hate contention & I disdain the victory" (*NL* 304, 12 Jan. 1823)—can at times be only its reverse side, its penchant for passivity. The escapism which characterizes the Dionysiac Eros and which Mary criticized as weakness in Victor-Percy is a basic response of her own. "I only find relief from the sadness of my position by living a dreamy existence from which realities are excluded" (*MSL* 2:87, 30 Oct. 1834). Although she is speaking here in the dire time after Percy's death, Mary has been using dreams to refashion life since at least 1815, when she "dream[ed] that my little baby came to life again" (*J* 41, 19 Mar. 1815). Further disasters make her sound all too much like the deluded Victor seeking consolation in the nocturnal visits of the dead.

> Visit me in my dreams to-night, my beloved Shelley . . . and the event of this day shall be forgotten. . . . Last night, dear Jane [Williams] I dreamt of them [Percy and Edward]. . . . Would that I could dream of them thus every night & I would sleep for ever. (*J* 188, 24 Feb. 1823; *NL* 307, 12 Jan. 1823)

From this dream state to the verge of solipsism is a short step. "Solitary as I am, I feed & live on imagination only. . . . the mind is no longer a mirror in which outward events may reflect themselves, but becomes itself the painter and creator" (*NL* 312, 19 Feb. 1823; *J* 183, 19 Oct. 1822).[9]

Moreover, having insisted upon the lethal consequences of Promethean passivity, Mary stands self-indicted. She knows in her heart that the deaths of Clara and William cannot be blamed solely upon Percy. Orthodoxy as well as feminism allowed and in fact required a woman to act decisively, even to the point of defying her husband, upon one occasion—when the children were threatened. That the wife-mother must opt for mother over wife is established in innumerable advice manuals, melodramas, and novels.[10] Mary could not help knowing that, especially in the case of Clara, she should have put her foot down. Percy's inclinations to irresponsibility, along with his infatuation with Byron and his devotion to Claire, weigh in the balance against Clara's general debility and her raging fever, the punishing carriage ride and the Italian heat. Mary should have stayed in Este. But dutiful wife wins out over devoted mother. She heeds her husband's summons, and Clara dies.

Passivity also contributes to William's death. Knowing the Roman climate is particularly dangerous as summer nears, Mary writes that "we already begin to feel or think that we begin to feel the effects of the Roman air—producing colds—depression & even fever to the feeblest of our party, so we emigrate a month earlier than we intended—& on the seventh of May leave this delightful city" (*MSL* 1:68, 26 Apr. 1819). Yet on May eleventh the Shelleys are still in Rome. "You [Maria Gisborne] will think us strange people that we stay on another month in Rome" (*NL* 97, 11 May 1819). What keeps them? "We have met an old friend ([the Irish radical and portraitist] Miss Curran), and that has induced us to stay longer." Then reality intrudes. "We leave Rome tomorrow week. . . . the heat of this southern climate disagrees with William—He has had a dangerous attack of worms and it is only yesterday & today that he is convalescent—We are advised above all things to pass the summer in as cool a place as possible" (*MSL* 1:71, 30 May 1819). Failing in this case to oppose Percy's other extreme—not his will but his lethargy—Mary has waited too long and William dies. Then amazingly, Mary, having fatally exposed her first son to the Italian summer, does the same thing with Percy Florence. "I shall soon leave Italy—heat does not agree with my boy—nor wd I not [sic] have risked this summer had not I seen S getting better" (*MSL* 1:177, 26 July 1822). Again wife prevails over mother.

Although Byron is hardly one to cast the first stone, his criticism of the Shelleys' childrearing is telling. "I so totally disapprove of the mode of Children's treatment in their family. . . . Have they *reared* one? . . . The Child [Allegra] shall not quit me again to perish of starvation and green fruit" (Buxton 117–18). Byron does not single out Shelley. "Their" and "they" indict both parents. One reason why Mary never recovers fully from William's death is that she cannot escape her role in it. A quarter-century after the relative triviality of Amelia Curran's company and portraits had kept her in Rome, Mary returns to the theme of Italian heat and children's deaths.

> We feared the south of Italy, and a hotter climate on account of our child [Percy Florence]; our former bereavement inspiring us with terror. . . . human life, besides its great unalterable necessities, is ruled by a thousand lilliputian ties that shackle at the time, although it is difficult to account afterwards for their influence over our destiny. (*CP* 636)

What Mary confessed to Jefferson Hogg in 1823—"you know my character sufficiently to be aware how deeply it is tinged with irresolution & an incapacity of action" (*NL* 316, 28 Feb. 1823)—she is still confessing to in 1835. "I know that however clever I may be there is in me a vacillation a weakness, a want of 'eagle winged' resolution that appertains to my intellect as well as my moral character" (*MSL* 2:98, 11 June 1835). The mother who was willful enough to match Percy Florence's determination to "go thro' fire and water" admits herself too weak to equal his decisiveness. "He can say *NO*, which I cannot do" (*MSL* 2:88, 17 Nov. 1834).[11]

What makes Mary particularly adept at recognizing and criticizing her own weakness is her lifelong exposure to feminism. "Jane [Claire] states her conception of the subterranean community of women. . . . Hogg comes; talk of law; of the different intercourse of the sexes. . . . a discussion [with Charles Clairmont] concerning female character" (*J* 18, 7 Oct. 1814; 29, 11 Dec. 1814; 30, 19 Dec. 1814). Mary repeatedly reacts as a feminist against womanly weakness. When Mrs. Clairmont forbids Fanny to come downstairs, Mary says, "Fanny, of course, behaves slavishly" (*J* 30, 17 Dec. 1814). The specter of slavery prompts Mary later to admonish Hunt, "you & Mrs. Hunt must leave off calling me Mrs. S for I do not half like the name" (*MSL* 1:19, 2 Mar. 1817). At William's death, Mary is threatened by another type of slavery, a resignation particularly hallowed in women. "I might say, 'Thy will be done,' but I cannot applaud the permitter of self-degradation, though dignity and superior wisdom arise from its bitter and burning ashes" (*J* 168, 8 Feb. 1822).

Despite her feminist reactions, however, Mary Shelley sees passivity as a trait essential to womanhood itself. "She [Lady Jane Shore] was all woman, fearful of repulse, dreading insult, more willing to lie down and die, than, fallen and miserable, to solicit uncertain relief. . . . she [Ethel] fled from the idea of going thither,—as it is the feminine disposition often to do" (*Perkin Warbeck* 2:134; *Lodore* 2:6). Mary's own moments of weakness must thus be seen in the context of her view of womankind. On the one hand she is absolved of responsibility, since her failing is genetic. On the other hand she is included in the indictment of the whole culture which produces many ineffectual Ethels and few independent Fannys. Although she definitely directs blame at Percy for William's death—"we came to Italy thinking to do Shelley's health good. . . . a most excellent English surgeon . . . allowed that these [William's fatal worms] were the fruits of this hateful Italy" (*MSL* 1:74, 75, 19 June 1819)—Mary knows that she concurred in the Italian trip, as she partook of Percy's Roman lethargy. The deaths of both children, occurring after the publication of *Frankenstein*, find expression in the violent self-hate of *Mathilda*, but self-criticism and guilt have been with Mary since 1815. The children's deaths are only the most anguishing consequence of what has characterized her union with Percy from the start—her wifely readiness to accommodate the family to her husband's demands. She knows the rigors of travel, the dangers of new climates and diets, the chanciness of foreign doctors; yet she exposes the children to all these for Percy's sake. "[The English tourist] gives foreigners a lively belief that we islanders are all mad, to migrate in this way, with the young and helpless, from comfortable homes, in search of the dangerous and comfortless" (*Falkner* 1:137). Harsh as this is on Falkner-Shelley, the islanders are "we . . . all." Mary went along with Percy.

*

Mary Shelley's very sense of the weakness in herself and womanhood makes her defensive in *Frankenstein*. After admitting that women are no more immune than men to weakness, she insists self-justifyingly that women are less weak. What destroys them is not effeminacy but a world impossibly strong. Thus as we explore Mary's demonstrations of weakness in *Frankenstein*, we must be more attuned than most criticism has been to the careful controls which prevent readers from responding to women in the severe and even derisive way we did to Victor the anxious bridegroom.[12] We must be particularly careful because extreme weakness is the very thing which critics charge Mary's women with. Justine, Caroline, and Elizabeth all act in ways which leave them open to criticism; none exhibits the perfection conventional with the good women of melodrama. In defining their weaknesses, however, we must avoid melodramatic simplifications.

With Justine the question is not whether she is weak but whether Mary Shelley sees that weakness as Justine's critics do, as symptomatic of the inadequacies of true womanhood. "Justine and Elizabeth have learned well the lessons of submissiveness and devotion. . . . Their model behavior similarly lowers their resistance to the forces that kill them" (Ellis 133). The lumping together of two characters as different as Justine and Elizabeth calls Ellis's criticism into doubt, and our experience of the text confirms that doubt. Before we learn of Justine's incriminating behavior, we are made to feel the weight of evidence against her. "This picture . . . was doubtless the temptation which urged the murderer to the deed. . . . even now Elizabeth will not be convinced [of Justine's guilt], notwithstanding all the evidence. . . . several circumstances came out, that have almost forced conviction upon us" (67–68, 74). My point is not that we, who already know of Justine's excellence, are

182

persuaded of her guilt, but that the Genevese are. The cards seem stacked formidably against Justine from the start.

Then, the courtroom scene minimizes her weakness.

> The appearance of Justine was calm. . . . she appeared confident in innocence, and did not tremble, although gazed on and execrated by thousands. . . . She was tranquil, yet her tranquility was evidently constrained; and as her confusion had before been adduced as a proof of her guilt, she worked up her mind to an appearance of courage. . . . A tear seemed to dim her eye when she saw us; but she quickly recovered herself, and a look of sorrowful affection seemed to attest to her utter guiltlessness. . . . Justine was called on for her defence. As the trial had proceeded, her countenance had altered. Surprise, horror, and misery were strongly expressed. Sometimes she struggled with her tears; but when she was desired to plead, she collected her powers, and spoke in an audible although variable voice. (77, 78)

Besides bearing up well under considerable pressure, Justine explains part of what seemed weak in her previous conduct. Her initial bewilderment "was not surprising, since she had passed a sleepless night, and the fate of poor William was yet uncertain" (78–79).

Our primary experience in the courtroom is not of Justine as weak, but of Justine as victim. Arrayed against her are five formidable forces. Besides the populace incensed by "the enormity she was supposed to have committed" (77) and the "timorous" friends who "supposed her guilty" (79), there are the plot of the novel, the power of the church, and the machinery of the law.

"I know . . . how heavily and fatally this one circumstance [the miniature] weighs against me, but I have no power of explaining it . . . when I have expressed my utter ignorance, I am only left to conjecture concerning the probabilities by which it might have been placed in my pocket. But here also I am checked" (79). Justine proves incapable of saving herself, but the cause of her failure affects our response to it. Her bafflement confirms less her analytical weakness than the weakness of analysis itself. Justine has been victimized by the very plot of the novel. How could she imagine that an eight-foot-tall, man-made monster had sneaked up and slipped the miniature into her pocket? Mary's structuring of the action is also a factor

183

when we reach Justine's weakest moment. That she might have shown spunk enough to refuse to confess, is true; but Mary does here what she need not—delays the confession until *after* the verdict. Had she wanted to indict true woman for passive weakness, Mary would have made Justine's fate dependent upon her giving in. Instead the young woman holds out as long as acquittal remains a possibility.

Moreover, Justine's giving in seems less weak when we learn of the other forces arrayed against her. "My confessor has besieged me; he threatened . . . excommunication and hell fire in my last moments" (82). Focus shifts away from the nature of true woman and onto that conventional target of gothic opprobrium, the Romish clergy. (How far Mary is going out of her way to invoke conventional anti-Catholic responses is shown by the illogic of events here: the last thing we would expect to encounter in Geneva, the bastion of John Calvin, is Catholic coerciveness.) Justine seems doubly beset because the clerical Father is carrying on the browbeating practiced by her fanatical mother. That sympathy which a victim of Catholicism is guaranteed with British readers is, moreover, augmented by Mary's implication of another force which her audience traditionally distrusts, the judiciary.

> "When one creature is murdered [says Elizabeth], another is immediately deprived of life in a slow torturing manner; then the executioners, their hands yet reeking with the blood of innocence, believe that they have done a great deed. They call this *retribution*. Hateful name! When that word is pronounced, I know greater and more horrid punishments are going to be inflicted than the gloomiest tyrant has ever invented to satiate his utmost revenge."
> (83)

Set off against state and church and venal individuals, true woman is presented not as debilitatingly weak but as touchingly vulnerable. Justine sounds like Mary Shelley herself when she cries out, "I had none to support me" (82).

While recognizing the force of external coercion we must, however, be careful of simplification. Justine's confession is not superfluous. By making it indispensable to the young woman's sentencing ("none of our judges like to condemn a criminal upon circumstantial evidence" [81]), Mary Shelley reveals in true woman not a "feminine" weakness which destroys her but a radical purpos-

184

iveness which releases her. Woman in the spirit of Eros spites and flees what Justine calls in 1831 "a sad and bitter world" (246). Rather than finding with Moers that Justine "accepts guilt with docility" (99), I agree with Knoepflmacher that Justine's "passive death becomes . . . a retaliation" (11).

There is thus in true womanhood an inevitable mix to which our response has been carefully controlled. Justine does not seem self-destructive in any simple, petulant sense; she is only self-victimized enough to be understandably human. Confronted with a plot as perfect in its criminal as in its novelistic aspect, Justine is a sympathetic sacrifice to forces inhumanly powerful. When she asks "what could I do?" (82), Mary Shelley has made sure that we can only answer, Not enough, poor thing.

About Caroline, Ellis says that "when Victor tells us that 'My father directed our studies, and my mother partook of our enjoyments,' he unwittingly suggests much about Caroline's reduced sphere of action" (131). This criticism presupposes what must be proven, that Mary Shelley sees woman's sphere as "reduced." First let's read the whole passage which Ellis has excerpted carefully from.

> Such was our domestic circle, from which care and pain seemed for ever banished. My father directed our studies, and my mother partook of our enjoyments. Neither [i.e. none] of us possessed the slightest pre-eminence over the other; the voice of command was never heard amongst us; but mutual affection engaged us all to comply with and obey the slightest desire of each other. (37)

That the father is a director without being a dictator makes him first among equals. Such a family structure will not appeal to every reader today, but as critics we must ask whether Mary Shelley sees the Frankensteins' relationships as inadequate. Does *Frankenstein* encourage us to believe either that Caroline desires a wider sphere of action or that she should? Ellis refers to Caroline's "lifelong subservience" (141), but is that how her life seems?

> With what delight do I even now remember the details of our domestic circle, and the happy years of my childhood. Joy attended on my steps—and the ardent affection that attached

> me to my excellent parents, my beloved Eliz-
> abeth, and Henry, the brother of my soul, has
> given almost a religious and sacred feeling to
> the recollection of a period passed beneath
> their eyes, and in their society. (31)

It is difficult to find criticism by Mary Shelley here. Her words seem
imbued with the same orthodoxy which would later prompt her to
say that women "have no public career—no aim nor end beyond
their domestic circle; but they can extend that, and make all the
creations of nature their own, to foster and do good to" (*Lodore*
3:297). That Mary sees Caroline's status and sphere as anything but
subservient and reduced is emphasized by two details. Caroline's
maiden name, "Beaufort," balances the beauty and the strength of
an ideal androgyny, particularly since Mary chooses the masculine
"beau" rather than the feminine "belle" for her woman. Mary then
is careful to hang Caroline's portrait in the very place in Alphonse's
home that the portrait of Mary Wollstonecraft hung in Godwin's—
over the mantlepiece in the study.

This does not mean that subservience is absent from the portrait
of Caroline. Alphonse chooses to have his wife portrayed pros-
trated over her dead father. The overbearing inference to be drawn
from this ostensible testament to Caroline's capacity for devotion—that she must be equally devoted to Alphonse, especially
since he saved her from the poverty which destroyed M. Beaufort—
redounds against Alphonse, however, not against Caroline or Mary
Shelley. If Caroline is to revere him as she did her dead father, then
he too is moribund. Thus the subservience in the portrait reflects
less Caroline's desire to abase herself in conventional fashion than
the male need for such abasement. The portrait expresses more of
Alphonse than of Caroline, and more of Mary Shelley's reaction to
men than to women.

This does not mean, however, that even Caroline is entirely free
from weakness. Mary adds in 1831 the following powerful passage:

> On the evening previous to her [Elizabeth]
> being brought to *my* home, *my* mother had
> said playfully,—'I have a pretty present for *my*
> Victor—to-morrow he shall *have it.*" And
> when, on the morrow, she presented Elizabeth
> *to me* as her promised gift, I, with childish se-
> riousness, interpreted her words literally, and
> looked upon Elizabeth as *mine—mine* to pro-
> tect, love, and cherish. All praises bestowed on

her, I received as made to a possession of *my own*. . . . till death she was to be *mine only*. (235–36; my italics)

Nine possessives in eight lines. "Have it . . . [presented] to me . . . mine . . . mine . . . my own . . . mine only" emphasize weakness in true woman by making Caroline the source of a tendency which we have seen in Victor, Walton, and Shelley—the tendency to view women as possessions. The dehumanizing nature of this tendency is reflected in the diction. The "present" who is Elizabeth is "it." Frankenstein tries to soften "Elizabeth as mine" by adding "mine to protect, love, and cherish," but, as usual, what is said first is felt deepest. Elizabeth is first and foremost a possession. The rest, protection and love, seem at best afterthoughts and at worst tokens. Like Percy who felt while describing Mary's "excellencies as if I were an egotist expatiating upon his own perfections," Victor considers all praises bestowed upon Elizabeth "as made to a possession of my own."

What distinguishes the "pretty present" passage from other instances of male possessiveness in *Frankenstein* is the implication of mother. Mary Shelley could easily have given Caroline's speech to Alphonse. She does not do so because maternal present-giving has profound consequences for daughters and sons. Instead of being strong enough to insist upon the daughter as an integral other who is independent of male pleasures, Caroline weakly succumbs to conventional stereotyping and presents Elizabeth as the male's "pretty present," his plaything not his complement. Mother is also weak in clinging to the son. As present-giver she perpetuates the boy's dependence upon her by reducing adult sexuality to one more pleasure which the all-bountiful and thus perennially useful mother can bestow. The first possessives in our passage, "my home," "my mother," and "my Victor," confirm the strong mother-son bond which will determine Frankenstein's view of Elizabeth as an intrusive rival for parental affection and a presumptuous aspirant to maternal status.

Elizabeth exemplifies for several critics the weakness of true womanhood. "[Elizabeth's] self-effacing behavior throughout the novel is singularly ineffectual in actual crisis situations" (Ellis 132). In what way? "Elizabeth [after Justine's arrest] is uninterested in pursuing the truth: that the 'evidence' that convicts Justine has been planted" (132). This makes it sound as though Elizabeth knows "the truth" and declines to pursue it. But how could she, any more than Justine, imagine the "true" alternative to the prosecutor's explanation of "the facts"? Ellis insists that "the description of Justine's apprehension makes this oversight seem truly incredible" (132). Why? Because the miniature's discovery by "two servants is certainly one [thing] that might reasonably arouse suspicion" (132). Thieves and murderers often retain incriminating evidence, which is often discovered by someone. Besides, how could "suspicion" at the discovery lead to the monster, lead anywhere but to the theory that the two servants themselves planted the miniature on Justine after stealing it from William? Two innocents would be convicted instead of one.

Confronted with a near-perfect crime, we see that rationality itself, not Elizabeth or true womanhood, is the real weakness. Miss Marple could not have solved this mystery. Which is crucial to our experience of Elizabeth. If the real truth were right there before her, Elizabeth's failure to grasp it would be damning indeed. But our sense of weakness in Elizabeth is carefully controlled by the impossibility of her task. The young woman does, as Swingle says, follow Victor's lead (62); she is by no means immune to true woman's reliance upon assertive males. But I react to that reliance in Elizabeth less harshly than Swingle does because of the irony here. In trusting Victor, Elizabeth is trusting the right man. He is exactly the one to save Justine. When Elizabeth later castigates the "pretended friends" who are too cowardly to stand up for Justine, she unknowingly adds to our sense of Victor's responsibility. Since we see that reliance upon herself could not possibly have brought Elizabeth to the truth about this perfect crime, we tend to minimize her responsibility and to focus upon the character whose unique vantage point could reveal "the truth." Promethean man's guilt makes true woman's dependency seem minor.

Critics of Elizabeth have additional problems when they switch from her supposed weakness and describe Mary Shelley's supposed alternative.

> Safie has asserted her independence from her Turkish father in the belief that she will be able, in a Christian country, "to aspire to higher powers of intellect, and an independence of spirit, forbidden to the female followers of Mahomet." She has no idea, in other words, that what she has done would be unthinkable to Elizabeth Lavenza and her virtuous nineteenth-

century middle-class counterparts. (Ellis 125–
26)

What Safie has sought *is* virtuous nineteenth-century middle-class
domesticity. She flees to what Elizabeth already has, to where Elizabeth already is, not only geographically but also culturally and
emotionally. Culturally the "powers of intellect" which Safie aspires to are "higher" than Mahometan standards, but they are not
higher than European. Safie has no desire to enter the university; the
character who laments woman's exclusion from higher education is
Elizabeth (151). Safie's reading at home with her tutor-lover Felix is
hardly a radical undertaking (especially since Mary establishes
pointedly that Safie learns slower than the monster [114]!). Emotionally Safie lives out Elizabeth's own scenario: union with the man
of her dreams and happiness in the house of his father. Defying the
heavy father is plucky, but not unprecedented. It is a staple of heroines in melodrama and of Harriet Westbrooks and Mary Godwins in
life. Safie achieves the domestic ideal that Elizabeth can only long
for, but we cannot attribute the women's success and failure to their
relative emancipation from womanly weakness.

So melodramatic an expedient as Safie's plucky journey is not
available to Elizabeth, any more than it is to Safie once she has set-
tled into domesticity with Felix. The primary constraints upon Elizabeth, however, are less environmental than psychological, and less
female than male. The real journey for her and for Safie is from isolation to communion. "Had Elizabeth been encouraged 'to aspire to
higher powers of intellect, and an independence of spirit,' she might
have followed Victor to Ingolstadt and perhaps even have insisted
that he provide the Monster a companion for his wanderings" (Ellis
141). Elizabeth deserves higher education, but the barrier to Ingolstadt is not primarily the cultural one of entrance requirements
and family attitudes. Whereas Felix wants Safie to join him, Victor
wants Elizabeth to stay behind. She cannot link up with Frankenstein beyond the hearth because he flies the hearth partly to escape
her. He flees to the university and to science for the same reason
that men down through history have gone off to the hunt and the
battlefield, in order to reach a male realm beyond the call of woman
and the confines of home.

Frankenstein's emotions are reflected obliquely in Safie's epithet,
"the Arabian," which links her with "the Arabian" Sinbad mentioned by Victor. Both Arabians are travelers, but the chief function
of the link is to associate Safie with Sinbad's story (wife destroys

husband) and thus to implicate her in Victor's distrust of womankind. The emotional logic here, however bizarre, is that since Victor fears Sinbad's wife he would not like this Arabian woman either. Safie is thus no alternative to, or model for, Elizabeth. Though she is a safe-y—Mary could have used the more expectable name "Sofia" or "Sofie" if she hadn't wanted the pun[13]—Safie and all women seem dangerous to Victor no matter how safely orthodox they seem to us. Thus weakness does indeed restrict Elizabeth to hearth and home, but the weakness is the Promethean's.

"Victor discovers a flaw in the wall that keeps his hearth untouched by evil from the outside: you cannot take its protective magic with you when you leave" (Ellis 136). Victor's psychological state is almost exactly the reverse of this. To his complaint that "I had often, when at home, thought it hard to remain during my youth cooped up in one place, and had longed to enter the world, and take my station among other human beings," Ellis responds, "unfortunately for him, these other human beings turn out all to be male" (136). Victor flies the coop of domesticity in order to reach males. His room at Ingolstadt is called a "cell" because monastic and eventually criminal reclusion, the antithesis of family integration, is essential to the growth of his artificial cell, his monstrous sel-f.

Primary responsibility rests once again with Victor. Safie as foil for Elizabeth functions less to show up any very culpable weakness in true woman than to show off the dependence of every woman upon her lover. Safie could not succeed so sweepingly if she had a Frankenstein to contend with; her Turkish father is, by comparison, a piece of baklava. Juxtaposing Safie and Elizabeth in terms of passivity goes beyond denying the Arabian any real superiority over the European, and even reveals a way in which Elizabeth is *less* passive.

The moment when she seems weakest, her death, is when we see most deeply into her unconscious intricacies. How does Elizabeth respond once she senses, however unconsciously, what she cannot entirely miss—that her loving motion out toward Victor is not matched by him, that the lover may be everything to her but she, like Mary Shelley, is not everything to him? Answering this important question entails asking an apparently trivial one. Why is Elizabeth described on the bridal bier as "relaxed" (193)? Her dead body has already been characterized adequately as "lifeless and inanimate." Just as these adjectives convey more than physical facts, convey Victor's deep antagonism to woman as reproductive clay, the adjective "relaxed" reveals *Elizabeth's* depths. What we are seeing is not a minutely rendered photograph of death but a subtle tableau of passion. To understand Elizabeth's strange ordeal on the wedding night, we should begin with events earlier in the day.

Crossing the lake after the marriage ceremony, Elizabeth admonishes Victor to "observe . . . the innumerable fish that are swimming in the clear waters where we can distinguish every pebble that lies at the bottom" (190). The moment seems conventional enough: true woman reveals a lucidity of vision and a purity of depths appropriate to her role as bride-guide. But once Mary Shelley has encouraged our tendency to see stereotypically, she again educates us in life's sterner complexities.

> Thus Elizabeth endeavoured to divert her thoughts and mine from all reflection upon melancholy subjects. But her temper was fluctuating; joy for a few instants shone in her eyes, but it continually gave place to distraction and reverie.
> The sun sank lower in the heavens. (191)

A passage which initially seems to foster stereotypes by showing the angel ministering to her man ends by blurring role distinctions. "Fluctuating" moods and "distraction and reverie" are Victor's stock-in-trade, yet they characterize Elizabeth here. Bride as well as groom is associated with the lake's depths ("we" can see), and each is implicated in the turbulence which increasingly complicates depth perception.

> We went to a balcony that overhung the lake and contemplated the lovely scene. . . . The wind, which had fallen in the south, now rose with great violence in the west. The moon had reached her summit in the heavens, and was beginning to descend; the clouds swept across it swifter than the flight of the vulture, and dimmed her rays, while the lake reflected the scene of the busy heavens, rendered still busier by the restless waves that were beginning to rise. Suddenly a heavy storm of rain descended. I had been calm during the day; but so soon as night obscured the shapes of objects, a thousand fears arose in my mind. (192)

The agitated depths, plus the vulture and the wind from the deadly west, reflect Frankenstein's inner turmoil unquestionably. But if Mary Shelley had wanted only this, she could easily have had Victor view the scene by himself after Elizabeth retires, or could have located the point of view exclusively in his consciousness by placing the "I" sentence before the wind description. Instead we see the scene through the "we" on the balcony, as we did through the "we" on the boat earlier. Bride as well as groom is implicated in the turbulent night.

Does the descending of the feminine ("her") moon suggest more than Elizabeth's decline into death, suggest her descent into the now black depths? Since she shares moon imagery with the monster throughout the novel, are they descending together into those watery depths which he will actually enter at her death? Are the moon's rays dimmed not only to show Elizabeth extinguished by murder but also to suggest the decreasing of lucid guidance as night darkens? Can bride as well as groom be sensing on some deep level the monster's advent, with fear and longing? Elizabeth is open to that advent. And we must understand why before we can understand the power of the word "relaxed."

Elizabeth is alone in the bridal chamber because Victor "earnestly entreated her to retire" (192). The word "retire" means more than to go to bed; it means to withdraw. Unconsciously the Erotic Victor wishes Elizabeth to withdraw into sleep solitary and permanent. "Earnestly" emphasizes his dualism: the good husband of Agape urges his wife's safety; the assassin maneuvers her into vulnerable isolation. Elizabeth as good wife heeds her husband's wishes without a murmur, but she has already been an advocate with Ernest and with Elizabeth. Is she now acting earnestly with Victor too, responding to Eros as well as Agape? That passivity can be a mode of action is soon suggested by diction: " . . . the room into which Elizabeth had retired" (193). "Retired" recurs, but with a difference. Earlier Elizabeth was the object of the verb phrase "entreated . . . to retire"; now she is the subject of the verb "retired." Earlier Elizabeth was banished from Victor's presence; now she withdraws from it. Mary Shelley is using repetition here to suggest what she will dramatize fiercely in her next novel, *Mathilda*—the plight of a heroine whose male proves incapable of bursting through his weakness and sweeping her up in the raptures that she deeply desires. When Victor sends off to sleep alone a bride who manifests no sexual reticence, we must watch that woman carefully.

What we do not see is a "pose straight out of Fuseli's 'The Nightmare'" (Joseph 109). As in Fuseli, the woman's head is down, no longer in the celebrated position of regnant reason, but Mary Shelley has added a crucial detail. "Her . . . features half covered by her hair" (193). Woman no less than man reveals a dark half. "Half" receives particular emphasis here from its unlikeliness. With the head hanging down, the hair would hang down too, away from the face rather than covering it. The hair of Fuseli's woman hangs this way, and Mary herself presents the more expectable pose in *The Last Man*: "Idris . . . had fallen [unconscious] from the seat to the bottom of the carriage; her head, its long hair pendent, with one arm, hung over the side" (258). Idris is not characterized by Elizabeth's unlikely half-half coiffure because she is not self-divided. Hair functions in *Frankenstein* as the blind horse does in Fuseli—to indicate how night dethrones the rational head and brings into prominence the animal unconscious. But by using hair rather than grotesques like the blind horse and incubus, Mary insists that the animal is in no way an external force characteristic of the monster only. Hair is as intrinsic to the heroine as her angelic face.

The angel's passive obedience to an inadequate male has brought her to the animal in herself and in an other. On some deep level, bride as well as groom has sensed incompatibility, and has sought the monster. This incompatibility between supposedly complementary lovers is what accounts for the word "relaxed." Elizabeth's body is "relaxed" while her face is "distorted" because she as monster-woman has found physical satisfaction in a release of passion which Victor can see only as disfiguring in angelic woman. Having shown no fear of the wedding night with Victor, Elizabeth has gone on subconsciously beyond her dysfunctionate bridegroom and has confronted masculinity itself.

That this confrontation results in her death does not constitute a criticism of Elizabeth's passive sexuality. She is killed not by her (very proper) sexual instinct but by the male principle in its extreme, monstrous form—machismo untempered by the sympathy generated by a feminine complement. In turn, the very fact that Elizabeth must confront *extreme* maleness is caused by the extreme weakness, the effeminacy, of her supposed protector, the anxious bridegroom.

The death that Elizabeth confronts is, finally, what her Erotic side has sought all along. She wants out of a world where the men are Victors and the alternative is monstrous. As she told Justine, "I cannot live in this world of misery" (84). Hair across the face of a woman lying dead upon a bed comes to Mary Shelley not from Fuseli but from life. During the formative months of *Frankenstein*, Mary learns of the suicide of Fanny Imlay, her long brown hair about her face" (Dowden 2:57). In her "relaxed" posture Elizabeth has learned the lesson of the Dionysiac Eros: sex and death are more than simply related, they are one in the final peace they bring. Mary would have focused exclusively upon the brutality of strangulation if a horror like Victor's were to be our only reaction. Instead she adds "relaxed." Since we have been told already that "a cloud that passes over the fair moon, for awhile hides, but cannot tarnish its brightness" (84), we sense with "relaxed" that the clouds which obscured the moon two hours earlier were indeed transitory. Earlier Elizabeth, like Mary Shelley, invoked death as an escape from life's savagery. "Alas! I would I were in peace with my aunt and my lovely William, escaped from a world which is hateful to me, and the visages of men which I abhor" (83). Now the "shriek" which suggests ecstasy as well as agony has left Elizabeth relaxed. She may well have proven herself far more active than Safie, have gone on a far scarier journey to reach her male, and may have indeed found the one peace that surpasseth domesticity.

7

Value and Viability

"Oh Death," she sang, "oh leave one singer to mourn."

Katherine Anne Porter

. . . and felt she had finally gotten to the beginning of something she couldn't begin.

Flannery O'Connor

WHERE DOES MARY SHELLEY'S COMPLICATED VIEW OF WOMEN LEAVE her at the end of *Frankenstein*? Where it does not leave her is disaffiliated from womankind as "the very antithesis of the common womanly ideal" (Brown 168). Still less does it warrant Grylls' contention that Mary shared Percy's inability "to be comfortable members of a community . . . even of a home circle . . . because [of] . . . the conflict there was in her nature between the feminine and the artist" (xiii). The *integration* of all of woman's components is what Mary Shelley insists upon, even as she passes upon that integrated self a judgment more damning in some respects than Grylls'.

> My belief is—whether there be sex in souls or not—that the sex of our [woman's] material mechanism makes us quite different creatures [from men]—better though weaker but wanting in the higher grades of intellect.

> We women are of the earth, earthy. . . . that spark from heaven genius is not granted to the sex.

> . . . the heavenly fire, which is to ferment the clay, is not given in equal proportions [to women].

> The woman of large capacity can seldom rise beyond the absorption of ideas; her physical

195

> conditions refuse to support the energy re-
> quired for spontaneous activity. . . . This, more
> than unfavorable external circumstances, is,
> we think, the reason why woman has not yet
> contributed any new form to art, any discovery
> in science, any deep-searching inquiry in
> philosophy.

Here are arguably the foremost women intellectuals produced by
Britain from 1780 to 1880: Mary Shelley, Mary Somerville, Mary
Wollstonecraft, Mary Ann Evans.[1] Their sincere deprecation of their
wonderful minds shows how deeply ingrained traditional stereotyping was, how difficult most contemporaries found it to believe in
the sexual equality espoused by Percy Shelley and J. S. Mill. We may
not like to hear brilliant women deprecate themselves and their sex,
as we may not like Mary Shelley saying that woman's highest role is
to be wife or mother of some great man. But the fact remains that
Mary's more radical moments—her insistence upon woman's capacity for a willfulness extreme enough to prove homicidal, her dissent from any theory of education so domestically oriented that it
hampers a woman's ability to act and think, her distrust of any standard of devotion so idealized that it overestimates a woman's capacity (and desire) to compensate for her man, her impatience with any
view of roles so child-centered that it requires a woman to favor
mother over wife[2]—these moments are qualifications of her basically, and to us at times devastatingly, orthodox view of the sexes.

What all this means for *Frankenstein* is that the novel will com-
plicate, but will not alter fundamentally, the doctrine of female superiority. True woman is flawed, but Promethean man is more so. In
most women, Agape predominates; in all too many men, Eros. Elizabeth may harbor homicidal drives, like Mary and us all, but Victor,
like Percy, kills. Elizabeth for all her limitations is capable of life,
and Victor for all his genius is not.

Mary's standard for evaluating the sexes is thus as practical as her
attitude toward death and limitation. As she tends to forgo concern
with the mortality which she cannot escape and to focus instead
upon the limitations which she might remedy or circumvent, so
with the sexes she sets up the workable, the practical, as her standard. Woman's traditional strengths, the domestic virtues, are re-
affirmed because they foster the largest amount of happiness possible in our largely unhappy world. It is as a practical standard, not a
perfect ideal, that these domestic virtues help us to evaluate Promethean and non-Promethean characters in the closing frame of

Frankenstein. What makes practicality a complex standard here is that Mary's very insistence upon the workable requires her to acknowledge any limitations to the efficacy of her standard. At stake at the end of *Frankenstein*, in other words, is not only value but viability, not only whether a standard is good, but whether it is effective. Mary questions the domestic virtues at the same time that she valorizes them. This skeptical, self-reflective aspect of *Frankenstein*, this doubting of the viability of value, is what gives to Mary Shelley's novel and mind their dour intricacy.

THE LAST OF THE PROMETHEANS

The basic conservativism of Mary Shelley's view of the sexes bears directly upon the scholarly controversies over the end of *Frankenstein*, particularly upon optimistic interpretations of Victor as "heroic" and of Robert as "redeemed." Kiely speaks for many readers when he says of Victor: "though a good and gifted person before his 'ruin,' it is really afterward, by means of the uniqueness and depth of his suffering, that Frankenstein achieves superiority over other men" (158).[3] Is suffering sufficient for superiority? Mary Shelley agrees with her Falkner that "he who conquers himself is, in my eyes, the only true hero" (*Falkner* 2:6). Suffering is a means, a fire which traditionally burns away the dross of self-deception and leaves behind the ore of self-knowledge. "I had an obscure feeling," Victor Frankenstein says, "that all was not over" (87). The dark drives which he cannot face fully he cannot ignore entirely. After William, Justine, and Henry are dead, Frankenstein recognizes that "other victims await their destiny" (174); yet he does nothing to prevent that destiny, the deaths of Elizabeth and Alphonse. That "there is something at work in my soul, which I do not understand" (231) is an 1831 highlighting of the 1818 intimations of morality. To help us judge how much self-awareness the Prometheans achieve, and thus how much "superiority over other men," Mary Shelley in the moments before the closing frame encourages us to question whether suffering has increased Victor's self-knowledge.

With Elizabeth dead, Victor "lay on a bed, hardly conscious of what had happened" (194). At issue is that responsibility for action which dogged Percy Shelley's life and shaped his art from the semiconscious protagonists of *Zastrozzi* and *St. Irvyne* onward. To show that Frankenstein is not only dazed by the awful events but unconscious of their psychosexual nature, Mary Shelley insists upon his lack of illumination. "I was bewildered in a cloud of wonder and horror," he says, "reflecting on my misfortunes, and their cause"

197

(194). Causation is indeed the issue. But since no sense of personal responsibility results from Victor's reflections—"I began to reflect on their cause—the monster" (196)—he cannot recognize the deep drives of "ardent desire" (202) which attract him to his creature. "My eyes wandered round the room, as if to seek something that I had lost" (194). "Something," not "someone." While the conscious Victor of Agape is seeking Elizabeth, his Erotic unconscious has already dismissed her as some thing (insect, clay) and is already attracted to the monstrous thing "lost" now in the depths of the lake and the night. At the moment of Frankenstein's greatest suffering, Mary Shelley emphasizes his self-delusion in order to qualify his heroism and our sympathy.

Nor does Victor help his cause by playing up the suffering. "No creature had ever been so miserable as I" (195). The Shelleyan ring to the self-pity here is emphasized in 1831 when Mary has Victor describe himself with one of Percy's favorite self-characterizations. "The wounded deer dragging its fainting limbs to some untrodden break, there to gaze upon the arrow which had pierced it, and to die—was but a type of me" (247). This Promethean sense of martyrdom soon leads Victor to outright self-canonization. "There was a phrenzy in my manner, and something, I doubt not, of that haughty fierceness, which the martyrs of old are said to have possessed" (198). Do we actually experience Victor this way? "Doubt not" is doubt-producing. And the combination of self-congratulation and self-pity here make the martyr's self-knowledge seem limited indeed.

We cannot rule out victory for Victor, however, because the closing frame changes the nature of the battle. Once the chance for action has passed, perception becomes event, and self-knowledge is heroism. With no more women to slaughter, can the Prometheans at last recognize the horror of Eros and achieve that self-conquest which fosters androgyny in the psyche and reintegration with the community?

Kiely is half correct when he says that for Victor "the death of Elizabeth is the end of everything for him" (169). It is also the beginning. Just as Robert Walton can undertake his pursuit of the pole because of a legacy received upon the death of his "cousin" (11), Victor profits by the death of his cousin, Elizabeth. The real legacy for both men is freedom. Victor's Erotic pursuit of the monster begins after the deaths of Elizabeth and Alphonse because only then can he attempt to join with himself to create the hermaphrodite of spurious immortality.

The extremes of passive weakness and hyperactive will persist in him. Passivity characterizes even so apparently frenetic an act as the pursuit of the monster, because the motivating force is external. "I pursued my path towards the destruction of the daemon, more as a task enjoined by heaven, as the mechanical impulse of some power of which I was unconscious, than as the ardent desire of my soul" (202). Victor's appeal to "heaven" indicates both the persistence of his sky-aspiring inclinations and their covert function—to hide the "ardent desire" of which he remains "unconscious."

The self-deception revealed here grows to ludicrous proportions as the passive pursuit continues. Victor's narrative is laced with details particularly damning because he is unconscious of them. After Victor indicates where he imagines the external aid is coming from ("a spirit of good followed and directed my steps. . . . I may not doubt that it [food] was set there by the spirits that I had invoked to aid me" [201], the monster defines the real situation. "My power is complete. Follow me. . . . You will find near this place, if you follow not too tardily, a dead hare; eat, and be refreshed" (202). The undercutting here, which Victor misses, is especially obvious to us because the creature has already proclaimed the absurdity of Promethean pretensions.

> "I [Frankenstein] call on you, spirits of the dead; and on you, wandering ministers of vengeance, to aid and conduct me in my work."
> . . . I was answered through the stillness of night by a loud and fiendish laugh. (200)

Does light dawn for benighted Victor? Does he know himself, or at least know doubt? "Surely in that moment I should have been possessed by phrenzy, and have destroyed my miserable existence, but . . . " There is always a "but" for Victor, always a self-justifying rationale for ignoring the truths about himself which have momentarily surfaced. " . . . but that my vow was heard, and that I was reserved for vengeance" (200). How does Victor *know* that his vow is heard? Instead of corroborating his claim existentially, Mary Shelley undercuts it stylistically. "Reserved for vengeance" means one thing to monomaniacal Victor and another to us. While he imagines himself as a Shelleyan Assassin sanctified for heavenly wrath, we see the limits to assassins. Men who seek to wreak vengeance are "reserved for" it, are set aside to receive it. The death which Victor plans for the creature is reserved for him as Mary takes her revenge upon vengeful males.

Passive Victor is, of course, no more aware of the pun on "reserved for" than he is of his situation. He persists in beliefs both ludicrously out of keeping with the reality of a "pursuit" orchestrated by the creature and unconsciously appropriate to the effeminately dependent half of a riven psyche. "I knelt down, and, with a full heart, thanked my guiding spirit" (203). The man who has sent forth horrors from his fancy now moves increasingly into, rather than away from, his fantasies. "During the day I was sustained and inspirited by the hope of night: for in sleep I saw my friends, my wife, and my beloved country" (202). Eventually the realms of reality and illusion reverse completely. Like Percy Shelley, who saw the air "peopled with the spirits of the departed" and found that "a train of visionary events arranged themselves in my imagination until ideas almost acquired the intensity of sensations" (Hogg 2:549; *PSL* 1:402, 4 Oct. 1814), Victor "enjoys one comfort, the offspring of solitude and delirium: he believes, that, when in dreams he holds converse with his friends . . . they are not the creations of his fancy, but the real beings who visit him from the regions of a remote world" (208). How can so deluded a solipsist have admired "superiority over other men"?

Having revealed the persistence of weakness during the pursuit, Victor on board ship reintroduces the issue of ego-centric will. Can he forgo inexorability and gain self-knowledge? He has several opportunities. What, for example, is his final attitude toward the monster? Earlier denunciations of its "delight in death and wretchedness" (165) are repeated now as Frankenstein reviles the creature for "unparalleled malignity" (215). The Victor of Eros makes of the monster what he did of woman, a reflection of his own needs. He needs now to shift primary responsibility for the horrific events onto the creature so that the creative will can avoid indicting itself as co-conspirator.

Self-knowledge remains possible, however, because Victor aboard ship questions his own responsibility for the havoc. "During these last days I have been occupied in examining my past conduct" (214). The whole novel comes back before our eyes so that we can reexperience Victor's past failures and evaluate his present awareness. "Examining my past conduct" does not, however, prompt him to ask the questions which occur to us and might enlighten him: why he failed to guard Elizabeth, to save Justine, to warn William and Henry, to warn the world. As though he were motivated solely by Agape's love of neighbor, Frankenstein accepts as unimpeachable his treatment of his friends, and he uses it to justify his mistreat-

200

ment of the monster. "My duties towards my fellow-creatures had greater claims to my attention" (215). Since Victor's *in*attention to the safety of his fellow is manifest, he seems to have learned little.

This is also the case when he recalls his destruction of the monstress. That she might have bred more monsters is a rationalization, not a reason. Since Victor was assembling her organ by organ, he could create her barren and still assure happy conjugality. But no, "she might become ten thousand times more malignant than her mate" (163). This seems viciously sexist. We do not see any scientific reason to believe Victor correct, and we do see a psychological reason for him to believe himself correct. He shares in the misogyny of the Erotic Shelley which made deformed women uglier than deformed men, "ugliest of all things ugly," in *Prometheus Unbound* (3. 4. 46). Does Frankenstein aboard ship recognize the error of his rationalizations? "I did right. . . . He shewed unparalleled malignity and selfishness" (215). The illogic here is patent. The creature was malignant because he was lonely; therefore the creation, not the destruction, of a mate would have been "right." We are particularly confident of our viewpoint here because Victor persists in his Shelleyan self-justifications. Having proclaimed earlier, "I was guiltless" (160), he now concludes, "I have been . . . examining my past conduct; nor do I find it blameable" (214).

Victor now has one last chance for insight. What advice will he give the other Promethean, Robert Walton? Should Robert imitate Frankenstein, or reject the sky-aspiring for the native-earth way? This question presupposes others: why does Victor tell his story to Robert in the first place? Does Victor know why? The answer is less simple than critics make it. "He tells his story to dissuade Walton from ruining himself similarly through excessive ambition. . . . the whole story is obviously intended to teach him where his quest for preeminence actually leads" (Kiely 167; Tropp 15). Why Victor tells his tale will, in effect, determine whether he is ultimately superior. Only by carefully tracing the pendulum swings of his explanations can we define his relation to the chief moral values of *Frankenstein*, the self-conquest and communal responsibility which result from self-awareness.

Initially Victor is noncommittal. "I do not know that the relation of my misfortunes will be useful to you, yet, if you are inclined, listen to my tale. . . . it will afford a view of nature, which may enlarge your faculties and understanding" (24). Soon he expresses the "native" ideal which I quoted earlier. "Learn from me, if not by my precepts, at least by my example, how dangerous is the acquirement of knowledge" (48). Danger obtrudes from another quarter when a subversive reason for telling the tale emerges in the closing frame. "Swear to me, Walton, that he [the monster] shall not escape; that you will seek him, and satisfy my vengeance in his death" (206). Whether or not Victor unconsciously planned it this way all along, his tale has become a covert argument, a rhetorical attempt to persuade Walton to continue Victor's quest. Acquiring Frankensteinian "knowledge" of the monster could prove "dangerous" indeed.

Victor then seems to pull back. "Yet, do I dare ask you to undertake my pilgrimage, to endure the hardships that I have undergone? No; I am not so selfish" (206). However sincere Victor may be on one level, his Erotic drives phrase the prohibition in macho terms of pilgrimage and endurance which inevitably excite an aspiring overreacher like Robert. The very appearance of "selfish" signals a covert judgment by Mary Shelley (and an unconscious admission by Frankenstein) which the "not" cannot negate. We are thus prepared for Victor's reversing field again: "Yet, when I am dead, if he should appear . . . swear that he shall not triumph over my accumulated woes" (206).

To Robert's subsequent questions about creating a monster, Victor reacts properly. "To what do your questions tend? Peace, peace! learn my miseries, and do not seek to increase your own" (207). Can Victor maintain this control on his deathbed? At first he seems to fail. "When actuated by selfish and vicious motives, I asked you to undertake my unfinished work; and I renew this request now, when I am only induced by reason and virtue" (215). After two hundred pages of motives often vicious and always intricate, we are suspicious of claims to reason and virtue. But now Victor pulls back, and achieves his finest moment in the novel. "My judgment and ideas are already disturbed by the near approach of death. I dare not ask you to do what I think right, for I may still be misled by passion" (215). If Victor were to die at this moment, he would indeed be heroic. Having always been disturbed, like Shelley and Byron, by the near approach of death, Victor could warn Walton back from this abyss only by acquiring both self-knowledge and communal concern. Victor would have conquered himself.

Mary Shelley makes sure, however, that he survives for one more paragraph. Most readers, disagreeing with what I feel is Tropp's correct recognition that "Victor's last words betray his ignorance of the meaning of his own destruction" (82), find in these words a continuing ambivalence. Small maintains that the "last speech . . . leaves everything unresolved" (188); Levine, that "the novel will not resolve the issue" (b 10); Dussinger, that "in his last breath he urges Walton contradictorily" (53); Swingle, that "at the last moment he admits that Walton had best think the evidence through for himself" (54–55). What does Victor actually say?

> "Seek happiness in tranquility, and avoid ambition, even if it be only the apparently innocent one of distinguishing yourself in science and discoveries. Yet why do I say this? I have myself been blasted in these hopes, yet another may succeed." (215)

The native ideal of "tranquility" and the Promethean goal of victory are initially juxtaposed, as Agape and Eros battle in Frankenstein to the end. But Mary does not vacillate between her ideal and Percy's. The *final* words of Frankenstein are not ambiguous. If he had died after "ambition" or even after "discoveries," he would have sided with Mary. But he goes on to pledge allegiance to Percy. "I have myself been blasted in these hopes" is very different from "I have blasted myself by these hopes" or "my hopes have blasted me." Victor's "blasted" is in the passive voice because he persists in passivity, in seeing himself victimized by external forces. Personal responsibility, like self-knowledge, remains largely absent. "Another may succeed" indicates Victor's inability to learn the general lesson of his life. He admits only that *he* was inadequate to his dream: he sees nothing inherently fatal and thus vicious in the dream itself. Frankenstein has missed the point of *Frankenstein*.

This brings us to Victor's death and to the question reiterated by readers for decades: why does Victor expire before the monster arrives? Why does Mary Shelley pass up an apocalyptic confrontation of pursuer and pursued like the one staged by Godwin in *Caleb Williams*? There are at least two reasons. One is that the confrontation *cannot* occur. With the father destroyed, maleness is precluded. Killing the father castrates the son, so there is in effect no monster left for Victor. Frankenstein must expire in that solitude which is the ultimate and only offspring of narcissism.

A second reason has to do with the Promethean's paradoxical relationship to death. Frankenstein does not simply die before the monster arrives, he verily fades away. Mary Shelley could have had him rage forth against the monster or perish in some other active way. He fades off because the ultimate consequence of thanatophobia is suicide. Guilt is fatal. However wildly Victor wants to gain immortality by melding his riven elements through union with the monster, he loathes self-union even more. Victor does not simply die, he quits living. Death alone can assure an end to the sufferings of a life become impossible. Mary Shelley insists that at the deepest level everyone, including Prometheans, shares her need for complementarity.

Victor, in death, does not achieve superiority over other men. Mary Shelley's standard of victory, her ideal of self-knowledge, denies him the status of hero. I agree with Kiely's moderated claim that "*Frankenstein* is neither a pure hymn of praise to Godwin and Shelley nor a simple repudiation of them" (172), but I cannot conclude with him that "still, Frankenstein remains the hero throughout" (156). If we heed Victor's own advice to Walton and learn not from his "precepts" but from his "example" (48), not from his assertions about himself but from our experience of that self, we must dissent from Griffin's conclusion that "Frankenstein's quest is successful" (50–51) and from Levine's claim that "the ambition [of the over-reacher] is heroic and admirable" (b 10) and from Kiely's assertion that "the fault is the world's or society's, but not his" (157). Victor ends deceived about both the past and the present, about his responsibility for the chaos and about his role in the pursuit.

Rather than unite his male and female elements in a moderating androgyny, he experiences a bifurcation so extreme that the polarized elements come full circle and blur in perverse, hermaphroditic confusion. The willful proves ineffectual; the weak, relentless. Victor neither balances the masculine and feminine elements in his psyche nor integrates himself with society. Rather than a conqueror of the self, Victor seems at best the pathetic victim of drives which he cannot control nor even acknowledge. What he achieves is not superiority over others but isolation from them. Prometheans who cannot love women cannot love men either. Even in pursuit of males, they subordinate love to will. The Frankenstein who will sacrifice Robert as he did Elizabeth proves by his last words that he is no victor.

*

Is Robert Walton "redeemed"? The question is important because if Robert can learn what Frankenstein has not, there may yet be hope for Prometheans. Walton unlike Victor turns south toward warmth. But this physical motion must have a psychological counterpart before he can actually practice Agape's love of neighbor and achieve the "redemption" celebrated by many critics. Why does Robert turn back? Knoepflmacher feels that Walton "refuses to bring death to his crew" (107); Tropp, that he learns that "exploration must begin with true concern for his fellow men" (82); Hill, that he "heeds" his crew and "consents" (156). But is this so? Robert admits that he turns back because he is forced to. "The fears I entertained of a mutiny" (211) are realized, and Robert yields to intimidation. The weakness which characterized him as failed androgyne in the opening frame persists to the end.

So does willfulness. Robert resentfully sees his crew as unmanly, as "unsupported by ideas of glory and honour" (213).[4] What we see is a maturity which allows the crewmen who initially shared his adolescent enthusiasm to achieve Margaret-Mary's perspective upon Promethean pursuits. Walton, however, persists in the Victor-Percy view of such pursuits as heroic. The panegyric on manliness which Victor delivers, and which Mary Shelley undercuts with allusions to Dante and Milton, is so moving to Robert that he soon echoes the macho idealism of Victor-Ulysses-Satan. "I had rather die, than return shamefully" (213). Has Walton really learned the "consequences" of the "error" of "excessive 'masculinity'" (Scott 189)?

There may yet be hope, however, because Walton adds, "thus are my hopes blasted by cowardice and indecision" (213). Whose cowardice and indecision? If the crew's, then Robert is imitating Victor in blaming external forces for blasting him. But if Robert is facing up to the limitations of machismo as Victor never did, he is sustaining that capacity for self-knowledge which allowed him to recognize some of his limits in the opening frame. Having his will "blasted" at the end may purchase still more of the self-awareness indispensible to heroism.

This possibility remains alive until the next sentence. "It requires more philosophy than I possess, to bear this injustice with patience" (213). What injustice? Robert has failed because his goal is unrealistic and his prowess inadequate. The very mention of justice recalls the monster's just demands upon Victor, the unjust sentencing of Justine, the unjust treatment of Safie's father and the De Laceys, plus Walton's own admission of the "justice" (211) of the crew's demand. In context, Robert's sense of personal injustice seems as self-pitying and benighted as Victor's. His humiliation does not, moreover, constitute a "healing crisis" (Scott 200), because his actions do not indicate a "new awareness of himself and new knowledge of his culture" (Tropp 8). In his continued self-delusion, Robert remains the acolyte of Victor Frankenstein, whose fantasy about visitations from "a remote world . . . gives," according to Walton, "a solemnity to his reveries that render them to me almost as imposing and interesting as truth" (208). No wonder that Robert's later parroting of Victor's argument makes the creature exclaim, "do you dream?" (217).

Willful Robert has not "renounced fantasy" (Scott 180), and he has no more renounced the Erotic use of people than Victor did. In the opening frame, Frankenstein revealingly called friendship an "acquisition" (23). Percy Shelley spoke in similar terms of Mary:

> I speedily conceived an ardent passion to pos-
> sess this inestimable treasure. . . . at length I
> possessed the inalienable treasure. . . . I pos-
> sess this treasure. . . . I do not think that I am
> less impatient now than formerly to repossess
> to entirely engross my own treasured love.
> (*PSL* 1:403, 4 Oct. 1814; 1:413–14, 28 Oct.
> 1814)

Possession is sufficiently basic to Walton's view of relationships that he immediately saw Victor as "a man . . . I should have been happy to have possessed" (22). In the opening frame, Robert repeatedly defined friendship acquisitively, not as reciprocal give-and-take, but as a one-way demand that the friend "sympathize . . . approve or amend . . . repair . . . regulate . . . sympathize . . . direct . . . confirm and support" *me*. Now in the closing frame the friend is still defined instrumentally. "I have lost my hopes of utility and glory;—I have lost my friend" (213). The loss of friendship comes second to the loss of glory. And what costs Robert the glory is the friend's dying! Even after he has learned of the horrors perpetrated by the monster, Walton repeatedly presses Frankenstein for the specifics of monster-making. "Are you mad," cries Victor, "whither does your senseless curiosity lead you?" (207). The only critic to notice Robert's rapacity here attributes it simply to his being "naturally inquisitive" (Glut 15). Robert is naturally acquisitive. He cannot resist wanting Victor's power for his own glory. Walton too has missed the point of *Frankenstein*.

The Walton who does not opt for love over knowledge cannot, I feel, escape isolation through the agency of a good woman, as Knoepflmacher sees him doing. "The memory of this civilizing and restraining woman [Margaret], a mother with 'lovely children,' helps him resist Frankenstein's destructive (and self-destructive) course" (107).[5] Robert in fact continues to share Frankenstein's *dis*-affiliation from women. In the last paragraph addressed directly to Margaret, Robert repeats his earlier insistence upon the limits of heterosexual communion. "What can I say, that will enable you to understand the depth of my sorrow?" (216).

The continuing gap between Robert and woman is not closed by his movement south. He is paralleling Frankenstein geographically and psychologically. Victor came south from Ireland to wed Elizabeth, but emotionally he never left the north. Destroying the monstress kept him bound to the monster. The monster's following Victor south indicated the tenacity of their male bond, the impossibility of any real union between Promethean and woman. Thus Victor's honeymoon trip south from Geneva to Lake Como began with the newlyweds going *north* to Evian.[6] Elizabeth died without ever turning south because Victor had been heading north all along—first to Ingolstadt, then to Britain, finally to the pole. Robert Walton's move south remains only geographical because he too leaves unfinished business in the north. His bond with Victor is sealed by Victor's death, in the same way that destruction of the monstress sealed the Victor-monster union. The monster remains alive at the end of Walton's narrative, as he did after his mate's destruction, to indicate the persistence of male forces which cannot be satisfied by southerly motions toward women. Such journeys are no more part of Robert's true psychological orientation than they were of Victor's; Walton too has been heading north all along in his own three-stage progression. First he went with "whale-fishers on several expeditions to the North Sea" (11); then by himself to St. Petersburgh and Archangel; finally with his crew to the pole. From that undiscovered country no Promethean ever returns.

The limits of *male* communion are manifest in Walton at the end of the closing frame. He confirms what Victor has established, that males who cannot unite with women cannot unite with men either. Robert's isolation is made complete not by the death of Victor (which Robert could not prevent), but by the exile of the creature (which he could). Robert is given at the end of the novel what he has sought throughout, a male friend. The creature is now wise enough in the ways of life and books to provide "support." He is the proper teacher because suffering has burned him freer of self-deception than any male in the novel. He knows the full depths of the heart's terrible passions, yet he remains capable of heartfelt tenderness. Walton, however, is incapable of connection. Having begun his confrontation with the monster by parroting Victor, he ends reduced to silence. This silence can at best mean only that Robert understands how wrong Frankenstein has been. That Robert goes on to recognize and be transformed by how right Mary Shelley is, can be maintained only by adding to the scene what she pointedly omits. How easy it would have been to show Walton seeing the light; just one sentence, even one image, would suffice. But there is no clear sign that Robert is redeemed, and there is the inescapable fact that he lets the creature go.[7]

Optimistic claims that Walton is "redeemed by connections with family, community, and human feeling" (Hill 341) lack firm grounding in either probability or text. "The allusions to the *Comedia* suggest that, just as Dante the voyager was enlightened by learning of Ulysses' distemper, so may Walton have been enlightened by Victor's" (Scott 200). Is it probable that so important an issue as the final status of the last Promethean would be left by Mary Shelley to depend upon allusions which her popular reading public would surely have missed? Hill rescues Robert with a textless "somehow": "Walton somehow turns away from repressive pursuit into madness and reasserts the human condition" (356). What is more regressive than going backwards, particularly when the geographical motion is back psychologically toward a woman who is not a bride for the future but a mother surrogate from the past? Mary Shelley could so easily have had Robert mention the existence of a fiancée, or could have made Margaret his wife, if she had wanted to hold out hope for Walton's conjugal and communal integration. He does not *expect* to find consolation in England (Hirsch 410); he says only that he "may" find it (216). Likewise with the "friends" he is supposedly returning to: in the opening frame Robert gave no sense of strong ties, or of virtually any ties, to anyone in England except Margaret; he certainly lacked there the male friend he craved. How, then, can Robert's emotional ties to friends be experientially powerful for us in the closing frame? And if they are not powerful, how seriously can we imagine that Walton will be integrated into the ordinary, orthodox life "for which" he has been "fit all along" (Hill 356)?

What Robert has been fit for all along is failure. His early failure with poetry (11) only intensified his desire to overreach. Now he has failed again. His lifelong recourse has been to a repression of ambition and a suppression of frustration that perpetuated adolescent dreams. Why would his greatest failure affect him differently? Such self-knowledge as he does possess has tended less to fruitful insight than to increased self-hate. The Robert who began by castigating himself as "more illiterate than many school-boys of fifteen" now "come[s] back ignorant and disappointed" (213). Robert will again share physical propinquity with Margaret, as Victor and Percy rejoined Elizabeth and Mary after various pursuits. But communion is limited for Promethean males who slenderly know themselves. Mary knew it in her heart.

VIABILITY

I said earlier that in contrasting Victor with other characters Mary Shelley ran the risk of becoming a Promethean herself, of idealizing the characters who embodied her values. A comparable risk occurs at the end of *Frankenstein*. By judging Robert and Victor so darkly, Mary again risks taking too absolute a stand. She must not overrate her values. *Frankenstein* is an angry book, but it is not righteous, because sorrow tempers its last moments. "Darkness and distance" characterize Mary Shelley herself, for she cannot help recognizing that the value of a moral standard is not enough. What counts finally for a woman resolutely not philosophical is the viability of value, the standard's efficacy in the world. Having qualified the domestic virtues already by revealing a dark Erotic side to woman, Mary takes the further risk of recognizing these virtues for what they are—an operational force, not an abstract ideal. The optimism, however qualified, which characterizes most interpretations of the end of *Frankenstein* is justified only to the extent that Mary's values prove viable.

Optimism seems particularly warranted by two of the novel's non-Promethean males. Felix De Lacey is, as we have seen, the antithesis of Victor Frankenstein. Felix stays home with his beloved father and unites with his female complement. Mary Shelley's approval appears in his name. "Felix" versus "Victor," happy versus triumphant. Lest there be any doubt about the source and worth of the happiness, Mary spells it out in Felix's full name. "Felix de lacer": "happy of ties."

The persistence of domestic ties is further emphasized by an aspect of *Frankenstein* overlooked consistently by critics. The endurance of Ernest. Why is the monster allowed to kill all the other Frankensteins and not him? Ernest is not, like Ishmael, the narrator who must remain to tell the tale. Why does he survive? Why, in fact, is Ernest in the novel at all? To answer these questions I must return to the order of deaths.

William	Justine	Henry	Ernest	Alphonse
			Elizabeth	Alphonse

Elizabeth and Ernest are the only members of the Frankenstein family who share an initial. Victor has two ways to reach Alphonse because his father has had two identities. Like the "A" character in the De Lacey household, Agatha ("good"), Alphonse ("noble") represents the good which Victor should be seeking. Unlike Agatha, however, Alphonse has manifested his excellence in two life styles. For years he remained a bachelor and devoted himself to the good of his native land; then he married and devoted himself to the good of his growing family. As Elizabeth offers Victor the family route to one kind of nobility, Ernest, who at twenty-two is more than old enough to have married if Mary Shelley wished it, offers the bachelor route. Mary's 1818 instinct to associate Ernest with farming links him to the "native" land, the earth ideal. Victor, however, is incapable of taking either the Ernest-bachelor or the Elizabeth-family route because his need is to destroy rather than bond with father.

Why then does the livid litany of corpses which marks his regression not include Ernest? For the same reason that Victor never meets and unites with the monster. Mary Shelley forbids it. There are limits to her tolerance because there must be a limit to Promethean will. Mary's own experience with Percy indicated how Promethean will could destroy wife-mother and children, but she cannot admit that that will is equally destructive outside of wedlock. The Dormouse must have her mousehole, the virtue of earnestness must endure. Ernest survives Victor because victory is self-defeating and earnestness, like happiness, is not.

*

The survival of earnest Ernest, happy Felix, good Agatha, and safe Safie is surely a point in favor of the viability of the domestic ideal and could lead to something like Hill's optimism about "hippocratic love." "The novel's nurses of both genders hold the promise of redemption from psychic tyranny in a turn outward from the self to others" (357). It must mean something, however, that the novel's healers—Caroline, Justine, Elizabeth, Henry, Alphonse—are all slaughtered. Mary's obvious respect for healing is a long way from "redemption," especially since even those characters who endure can hardly be said to prevail. Felix De Lacey is largely irrelevant to the main plots of *Frankenstein*. He and the other De Laceys play no part in Victor's or Robert's lives and offer no serious remedy to the Promethean malady from which they are blessedly immune. They could not stop Frankenstein if they encountered him, and he could not become one of them if he tried.

More serious limits to the efficacy of the domestic ideal are revealed through the non-Promethean males who do encounter Frankenstein. Henry and Alphonse cannot control Victor and sustain order any more than Elizabeth can. Henry is an excellent nurse; he responds sympathetically to nature and poetry. But these "feminine" traits do not make him effectively androgynous, do not make him the Knightly Man whom the nineteenth century envisioned as True Woman's complement. Henry fails as St. George. He can no more slay the monster than Percy's Agape can stop his Erotic will.

The domestic virtues prove ineffective in Alphonse in a different way. He trusts the system and comes to represent orthodoxy paralyzed. He urges Justine to throw herself upon the juridical process because he believes that the law is logical and the judges rational. But the legal system cannot adapt to the illogic of monstrous force, and rational judges can succumb to irrational passions. Alphonse also fails when he tries to deal with Victor's agonies.

> When I [Victor] assured him that the late events were the causes of my dejection, he called to his aid philosophy and reason. . . . This advice, although good, was totally inapplicable to my case. . . . [later] he endeavoured to inspire me with more philosophic sentiments. But his arguments drawn from general observation failed in reaching the core of my incurable disease. (86, 182)

Forms fail to handle particulars. Law, medicine, religion, politics— all institutions prove inadequate in *Frankenstein* because none can account for aberrations like the monster. Worse still, all exist not as pure forms but as practical devices dependent for their operation upon human beings potentially as aberrant as the monster.

Thus Alphonse, like Henry, can nurse Victor but cannot stop him. The domestic virtues participate in this failure, not because they prevent action in the outer world, but because they are finally part of that world. As one institution among many in the larger social configuration, home is one of many agencies entrusted with keeping the peace. The domestic virtues are to function as a gently admonitory force which can make a positive difference because humankind is basically functionate. Just a little shove in the right direction at the right time. . . . That men and women can be horrendously out of control, or that either sex can be prompted by Eros to shove in the wrong direction at the wrong time, is something which this culture does not, cannot allow for. The dream of reason that Shelley shared with Godwin and that orthodoxy, despite its reservations about these radicals, shared with them, proves to be at best a half truth. And the weakness of one half divorced from the other—

of head from heart, of male from female—is what *Frankenstein* is about.

*

This brings us to the monster. To what extent does he achieve the androgynous fusion which, as an indication of self-mastery, would establish his efficacy and warrant our optimism? We can certainly take the creature more seriously as an androgyne than we can any other character in *Frankenstein*. The fact that this huge and often willful male desires a female other indicates the endurance of the feminine component within him. "You must create a female for me, with whom I can live in the interchange of those sympathies necessary for my being" (140). When the monster says, "what I ask for is reasonable and moderate" (142), we agree because he is asking for Mary Shelley's domestic ideal—monogamous wedlock with a complementary mate. "The picture I present to you is peaceful and human" (142).

In the final scene, the monster's feminine component manifests itself not only in his overt grief for Victor, but in Mary Shelley's subtle staging of the tableau. "As he hung over the coffin, his face was concealed by long locks of ragged hair" (216). The link with Caroline leaning over her dead father would be enough to emphasize the monster's feminine aspect; the link with Elizabeth's hair-covered face shows that the creature has become less her victimizer than her self. Both characters are destroyed by Frankenstein's antidomestic will.

This flowering of the feminine in the monster does not, however, warrant Spark's optimistic conclusion that "they [Victor and monster] merge one into the other, entwined in final submission" (137). The plot, not to mention the whole psychological thrust, of *Frankenstein* stresses the final *dis*unity of creator and creature. Victor is dead, the monster is soon gone. Neither by his capacity for feminine sympathy nor by his powers of masculine will can the creature achieve the union which he seeks and which Spark celebrates. Male will is prominent in the last scene. Monster is victor: he outlasts Frankenstein and outargues Walton. But so what? He can render Walton speechless, but the defeat of rationalizations, misconceptions, and self-deceptions yields no practical gain. Since Robert cannot get beyond Victor enough to respond positively to this potentially new "friend," both survivors are doomed to exile.

Outlasting Frankenstein is an even hollower victory. The monster as Victor's projected masculinity can tower over him as fallen femininity in the last scene, but cannot escape a comparable fall.

212

The creator's dysfunction is the creature's state. Motivated by "the impotence of anger" (165), the monster "wasting in impotent passions" can feel only "impotent envy" (219, 218). Males cannot function without females. With "one vast hand . . . extended" (216), the monster reaches for connection for the third time. The union first sought by him on the creation night, when he proffered his hand to his creator, was transformed by Frankenstein into the perverse connection which Victor pursued after Elizabeth's death. The monster responded then by parodying in the bridal chamber his initial gesture of affection in Frankenstein's bedchamber. Now repeated with pathos, the monster's attempt at connection fails again, not simply because Victor is physically dead, but because he was never alive to complementarity. The death scenes of Victor and Elizabeth are linked by the hand gesture to show that, in a way which Kiely did not intend, Frankenstein's life did indeed end with Elizabeth's.

The two scenes are further associated by the creature's final act. He springs from the cabin window as he did from the bridal chamber. The murder which forever denied a complement to Victor has loosed a powerful force upon the world. The feminine element in the creature's psyche is now developed enough to prevent any further violence, but he cannot achieve true self-integration. Scott's recognition that "the novel describes Victor's fall as Androgyny Lost" seems right to me, whereas his admittedly guarded optimism does not. It [the novel] at least offers the prospect of an Androgyny Regained" (189). This prospect, which was dark with Frankenstein and Walton, is even darker with the monster. Since identity is social for Mary Shelley, union within the self requires union with another self. The monster as male can defeat Robert and as female can mourn Victor, but the two processes remain as separate as the polarized gender traits of Frankenstein or of Shelley. True integration of the masculine and feminine within requires the human intercourse which unites man with woman and individual with society.

Finally the monster is dysfunctionate for the same reason that Robert and Victor are. His story tells their tale: fail with father, and you will fail with female and male peers. Just as Victor's murderous rage at Alphonse precludes both marriage to Elizabeth and any comparable bond with Robert, and as Robert fails to achieve either glory or friendship after his father's deathbed repudiation of Promethean quests, the monster repeats the pattern. Like Walton, this son suffers permanent alienation at the paternal deathbed; like Walton and Victor, he never connects with a female complement or a male equivalent. We unquestionably feel for the monster an intense sympathy absent from our reactions to the other sons, because he is horribly victimized. Deathbed alienation occurs not because his father is correct like Walton's, but because Victor is intransigent like Shelley; union with a female complement is precluded not because the monster rejects it, but because his father does. Our sympathy with the creature cannot, however, obscure the fact that he does end alone. "Impotent" knells through his lamentations because he too is castrate.

How can society deal with this powerful and now permanently maimed will? Critics who discuss the monster's immolation presume what Mary Shelley manifestly withholds—proof that he actually dies. "The monster will immolate itself to save humanity from its own violence" (Knoepflmacher 107). If we are indeed saved, why are we denied the experience of this incarnate moment? Mary could easily have extended Walton's narrative by one sentence in order to have him glimpse later a glow on the horizon. Why she forgoes this is not explained by Levine's contention that "we cannot destroy the monster without destroying ourselves" (a 27). We cannot destroy the monster anyway. Eros is a force coeval with mankind, so the issue is not its death but its repression. The fire which the monster prophesies is the fire next time. He will endure until apocalypse because Erotic anguish endures till then. Eros abides out there in its own darkness, and we can either repress it until it explodes in murderous and finally impotent frustration or we can seek that self-knowledge which is the precondition of self-integration, and heroism.

*

The value of the domestic virtues for Mary Shelley derives from their superiority to anything else. Despite her inclination to society, Mary in 1818 knows that the larger world of institutional forms is impossible during her life with Percy. Law courts, money lenders, solicitors, reviewers and publishers, cliques, captious and vengeful in-laws . . . to these horrors, Mary prefers her alternative of "native" bliss, an island retreat with Percy Bysshe and Percy Florence and many books and a few (very few) friends (*MSL* 1:160, 7 Mar. 1822). Her commitment to home began of course in Godwin's chill and later fractious house; it endured through all her wanderings and lodgings; and it was realized in the peaceful mansion of Sir Percy and Lady Jane. Mary's journal entry for March 25, 1815, has never to my knowledge been discussed: "Day of Our Lady, the Virgin Mother of God" (42). Raised in a rationalist household far from Mariolatry, the young mother with her first baby dead three weeks is already pledging allegiance to her ultimate namesake, the mother who suffered the death of her firstborn and became the culture's emblem of domestic virtue.

Living with Percy increasingly convinces Mary, however, that the value of the ideal of home is not the primary issue. She can drag Shelley to an island, but can she make him well? At issue is less the value than the viability of domestic virtue. Mary knows that she cannot blame her difficulties solely upon a venal world; psychology is also at work. It will accompany Percy to whatever island. The most basic issue of *Frankenstein* is thus the extent to which psychic forces, particularly in men, are uncontrollable. Mary makes Alphonse's household superior enough to convince us that Victor is dissatisfied not with his family but with Family. Levine recognizes that " 'the amiableness of domestic affection' does nothing to satisfy Victor Frankenstein's ambitions" (b 14), but he concludes that the fault lies with the amiable affections. Mary's reservations about the bourgeoisie do not translate to the family in anything like the direct way that Marxist critics contend. Home for Mary transcends class. Domestic disruptions arise from conflicts elemental to the psyche.

Frankenstein is nowhere more a woman's book than in its frustration. Margaret Saville is, in this respect, the emblem of the novel. She never appears. She fails to get into the action—into the plot or into Robert's adult life—not because True Womanhood binds her to the home or even to vitiating concepts, but because Promethean men are incorrigible. Robert would not heed her before he left, and he will listen still less upon a return which proves her right all along. Mary was equally helpless with Godwin and with Percy, whenever it really mattered. By the time of Diodati she is analyzing, judging every minute, but she is still the silent figure who watched Coleridge years before from the silent corner. She still can only look powerlessly on as the precocious males of Diodati are doomed to leave the ghost story project unfinished and to die by suicide, drowning, and fever within a decade.

To imagine that "Victor is alienated from his 'child' [the monster] . . . by his desire to flee to the shelter of domesticity" (Ellis 142) is to read Mary Shelley's book and life backwards. Her men flee from her into the wild abandonment of ego and the inevitable collapse of prowess. Mary can rail inwardly at these men, but she cannot change them. And so she takes her only out—she tells the story of her generation. In a widening gyre she moves from Percy and Godwin as husband and father, to Percy, Godwin, and Byron as Prometheans, to all Romantic males, to (almost all) men as romantic.

215

Frankenstein raises the issue of "our infantine dispositions, which, however they may be afterwards modified, are never eradicated" (209) because regression, or rather the failure to mature, is Mary's theme. The male is too death-obsessed to escape tangled feelings for mother and father; he attempts escape through Promethean fantasies boyish and impracticable. Doubly shut off from reality and community, the over-aspiring male finds maturity particularly difficult in Mary's own era, when the career of Lord Byron and the general thrust of Romanticism have writ Prometheus across the sky. Can males caught between heaven and death mature into useful citizens and happy husbands? Can they grow up by coming down from adolescent reveries—without falling too far?

The endurance of the "good" survivors allows us some hope in answering this question, but not much. ". . . lost in darkness and distance." *Frankenstein* ends with obscurity and separation. The final note is, to my ear, less peaceful than elegiac. And the elegy is not for a dead monster (who is alive), but for Mary Shelley herself in her frustration. The valuable proves inviable. And what else is there? Darkness and distance, obscurity and separation, men whom she finally could neither forget nor control. What made them Promethean? Mary's inability to say is what undermines optimism. To say that her "critique of Percy's revolutionary ideology" is "unhostile" (Scott 202) is to ignore how much of her life is bound up in that critique. Whether or not an author so dedicated to complementarity would actually "hope for the evolution of a new consciousness: one which someday will be neither male nor even feminist, but quintessentially human" (Scott 202), I see in *Frankenstein* little indication of where that evolution might grow from. What in Godwin and Victor and Percy and Robert and Byron indicates any fundamental turning away from Eros and toward community?

Critical reliance upon Dante—"the poet who teaches us that by speaking out our repressed anger we can recognize, and thus correct, not only our own distemper but that of our civilization"[8]— presupposes a basically Freudian optimism (ye shall know the truth and the truth shall make ye well). How can Mary Shelley sustain such optimism in the face of Prometheans who manage moments of self-awareness amid careers of self-indulgence? The rejection of therapeutic optimism characterizes not only Mary's novel but also her remaining years. As Knoepflmacher notes, Mary has revenge upon the Prometheans who so loved glory: she never writes their biographies, and she impedes other biographers while

216

life remains in her. She also carries revenge on Percy one step far-
ther. The ashes which are brought from England and buried beside
his in the Protestant Cemetery in Rome are Trelawany's, not
Mary's. By 1851 there are no financial barriers to either burying
Mary in Rome or returning Percy to England. But she chooses family. Nearly thirty years after Lerici she chooses to rest with mother
and father and Percy Florence, and she leaves Percy Bysshe to distance and darkness.

Revenge, as the monster knows, is finally a poor thing. It makes
poor fiction too. The fullest expression of Mary's rage at Promethean men occurs when their irresponsibility has wreaked its
worst havoc and before it has consumed itself in death and legend—
after *Frankenstein* and before 1822. Knowing by 1819 that Percy
will never be "everything" to her, Mary gets revenge. She stops re-
sisting her incestuous drives and reintroduces father. Small is correct that the greatness of *Mathilda* lies not in Mary's admission of
her incestuous desire for Godwin, but in her implication of her bond
with Percy in that desire (185). We can go a step further. The wonder
of *Mathilda* is not simply that Mary writes it, but that she sends it
to Godwin. Of course he is her agent in London, but more than pro-
fessionalism is involved. *Mathilda* is a love letter. Mary takes the
initiative here, as she did with Percy in the 1814 declaration of passion. By sending *Mathilda* to Godwin after the death of little
William has ended forever the full intensity of her union with Percy,
Mary is not only confessing to past incestuous passion, she is reaffirming it. However much Godwin has failed, he is again, is still,
her God. Father is restored to the primacy he enjoyed before the
suitor's incursion. The Percy figure, Woodville, is made ineffectual
in *Mathilda* to indicate what the father has surpassed in his intense,
if forbidden, passion.

Mathilda is poor fiction because going back to Daddy is poor judgment. However outré Mary's version of this daughterly motion, incest in *Mathilda* is a simplistic, finally sentimental response to her
involved ties to husband and father. Simplification of a more
orthodox sort lies ahead of Mary as novelist once Percy's death im-
poses the different but equally debilitating sentimentality of pulled
punches and qualified revelations. By 1820 greatness is already behind her. *Frankenstein* surpasses *Mathilda* in several respects. It is
more humane. It admonishes, not simply inveighs. Mary in 1818
holds out enough hope for the marriage that she holds up a dark
mirror for Percy to see himself in before it is too late. It is too late.

His response—to portray the Promethean son as moral perfection who assassinates father without ever bloodying his self-awareness—makes *Mathilda* inevitable.

Frankenstein also surpasses *Mathilda* by dealing much more amply with the intricacies of Mary Shelley's situation. Rather than simply indulging in pain and frustration, *Frankenstein* allows us, Mary's fellow creatures, to experience the flaying contrariety of her days. We recognize simultaneously that the domestic virtues will foster all the happiness which mortality is allowed, and that Promethean males will not allow this truth. Though these men are not *essentially* Erotic—they really do have a "double existence"—they finally cannot be essentially androgynous. Mary Shelley thus effects an ambivalence appropriate to her special brand of conservative radicalism. She is too orthodox to engage in that full-scale critique of tradition which her gothic heirs will practice. But she cannot close her eyes to the self-satisfying non sequitur of orthodoxy, the canonical but unfounded assumption that ours is a universe where what is valuable must therefore be viable.

In her frustration Mary Shelley does more than hate and rail. She tries to understand. And from this act I feel more hope than from all the optimistic straws that critics clutch at in her dark flood. There is heroism in the final vision of *Frankenstein*, not because Mary Shelley believes the world can be redeemed, but because she has tried to tell the truth. Her position seems hopeless. With her express-repress inclinations, she attacks men, but shows women fallible, and ends up apparently caught in the middle. Where she actually ends up is with a complexity of vision that constitutes moral androgyny. She combines the aggressive will necessary to indict bifurcation and a humane sympathy for our vulnerability to failure. She is implicated in the limitations of her characters, yet she transcends any character, even the monster, in her awareness of those limitations. What she says later of herself is true of her greatest literary effort. "Thus have I put down my thoughts. I may have deceived myself; I may be in the wrong; I try to examine myself; and such as I have written appears to me the exact truth" (*J* 206, 21 Oct. 1838).

In her introduction to the 1831 *Frankenstein*, Mary Shelley defines her goal and sets our challenge: to "speak to the mysterious fears of our nature" (226). The challenge derives from the verbal ambiguity here. Not only are there fears in us naturally; we fear our nature. Our natural inclination to fear makes us all the more fearful of what is fearsome in ourselves. By peeling back the first layer of meaning in Mary's words and finding another still more threatening layer, we readers are participating in her own determination to uncover the truth, however deep, however terrible. We join the author in what her Prometheans could never do: not Victor or Robert; and not Percy, even in *Alastor*, and not consistently in life. "Enough if every day I gain a profounder knowledge of my defects, and a more certain method of turning them to a good direction" (*J* 189, 19 Mar. 1823). Mary asked of the Prometheans no more than this. *Frankenstein* records their response. And hers.

Appendix A

Chronology of the Shelleys' Lives

1792   Percy Bysshe Shelley is born to Sir Timothy and Lady Elizabeth Shelley at Field Place.

1797   Mary Godwin is born to William Godwin and Mary Wollstonecraft (who then dies).

1801   Godwin marries (Mrs.) Mary Jane Clairmont.

1806   Percy meets Dr. Lind at Eton.

1810   Percy writes *Zastrozzi*. He also writes (with his sister Elizabeth) *Original Poetry by Victor and Cazire* which is withdrawn because of plagiarism. Percy goes to Oxford, meets Thomas Jefferson Hogg, with whom he writes *Posthumous Fragments of Margaret Nicholson*. Percy also writes *St. Irvyne*.

1811   Percy marries Harriet Westbrook.

1812   Percy's strange relationship with Elizabeth Hitchener; he writes *Queen Mab*. Mary first meets Percy and Harriet; he studies intensively under Godwin.

1813   Ianthe born. Percy separates from Harriet.

1814   Mary sees Percy again; they fall in love, meet at the grave of Mary Wollstonecraft. They elope (with Mary's stepsister Claire [Jane] Clairmont). Percy begins a narrative, *The Assassins*; Mary begins a novel, *Hate*. They return to England. Harriet gives birth to Percy's son Charles.

1815   Mary and Percy's first child, a daughter, is born, dies. Percy writes "To Wordsworth," *Alastor*, and possibly "On Love."

1816   Mary and Percy's son William is born; Claire initiates an affair with Byron. Mary, Percy, and Claire meet Byron in Geneva. At the Villa Diodati, Byron, Percy, Polidori, and Mary each agree to write a ghost story. Mary begins *Frankenstein*. Percy, Mary, and Claire return to England. Fanny Imlay (Mary Wollstonecraft's daughter by Gilbert Imlay) commits suicide. Harriet's suicide frees Mary and Percy to marry.

1817   Allegra, Claire's daughter by Byron, is born. The Shelleys, plus Claire and Allegra, settle at Marlow for the "garden year." The Shelleys' daughter Clara is born. Mary completes *Frankenstein*. Percy writes *The Revolt of Islam* and *Prince Athanase*.

1818   *Frankenstein* is published with Percy's preface; he also writes an unpublished review of the novel. Mary, Percy, William, Clara, Claire, and Allegra sail for Italy; Clara dies in Venice; Percy writes "Julian and Maddalo," "A Discourse on the Manners of the Ancient Greeks Relative to the Subject of Love," and "The Coliseum."

1819   William dies in Rome. Mary writes *Mathilda* (though it is not published for more than a century). The Shelleys' son Percy Florence is born in Florence. Percy writes *Prometheus Unbound, The Cenci,* "Peter Bell the Third," and "Notes on Sculptures in Rome and Florence."

1820   The Shelleys move to Pisa. Percy writes "The Witch of Atlas" and *Swellfoot the Tyrant.* His relationship with Emilia Viviani begins. Mary writes her verse dramas *Proserpine* and *Midas.*

1821   Edward and Jane Williams arrive; and Byron. Shelley writes *Epipsychidion* and "A Defense of Poetry."

1822   Trelawny arrives; Allegra dies; the Shelleys reside with the Williamses at Casa Magni at Lerici. Mary miscarries. Shelley and Williams drown. Mary writes "The Choice."

1823   Mary publishes *Valperga.* She returns to England with Claire and Percy Florence. She revises *Frankenstein* in the margins of Mrs. Thomas's copy of the novel.

1824   Byron dies.

1826   Mary writes *The Last Man.* Harriet's son Charles dies, making Percy Florence the heir to Sir Timothy.

1830   Mary publishes *Perkin Warbeck.*

1831   The revised edition of *Frankenstein* appears with Mary's own introduction.

1835   Mary writes *Lodore.*

1836   Godwin dies.

1837   Mary writes *Falkner.*

1839   Mary edits Percy's *Poetical Works* and *Essays.*

1844   Sir Timothy dies, Percy Florence succeeding to the title and estates.

1848   Sir Percy Florence marries Jane St. John.

1851   Mary Shelley dies.

Appendix B

Plots of Mary Shelley's Novels after 1818

Mathilda (1819). Mathilda's mother dies giving birth to her, and her grief-stricken father flees—leaving her to the care of his dour Scots sister. When he returns sixteen years later, Mathilda loves him devotedly, and he soon loves her incestuously. He flees in shame, and drowns in a storm. Mathilda withdraws in shame and grief to a Scots cottage where a young poet eventually breaks in upon her self-pitying solitude. Woodville talks Mathilda out of suicide, and tries to encourage her to live purposively. But while he is absent tending his sick mother, consumption strikes the heroine, and her last days are given to writing the manuscript *Mathilda*.

Valperga (1823). Euthanasia, orphaned possessor of the Apennine castle Valperga, must choose between the freedom of her beloved republic, Florence, and the attractions of her betrothed, Castruccio Castracani. He is the young Ghibelline whom exile by Euthanasia's Guelf party drives to seek fame on the battlefields of England and Flanders. He returns to Italy and gains control of Lucca. He soon degenerates into a tyrant, as Euthanasia (and Beatrice the religious fanatic whom he seduces and abandons) realize that he cannot love. He can only desire.

The Last Man (1826). Lionel Varney narrates the extermination of the human race by plague at the end of the twenty-first century. Two males dominate the action, Raymond and Adrian. Raymond determines to return England to monarchical rule (the last king, Adrian's father, permitted the country to become a democracy). Raymond's energy is dissipated by his untoward passion for Adrian's former beloved Evadne, by his inability to live happily with his devoted but often willful wife Perdita, and by his dreams of military glory. Raymond conquers Constantinople, but dies as the plague breaks out. Adrian gradually assumes leadership of the dwindling remnant of the earth's wandering populace. He is reconciled to his dominating mother, the ex-queen, whose willfulness is softened by the life and death of Adrian's exemplary sister, Idris. Adrian eventually drowns, and Lionel is left alone to ponder man's fate.

The Fortunes of Perkin Warbeck (1830). The hope of the Yorkists after Bosworth Field is Edward IV's son whom they hide away in Flanders and call "Perkin Warbeck." Loved platonically by the commoner Monina De Faro and successfully by the Scots aristocrat Katherine Gordon, Perkin marries the latter and spends the rest of his short life futilely trying to dethrone the clever but cold King Henry VII.

Lodore (1835). Ethel, the daughter of Lord Lodore and Cornelia Santerre, leaves England with her father (and without her mother) and settles for twelve years in America. After Lodore's death in New York, Ethel returns to England and marries Edward Villiers whose tangled finances lead the couple to bailiff-dodging and eventual incarceration. They are saved by Lady Lodore, who marries Edward's cousin, Horatio Saville, after her initial failure to recognize his excellences has precipitated him into an unhappy but short-lived marriage with an apoplectic Italian named Clorinda.

Falkner (1837). An orphaned girl, Elizabeth Raby, meets Rupert John Falkner at the moment when despair has brought him to the point of suicide. After saving his life, Elizabeth joins in his wanderings. His past, particularly his inadvertent part in the death of his beloved Alithea, comes to light as he and Elizabeth become increasingly involved with young Gerald Neville. Neville loves Elizabeth and respects Falkner (his own father is reprehensible), but he cannot rest until the murderer of his mother (Alithea of course) is punished. After many complications (including an unpleasant encounter with another inadequate father figure, Oswald Raby), Elizabeth manages to help Falkner acknowledge his guilt publicly, to help Neville forgive Falkner, and thus to help herself be united with both men (as wife to Neville and as permanently dutiful daughter to Falkner).

Appendix C

On Percy Shelley's Review
of *Frankenstein*

On *Frankenstein*

The novel of "Frankenstein; or, The Modern Prometheus," is undoubtedly, as a mere story, one of the most original and complete productions of the day. We debate with ourselves in wonder, as we read it, what could have been the series of thoughts—what could have been the peculiar experiences that awakened them—which conduced, in the author's mind, to the astonishing combinations of motives and incidents, and the startling catastrophe, which compose this tale. There are, perhaps, some points of subordinate importance, which prove that it is the author's first attempt. But in this judgment, which requires a very nice discrimination, we may be mistaken; for it is conducted throughout with a firm and steady hand. The interest gradually accumulates and advances towards the conclusion with the accelerated rapidity of a rock rolled down a mountain. We are led breathless with suspense and sympathy, and the heaping up of incident on incident, and the working of passion out of passion. We cry "hold, hold! enough!"—but there is yet something to come; and, like the victim whose history it relates, we think we can bear no more, and yet more is to be borne. Pelion is heaped on Ossa, and Ossa on Olympus. We climb Alp after Alp, until the horizon is seen blank, vacant, and limitless; and the head turns giddy, and the ground seems to fail under our feet.

This novel rests its claim on being a source of powerful and profound emotion. The elementary feelings of the human mind are exposed to view; and those who are accustomed to reason deeply on their origin and tendency will, perhaps, be the only persons who can sympathize, to the full extent, in the interest of the actions which are their result. But, founded on nature as they are, there is perhaps no reader, who can endure anything beside a new love-story, who will not feel a responsive string touched in his inmost soul. The sentiments are so affection-ate and so innocent—the characters of the subordi-nate agents in this strange drama are clothed in the light of such a mild and gentle mind—the pictures of domestic manners are of the most simple and at-taching character: the pathos is irresistible and deep. Nor are the crimes and malevolence of the single Being, though indeed withering and tremendous, the offspring of any unaccountable propensity to evil, but flow irresistibly from certain causes fully ade-quate to their production. They are the children, as it were, of Necessity and Human Nature. In this the direct moral of the book consists; and it is perhaps the most important, and of the most universal ap-plication, of any moral that can be enforced by ex-ample. Treat a person ill, and he will become wick-ed. Requite affection with scorn;—let one being be selected, for whatever cause, as the refuse of his kind—divide him, a social being, from society, and you impose upon him the irresistible obligations— malevolence and selfishness. It is thus that, too often in society, those who are best qualified to be its benefactors and its ornaments are branded by some accident with scorn, and changed, by neglect and solitude of heart, into a scourge and a curse.

The Being in "Frankenstein" is, no doubt, a tre-mendous creature. It was impossible that he should not have received among men that treatment which led to the consequences of his being a social nature. He was an abortion and an anomaly; and though his mind was such as its first impressions framed it, af-fectionate and full of moral sensibility, yet the cir-cumstances of his existence are so monstrous and uncommon, that, when the consequences of them became developed in action, his original goodness was gradually turned into inextinguishable mis-anthropy and revenge. The scene between the Being and the blind De Lacey in the cottage is one of the most profound and extraordinary instances of pathos that we ever recollect. It is impossible to read this dialogue,—and indeed many others of a somewhat similar character,—without feeling the heart sus-pend its pulsations with wonder, and the "tears stream down the cheeks." The encounter and argu-ment between Frankenstein and the Being on the sea of ice, almost approaches, in effect, to the expostula-tion of Caleb Williams with Falkland. It reminds us, indeed, somewhat of the style and character of that admirable writer, to whom the author has dedicated his work, and whose productions he seems to have studied.

There is only one instance, however, in which we detect the least approach to imitation; and that is the conduct of the incident of Frankenstein's landing in Ireland. The general character of the tale, indeed, resembles nothing that ever preceded it. After the death of Elizabeth, the story, like a stream which grows at once more rapid and profound as it proceeds, assumes an irresistible solemnity, and the magnificent energy and swiftness of a tempest.

The churchyard scene, in which Frankenstein visits the tombs of his family, his quitting Geneva, and his journey through Tartary to the shores of the Frozen Ocean, resemble at once the terrible reanimation of a corpse and the supernatural career of a spirit. The scene in the cabin of Walton's ship—the more than mortal enthusiasm and grandeur of the Being's speech over the dead body of his victim—is an exhibition of intellectual and imaginative power, which we think the reader will acknowledge has seldom been surpassed. (*JS* 6:263–65)

How much Percy Shelley saw *Frankenstein* as a judgment upon males and indeed upon himself is reflected in a document which has received surprisingly scant attention, his review of (as opposed to his preface to) the novel. "We debate with ourselves in wonder, as we read it, what could have been the series of thoughts . . . which conduced, in the author's mind . . . " Why does Shelley add the apparently unnecessary "with ourselves" and "in wonder" to the "we debate" which itself is redundant since he could have begun simply with the question "what could have been . . . ?" His puzzlement is inordinate to the ostensible issue of how a young woman could have written so horrific a story. "We cry 'hold, hold! enough!'—but there is yet something to come; and, like the victim whose history it relates, we think we can bear no more, and yet more is to be borne. . . . We climb Alp after Alp, until the horizon is seen blank, vacant, and limitless; and the head turns giddy, and the ground seems to fail under our feet." It is as revealing as it is symptomatic: Shelley makes Victor the "victim." Not victimizer, or co-victimizer, or even victim-victimizer. Percy did it all his life—generate dilemmas and then see himself as the one put upon. And so, when he acknowledges the potentially incriminating bond between himself and Victor—"like the victim . . . we"—Shelley can escape any implication in Frankenstein's enormities by ignoring their existence and focusing upon male pain. Percy as reader-victim is assaulted by Mary-author and as Victor-victim is assaulted by Mary's monster.

Then, having refused even to admit that a charge has been brought against him, Shelley escapes the trial of his male-hood entirely by two other, again symptomatic moves. "The head turns giddy . . . the ground seems to fail . . ." He faints. Recurring throughout his work, fainting has for Shelley the same significance that it has for Frankenstein. "When his conflicts become completely intolerable, Verezzi [a projection of Shelley's passive self in *Zastrozzi*] escapes from the predicament by losing consciousness or becoming delirious. Coma—death—is the only way out" (Chesser 26). Shelley's second mode of escape is equally characteristic. He directs attention away from Victor-Percy and devotes most of the rest of his review to the monster. This way he both takes the spotlight off a Frankenstein who cannot bear much examination if he is to remain simply "victim" and allows himself to draw a conclusion which will preclude implicating himself. "Treat a person ill, and he will become wicked" (264). That this is true of the novel and of life is beside the point. Shelley's truism oversimplifies grossly the moral issues in *Frankenstein* because it disregards Victor: what about all *his* victims? Who treated him ill? Shelley's truism also has another function. It is a warning to the author-wife: treat me as ill as you have by victimizing Victor, and I will repay in kind.

Notes

1. Among many examples of this trend see Shoshana Felman's contrast between Edmund Wilson's reductive Freudianism and a more complex reading which heeds Freud's own strictures against reductiveness ("Turning the Screw of Interpretation," in *Literature and Psychoanalysis*, ed. Shoshana Felman [Baltimore: Johns Hopkins University Press, 1983], 104–10). Wilson comes off better when Meredith Anne Skura shows him at times capable of a complexity like Freud's (*The Literary Use of the Psychoanalytic Process* [New Haven: Yale University Press, 1981], 62). Skura seeks to locate the limitations of Freudian ideas and criticism and to suggest ways to move beyond them. Frederick C. Crews is severer than Skura in attacking reductive tendencies, though *Out of My System* (New York: Oxford University Press, 1975) does not go so far as to deny all validity to psychoanalytic criticism. Murray M. Schwartz connects Freud with George Klein and D. W. Winnicott in sketching three lines of development away from "restrictive dismissive" criticism ("Shakespeare through Contemporary Psychoanalysis," in *Representing Shakespeare*, ed. Murray M. Schwartz and Coppélia Kahn [Baltimore: Johns Hopkins University Press, 1980], 21–32).

Among effective examples of the newer psychoanalytic criticism see Irwin; and the Lacan-Derrida-Johnson exchange over "The Purloined Letter" ("Seminar on 'The Purloined Letter,'" *Yale French Studies* 48 [1972]: 38–72; "The Purveyor of Truth," *Yale French Studies* 50 [1974]: 31–113; "The Frame of Reference: Poe, Lacan, Derrida," in *Literature and Psychoanalysis*, 457–505). By emphasizing relationships rather than roles, both Irwin and Lacan can place a character in all three positions of the oedipal triangle and can thus come closer to capturing the experiential complexity of Faulkner and Poe. To two other critics, Lorna Gladstone and Jeffrey Stern, I would like to express my gratitude for patient conversations which have educated and cheered me mightily. Their dissertations, "The Telling of the Wolf-Man's Story: A Rereading of the Relationship between Psychoanalysis and Literature" (University of Chicago, 1981) and " 'The Cause of Thunder': A Psychoanalytic Reading of Shakespeare's *King Lear, Pericles* and *The Tempest*" (University of Chicago, 1981), represent the new psychoanalytic practice at its finest. I want also to express my appreciation to the Psychoanalytic Interest Group at the University of Chicago and to the Workshop on Psychoanalysis and Literature at the Psychoanalytic Institute of Chicago.

For psychoanalytic readings of *Frankenstein* see Hill; Hirsch; Joseph; Kaplan and Kloss; Rubenstein; and Paul Sherwin, "*Frankenstein:* Creation as Catastrophe," *PMLA* 96 (1981): 883–903.

2. For birth trauma and primal scene see Moers, and Rubenstein; for Mary's ties to Godwin see Knoepflmacher; for her ties to Wollstonecraft see

chapter 5, note 1. More generally, *The Endurance of Frankenstein* is a milestone in *Frankenstein* criticism. It shows that scholars have at last taken Mary Shelley seriously as an artist and have seen her candidly as a human being. After *The Endurance* we can also assume a consensus on certain aspects of the novel: that Mary expresses through Victor Frankenstein her responses to Percy and Godwin; that the monster bodies forth both Victor and Mary; that Victor and the monster are in various respects "doubles." Comparable agreement about basic ties between Victor and Percy was summarized by Cameron a few years earlier: "Shelley used Victor as a pseudonym in *Original Poetry*; both [men] had sisters called Elizabeth; both read Albertus Magnus and Paracelsus in their 'votary of romance' periods then turned to science, especially electricity; Frankenstein's science teachers resemble Shelley's (Lind and Walker); Frankenstein too lamented the loss of early enthusiasms. Mary's ambivalence toward Frankenstein, whose Shelleyan desire to change the world ended in failure and hurt others, may reflect her ambivalence toward Shelley" (619). The most extensive examination of the Victor-Percy tie is Small's; see also Cantor, Holmes (332–33), and Scott. For the monster as expressing Mary Shelley see among others Gilbert and Gubar, Knoepflmacher, and Poovey.

Overall U. C. Knoepflmacher's essay and Mary Poovey's chapter seem to me particularly in tune with Mary's workings in *Frankenstein*. I only regret that the early stages of my work did not have the benefit of their fierce delicacy. The other studies which relate most to mine are Ketterer's, Massey's, and Gilbert and Gubar's. Ketterer is consistently suggestive about doubles; about the connection between incest, masturbation, homosexuality, and self-love; and about the monster as a character in his own right as well as a projection of Victor. Massey seems to me correct that the creature is Victor's "only true love" and that Frankenstein "would have wanted no other mate" (130), but I define the creature's importance to Victor as more immediate and physical than any "hypostatized thought that gives [Frankenstein] meaning" (131). I see Victor's female side expressed not primarily in his having a baby (Gilbert and Gubar 232), but in an overall psychological evolution to the feminine and on beyond to the effeminate.

3. "Advertisement" to *Mary. A Fiction* (New York: Norton, 1967; also Gainesville, Fla.: Scholars' Facsimiles & Reprints, 1960).

4. The readiest guide to the intention controversy up through the mid-seventies is David Newton–De Molina's *On Literary Intention* (Edinburgh: Edinburgh University Press, 1976). This type of work has little to say about the unconscious forces operative upon Mary Shelley, however. See David J. Gordon's *Literary Art and the Unconscious* (Baton Rouge: LSU Press, 1976). Also helpful is Gordon's exchange with Bloom in "Literature and Repression: Shavian Drama" (in *The Literary Freud*, ed. Joseph H. Smith [New Haven: Yale University Press, 1980], 184–85).

5. The severest critics of Shelley the man are Thomas De Quincey ("Notes on Gilfillan's Literary Portraits," in *The Collected Writings of Thomas De Quincey*, vol. 11, ed. D. Masson [Edinburgh, 1890] 354–76); William Hazlitt ("On Paradox and Commonplace," in *The Collected Works of William Hazlitt* [London: Dent, 1903], 6:148–49); J. Cordy Jeaffreson (*The Real Shelley* [London, 1885]); and Robert Metcalf Smith (*The Shelley Legend* [New York: Scribner's, 1945]). Smith was roundly attacked by Fred-

erick L. Jones ("The Shelley Legend," *PMLA* 61 [1946]: 848–90); Newman Ivey White (" 'The Shelley Legend' Examined," *SP* 43 [1946]: 522–44); and Kenneth Neill Cameron ("A New Shelley Legend," *JEGP* 45 [1946]: 369–79). These attacks are collected in *An Examination of "The Shelley Legend"* (Philadelphia: University of Pennsylvania Press, 1951).

For psychoanalytic studies of Shelley see Carpenter and Barnefield; Chesser; John V. Hagopian, "A Psychological Approach to Shelley's Poetry," *The American Imago* 12 (1955): 25–45; Milton L. Miller, "Manic Depressive Cycles of the Poet Shelley," *Psychoanalytic Forum* 1 (1966): 188–203; and Moore.

6. White establishes that both Shelleys share the express-repress tendency: "Mary, like Shelley, also felt the contradictory impulse both to conceal private discord and to 'remove a veil' from her 'pent mind' " (2:55). Others who note this attack-retreat tendency in Mary are Bowerbank, Knoepflmacher, Poovey, and Spark. Indirection as a basic female strategy is discussed by Gilbert and Gubar, and in various feminist works including Carolyn G. Heilbrun and Catharine R. Stimpson's "Theories of Feminist Criticism" (in *Feminist Literary Criticism*, ed. Josephine Donovan [Lexington: University Press of Kentucky, 1975).

7. Claire's description is cited by Holmes (240) from the Pforzheimer Library's unpublished revised MS of her journal. For Trelawny see his *Recollections of the Last Days of Shelley and Byron* (London, 1858), 171–72.

8. Unlike Bowerbank, Dussinger, and Ellis, who overemphasize Mary's radicalness, Knoepflmacher and Poovey argue convincingly that she rejected utopian visions for a more conservative, pessimistic view of experience. For various perspectives on Mary Shelley as a woman writer see Rachel Brownstein, "Portrait of the Artist as a Young Woman," *Book Forum* 2 (1976): 191–213; Gilbert and Gubar; and Weissman.

For work done on "Victorian" attitudes toward woman from the mid–eighteenth century through the 1870s see Mary Sumner Benson, *Women in Eighteenth-Century America* (New York: Columbia University Press, 1935; rpt. New York: AMS, 1976); Ruth H. Bloch, "American Feminine Ideals in Transition: The Rise of the Moral Mother, 1785–1815," *Feminist Studies* 4 (June 1978): 101–26; Katherine B. Clinton, "Femme et Philosophe: Enlightenment Origins of Feminism," *Eighteenth-Century Studies* 8 (1974–75): 283–99; Nancy F. Cott, *The Bonds of Womanhood* (New Haven: Yale University Press, 1977); Margaret George, "From 'Goodwife' to 'Mistress': The Transformation of the Female in Bourgeois Culture," *Science and Society* 37 (1973): 152–77; Muriel Jaeger, *Before Victoria* (London: Chatto and Windus, 1956); Linda Kerber, "The Republican Mother: Women and the Enlightenment—An American Perspective," *AQ* 28 (1976): 187–205; Marlene LeGates, "The Cult of Womanhood in Eighteenth-Century Thought," *Eighteenth-Century Studies* 10 (1976): 21–39; Gordon Rattray Taylor, *The Angel-Makers* (London: Heinemann, 1958); Poovey; Robert Palfrey Utter and Gwendolyn Bridges Needham, *Pamela's Daughters* (New York: Macmillan, 1936; rpt. London: Russell & Russell, 1972).

9. In the last decade, historians and critics have used a variety of methodologies and approaches to establish that people in the nineteenth century did not conform and subscribe to sexual stereotypes as rigidly as was once

thought. (For a study of and bibliography on this issue see my chapter "Science" in Helsinger, Sheets, and Veeder, 2:56–108.) The fact remains, however, that most people throughout the nineteenth century were substantially influenced by traditional gender stereotypes. Mary and Percy Shelley did not hold to every stereotype conventional in their time, as I will show; but Mary in particular was more conventional than some scholars today are inclined to admit. Though advanced thinkers in the eighteenth and nineteenth centuries from Mary Wollstonecraft to Sigmund Freud insisted that "there is no sex in mind," that "active" and "passive" are more tenable than "masculine" and "feminine," most of their contemporaries continued to divide emotional traits between the sexes. I reflect their practice in this book, because this book is about their practice.

10. Barbara Welter, "The Cult of True Womanhood: 1820–1850," *AQ* 18 (1966): 151–74; rpt. in her *Dimity Convictions* (Athens: Ohio University Press, 1976), 21–41. Though useful objections to and necessary qualifications of the concept of True Woman have been made, Welter's essay remains a helpful view of gender attitudes in the nineteenth century. For "domestic feminism," see chapter 1, note 3.

11. For other critics who see a continuity to Shelley's mind and habits see Harold Bloom, "The Unpastured Sea," in *The Ringers in the Tower* (Chicago: University of Chicago Press, 1971), 89; Olwen Ward Campbell 156, 170, 278; Hughes iii, 19, 218, 256; David Perkins, *The Quest for Permanence* (Cambridge: Harvard University Press, 1959), 154; George I. Richards, "Shelley's Urn of Bitter Prophecy," *KSJ* 21–22 (1972–73): 112–25. For those who find important changes see among others Hume; Jerome J. McGann, "The Secrets of an Elder Day: Shelley after *Hellas*," *KSJ* 15 (1966): 25–41; Gerald McNiece, *Shelley and the Revolutionary Idea* (Cambridge: Harvard University Press, 1969); and Frederick L. Beatty, *Light from Heaven* (De Kalb: Northern Illinois University Press, 1971).

12. The case for the Frankenstein summer as a happy time is made by Grylls (82); Mary Graham Lund ("Mary Godwin Shelley and the Monster," *University of Kansas City Review* 28 [1962]: 253–58); Nitchie (16); and Scott (185–87). The marital troubles of this period are emphasized by Cameron (297), Dunn (161), Fuller (180, 229), and Knoepflmacher (97).

CHAPTER ONE

1. Among many studies of androgyny see Joseph Campbell; Eliade; C. J. Jung, *Aion: Researches into the Phenomenology of the Self* (New York: Pantheon, 1959); Robert Kimbrough, "Androgyny, Old and New," *The Western Humanities Review* 35 (1981): 197–215; O'Flaherty; Singer; and Alan W. Watts, *The Two Hands of God* (New York: Braziller, 1963). Freud's lifelong concern with bisexuality makes him a substantial resource here. Besides the famous footnote to the section "Differentiation Between Men and Women" of *Three Essays on the Theory of Sexuality* (*SE* 7: 219–20) and the thirty-third lecture ("Femininity") in *New Introductory Lectures on Psychoanalysis* (*SE*, vol. 22) see Freud's discussion of the bisexuality of dreams in *The Interpretation of Dreams* (*SE* 5: 113–35); his argument for the bisexual aspects of hysteria in "Hysterical Phantasies and their Relation to Bisexuality" (*SE* 9: 155–66); his analyses of males fantasizing situations in which

they play female parts (not only little Hans's desire to have a baby, but also the Jones case history quoted by Freud in *The Psychopathology of Everyday Life* (*SE* 6:196); and the important sixth section of "A Child Is Being Beaten" (*SE* 17:195–204); see also the first section of "The Psychogenesis of a Case of Homosexuality in a Woman" (*SE* 18:147–54). For various other views of psychic duality, see Antoine Artaud, *The Theater and Its Double*, trans. Victor Corti (London: Calder & Boyars, 1970); R. D. Laing, "Complementary Identity," in *Self and Others* (Harmondsworth: Penguin, 1971), 81–97; and Robert J. Stoller, *Splitting* (New York: Dell, 1974). In the *Women's Studies* issue on androgyny, (no. 2, 1974) see Barbara Charlesworth Gelpi, "The Politics of Androgyny" (pp. 151–60) and Carolyn G. Heilbrun, "Further Notes toward a Recognition of Androgyny" (pp. 143–49).

Among studies with a more specific focus, the biblical and early Christian attitudes toward androgyny which shaped western thought up to our own time are examined in Wayne A. Meeks, "The Image of the Androgyne: Some Use of a Symbol in Earliest Christianity," *History of Religions* 13 (1974): 165–208; and Elaine H. Pagels, "What Became of God the Mother? Conflicting Images of God in Early Christianity," *Signs* 2 (1976): 293–303. Among expressly literary studies of androgyny, the most extensive in its range is Carolyn G. Heilbrun's *Toward a Recognition of Androgyny* (New York: Knopf, 1973). Among Renaissance writers Spenser, Shakespeare, and Milton have expectably received most attention from students of androgyny. For Spenser see A. R. Cirillo, "Spenser's 'Faire Hermaphrodite,'" *PQ* 47 (1968): 136–37; Donald Cheney, "Spenser's Hermaphrodite and the 1590 *Fairie Queen*," *PMLA* 87 (1972): 192–200; and Lorna Irvine, "Courtesy: An Androgynous Virtue," in *Spenser: Classical, Medieval, Renaissance, and Modern*, ed. David A. Richardson (Cleveland: Cleveland State University Press, 1977), 189–93. For Shakespeare see Robert Kimbrough, "Androgyny Seen Through Shakespeare's Disguise," *Shakespeare Quarterly* 33 (1982): 17–33; and Nancy K. Hayles, "Sexual Disguise in *Cymbeline*," *Modern Language Quarterly* 41 (1980): 231–47. Kahn discusses hermaphroditism in the context of male identity. An important contribution to and excellent bibliography on the extensive debate over androgyny in Milton are provided by Marilyn R. Farwell in "Eve, the Separation Scene, and the Renaissance Idea of Androgyny" (*Milton Studies* 16 [1982]: 3–22). Eighteenth-century androgyny is the focus of Raymond Furness's "The Androgynous Ideal; Its Significance in German Literature" (*Modern Language Review* 60 [1965]: 58–64). An overview of the nineteenth century is provided by A. J. L. Busst's "The Image of the Androgyne in the Nineteenth Century," in *Romantic Mythologies*, ed. Ian Fletcher (New York: Barnes & Noble, 1957), 1–96. In the Romantic period, Blake and Shelley are particularly concerned with adrogyny. For Blake see Bloom's work on sexuality, *Blake's Apocalypse* (Garden City, N.Y.: Doubleday, 1963); Hoeveler; Karleen Middleton Murphy, "'All the Lovely Sex': Blake and the Woman Question," in *Sparks of Fire*, ed. James Bogan and Fred Goss (Richmond, Calif.: North Atlantic, 1982), 272–75. For Shelley see Brown; Hoeveler; and William H. Marshall, "Plato's Myth of Aristophanes and Shelley's Panthea," *Classical Journal* 55 (1959): 121–23. In the Victorian period, the Brontës and Stowe feature androgynous characters repeatedly. For Charlotte Brontë see Helene Moglen, *Charlotte Brontë* (New York: Norton, 1976); and F. A. C. Wilson, "'The Primrose Wreath': The Heroes of Charlotte Brontë," *NCF* 29 (1974): 40–57. While Wilson denies androgyny to Emily Brontë, Gilbert and Gubar find it strongly operative (264–67). For Stowe see Elizabeth Ammons, "Heroines in *Uncle Tom's Cabin*," *American Literature* 49 (1977): 161–79 (rpt. in *Critical Essays on Harriet Beecher Stowe*, ed. Elizabeth Ammons [Boston: Hall, 1980], 152–165); and Crumpacker. Among twentieth-century women writers, Woolf has of course received the most attention. See among others Nancy Topping Bazin, *Virginia Woolf and the Androgynous Vision* (New Brunswick: Rutgers University Press, 1972); Elaine Showalter, "Virginia Woolf and the Flight into Androgyny," in *A Literature of Their Own* (Princeton: Princeton University Press, 1977), 263–97; and Barbara Fassler, "Theories of Homosexuality as Sources of Bloomsbury's Androgyny," *Signs* 5 (1980): 237–51. The importance of androgyny for H. D. has recently begun to receive the attention it deserves. See Susan Friedman's "Creating a Women's Mythology: H. D.'s *Helen in Egypt*" (*Women's Studies* 5 [1977]: 163–97) and *Psyche Reborn: The Emergence of H. D.* (Bloomington: Indiana University Press, 1981); and Rachel Blau Du Plessis, "Romantic Thralldom in H. D.," *Contemporary Literature* 20 (1979): 178–203. Androgyny in Isak Dinesen is discussed by Robin Lydenberg in "Against the Law of Gravity: Female Adolescence in Isak Dinesen's *Seven Gothic Tales*" (*MFS* 24 [1978–79]: 521–32).

Androgyny has not, of course, been treated in exclusively positive fashion. In the *Women's Studies* number, it is attacked by Cynthia Secor ("Androgyny: An Early Reappraisal," pp. 161–69) and Daniel A. Harris ("Androgyny: The Sexist Myth in Disguise," pp. 171–84). Presenting polar views of sexuality generally, Janice G. Raymond (*The Transsexual Empire* [Boston: Beacon, 1979]) and Robert May (*Sex and Fantasy* [New York: Norton, 1980]) reach the same conclusion about the inadequacy of androgyny. Other scholars who began as partisans of androgyny have become its critics. See particularly Mary Daly's *Beyond God the Father* (Boston: Beacon, 1973). How divergent critical views on androgyny are today was reflected at the 1984 MMLA meeting when Robin Riley Fast discussed H. D.'s power in terms of androgyny ("Androgyny and Poetic Process in H. D.'s Trilogy") and Sarah Friedrichsmeyer called for a move beyond what she saw as the inevitably polarizing and thus conflict-oriented nature of androgyny ("The Subversive Androgyne").

Criticisms of androgyny come down basically to the belief that it is essentially a male-oriented ideal. Either the feminine is subsumed into the masculine in the psyche, or the couple-as-androgyne precludes woman's functioning on her own in society. Both points are well taken, but neither relates to androgyny *as an ideal*. In the psyche, the feminine can of course be subsumed into the masculine, but it need not be. Hoeveler points readily to androgynous women in fiction who display strong masculine traits—Ariosto's Bradamant, Spenser's Britomart, Blake's Jerusalem, and Shelley's Cythna. More important are the many women in literature and life who do not approach the Amazonian and yet do display and develop "masculine" traits of decisiveness and daring, physical hardihood, etc. Androgyny, like the complementarity which it resembles, can unquestionably be used for chauvinistic ends. Men can appropriate the feminine, even as they can convert complementarity into a means of controlling women by restricting them to the quiescent, convenient virtues. But this need not happen. Complementarity as an ideal insists upon the equal value of both feminine and masculine traits. Androgyny as an ideal insists that men and women develop both sets of traits associated with the respective genders. This emphasis upon balance in the psyche is, moreover, what guards androgyny against the second criticism—that the ideal of the couple as androgyne prevents woman from acting independently. Androgyny is a psychic as well as a conjugal ideal, so woman, like man, must develop both sets of psychic traits sufficiently to enable her to function on her own. The couple as androgyne completes the psychic balance by allowing each lover to supply what the other has not yet developed fully. But such completion in no way precludes a development on each lover's part sufficient to allow for mature, effective conduct.

I would like to express my particular gratitude to a study of androgyny which reached me late in the evolution of this book: Diane Long Hoeveler's dissertation, "The Erotic Apocalypse: The Androgynous Ideal in Blake and Shelley." Though Hoeveler and I do not agree in our readings of some Shelley poems, and though I think she underrates Victorian struggles with gender roles, I admire her attempt to link androgyny to the traditions of Eros and Agape. She has anticipated me in this endeavor and I have learned from her. I also draw upon her work on Blake, and her distinction between androgyne and hermaphrodite.

2. This quotation is from Hale's much-neglected *Women's Record* (New York, 1855), 328. For more on Hale's particular blend of orthodoxy and radicalism, see my chapter "Religion" in Helsinger, Sheets, and Veeder, 2:168–74.

3. Domestic feminism is defined and discussed by Cott; Katherine Kish Sklar (*Catharine Beecher* [New Haven: Yale University Press, 1973]); and Smith; see also Crumpacker; Barbara Leslie Epstein, *The Politics of Domesticity* (Middletown, Conn.: Wesleyan University Press, 1981); Aileen S. Kraditor's introduction to *Up From the Pedestal* (Chicago: Quadrangle, 1968); and Carroll Smith-Rosenberg, "Beauty, the Beast, and the Militant Woman," *AQ* 23 (1971): 562–84.

4. I do not want to make Wollstonecraft seem too conservative. At her most radical she stood, as Barbara Taylor says, for the overthrow of the "pestiferous purple and all those who sheltered under it" (*Eve and the New Jerusalem* [New York: Pantheon, 1983], 5); see also Elissa S. Guralnick, "Radical Politics in Mary Wollstonecraft's *A Vindication of the Rights of Women*," *Studies in Burke and His Times* 18 (1977): 155–66. Even Wollstonecraft's arguments for motherhood are tied inseparably to her demand for rationality and education, since a silly or sensual wife will be a bad mother. But Wollstonecraft's political radicalism *is* complicated by her conservative view of woman, as Zillah R. Eisenstein notes. "Her acceptance of the separate spheres of male and female life, which defines the woman as mother in relation to the rearing of children within a new economy and which does not recognize the activity as economically rewarding and socially necessary, relegates woman to the very economic dependence she so hated and feared. . . . Her liberal *Feminist* position is at the same time both radical in its claims for woman and yet patriarchal. As a feminist she stands in conflict with the status quo by demanding 'rights'

for women as a sexual class. . . . She also embraces (unknowingly, in a sense) the basic political structuring of the status quo via her theory of motherhood" (*The Radical Future of Liberal Feminism* [London: Longman, 1981], 103). An example of Wollstonecraft's ties to the patriarchy appears when she discusses virtue relative to the sexes. "Let it not be concluded that I wish to invert the order of things; I have already granted, that, from the constitution of their bodies, men seem to be designed by Providence to attain a greater degree of virtue" (59). Wollstonecraft's distinction between "essence" and "degree" assures that, since the sexes are equal in essence, they share the same ability to *be* virtuous. But to allow that man's larger body enables him to attain *more* virtue is a concession which many radicals would not make. The more usual line of argument sees man's superior strength as a force which woman utilizes to make her superior virtue efficacious in the world. The extent of Wollstonecraft's ties to the patriarchy is discussed complexly by Poovey. "Wollstonecraft actually aspires to *be* a man" (57). Given the impossibility of this, "what Wollstonecraft really wants is to achieve," according to Poovey, "a new position of dependence within a paternal order of her own choosing. . . . In her utopia an entire army of father figures, both secular and religious, ensures happiness by anticipating every need" (67).

5. Besides Douglas, and Welter ("The Feminization of American Religion," in *Clio's Consciousness Raised*, ed. Mary Hartman and Lois W. Banner [New York: Harper & Row, 1974], 137–57; rpt. in Welter's *Dimity Convictions* [Athens: Ohio University Press, 1976], 83–102), see Ruth H. Bloch, "Untangling the Roots of Modern Sex Roles: A Summary of Four Centuries of Change," *Signs* 4 (1978): 237–52; and Crumpacker. For a summary of negative responses to the notion of the "feminization" of American religion and culture, and an attempt to define a middle position between Douglas and her critics, see David S. Reynolds, "The Feminization Controversy: Sexual Stereotypes and the Paradigms of Piety in Nineteenth-Century America," *NEQ* 53 (1980): 96–106. Despite unquestionable limitations to Douglas's hypothesis and argument, three facts remain, so far as I can see, incontestable: that increased emphasis upon the feminine was one feature of mid-century Christianity; that this emphasis was part of an overall awareness of the need to bring the feminine to bear upon the masculine in Anglo-American culture; and that this meant an increased prominence for androgyny as an ideal for both sexes. Reynolds in charting his middle way between Douglas and her critics establishes precisely that androgynous (he does not use this term) quality of mid-Victorian religion which I am arguing for. "The pious protestant was often a paradoxical mixture of courage and gentleness, reasonableness and warmth. . . . As an opponent of such doctrines as total depravity and predestination, the protestant exhibited 'masculine' strength and perseverance; as a foe of polemical rigidity, he or she showed a 'feminine' inclination to simplicity and warmth" (104). Reynolds then lists an entire page of "androgynous" protagonists.

6. Farnham is one of the most interesting, and most neglected, radicals of the Victorian women's movement. For more on her see my chapter "Religion" in Helsinger, Sheets, and Veeder, 2:201–6.

7. This process began in the mid–eighteenth century with what Wollstonecraft condemned—woman achieving angel status. I say "achiev-

ing" because more is involved in True Womanhood than the simple repression of female sexuality by insecure and/or rapacious males. Why would so many women celebrate and seek the angelic so enthusiastically? Were they simply duped and coerced by men into betraying their best interests? Victim theory, encouraged by Wollstonecraft's tendency to view women exclusively as products of men, and espoused by modern historians until the 1970s, has been countered recently by a more complex explanation. "The serviceability of passionlessness to women in gaining social and familial power should be acknowledged as a primary reason that the ideology was quickly and widely accepted. . . . On a practical level, belief in female passionlessness could aid a woman to limit sexual intercourse within marriage and thus limit family size. . . . The concept could not assure woman full autonomy—but what transformation in sexual ideology alone could have done so?" (Cott 235, 234, 236). Cott's contention that True Womanhood was less a simple victimization than a trade-off is supported by Bloch ("Untangling the Roots of Modern Sex Roles: A Summary of Four Centuries of Change," see note 5; Estelle B. Freedman ("Separation as Strategy: Female Institution Building and American Feminism, 1870–1930," *Feminist Studies* 3 [1979]: 512–29); Howard Gadlin ("Private Lives and Public Order: A Critical View of Intimate Relations in the U.S.," *Massachusetts Review* 17 [1976]: 304–30); Mary Beth Norton ("The Paradox of 'Women's Sphere,'" in *Women of America*, ed. Carol Ruth Berkin and Mary Beth Norton [Boston: Houghton Mifflin, 1979], 139–46); and Smith.

8. For detailed discussions of and bibliographies on the various campaigns which attempted to apply woman's virtues and standards to public life see Karen J. Blair, *The Clubwoman as Feminist* (New York: Holmes & Meier, 1980); Blanche Wiessen Cook, "Female Support Networks and Political Activism: Lillian Wall, Crystal Eastman, Emma Goldman," *Chrysalis* 3 (1977); Ellen Du Bois, *Feminism and Suffrage* (Ithaca: Cornell University Press, 1978); Barbara Leslie Epstein, *The Politics of Domesticity* (Middletown, Conn.: Wesleyan University Press, 1981); Estelle B. Freedman, *Their Sisters' Keepers* (Ann Arbor: University of Michigan Press, 1981); Aileen Kraditor, *The Ideas of the Woman Suffrage Movement, 1890–1920* (New York: Columbia University Press, 1965); William Leach, *True Love and Perfect Union* (New York: Basic Books, 1980); Elizabeth Pleck, "Feminist Response to 'Crimes Against Women,' 1868–1896," *Signs* 8 (1983): 451–70.

9. For links of androgyny, feminism, and fiction see the critics of fiction listed in chapter 1, note 1, plus Helen Waite Papashvily, *All the Happy Endings* (New York: Harper & Row, 1956; rpt. Port Washington, N.Y.: Kennikat, 1972); Ann Douglas Wood, "'The Scribbling Women' and Fanny Fern: Why Women Wrote," *AQ* 23 (1971): 3–24; and Douglas. See also Vineta Colby, *Yesterday's Women* (Princeton: Princeton University Press, 1974); Elaine Showalter, "Dinah Mullock Craik and the Tactics of Sentiment: A Case Study in Victorian Female Authorship," *Feminist Studies* 2 (1975): 5–23, and *A Literature of Their Own* (Princeton: Princeton University Press, 1977); Dee Garrison, "Immoral Fiction in the Late Victorian Library," *AQ* 28 (1976): 71–89; Moers; Barbara Welter, "Defenders of the Faith: Women Novelists of Religious Controversy in the Nineteenth Century," in her *Dimity Convictions* (Athens: Ohio University Press, 1976),

103–29; Mary Kelley, "The Sentimentalists: Promise and Betrayal in the Home," *Signs* 4 (1979): 434–46; Jane Tompkins, "Sentimental Power: *Uncle Tom's Cabin* and the Politics of Literary History," *Glyph* 8 (1981): 79–102; and Gilbert and Gubar. Another area where women and gender roles come together complexly is the sensation novel. For bibliography and discussion see my chapter on sensationism in Helsinger, Sheets, and Veeder, 3:122–45.

10. This may be less true in *Pamela*. Fielding certainly thought Richardson was equating virtue with woman, since *Joseph Andrews* was intended to rebut *Pamela* on just this question. But Sir Charles Grandison as male virgin is Richardson's counterpart to Joseph Andrews, and thus his own testament to the sexlessness of virtue.

11. LeGates overstates when she argues that "although she [Pamela] has successfully practiced her artful ways against her would-be seducer, Pamela is helpless against the artful ways of her fiancé . . . [who manipulates] Pamela much as Wolmar manipulates Julie. Pamela herself admits that Mr. B. chose her because 'he expected from me more humility, more submission, than he thought would be paid him by a lady equally born and educated.' . . . Thus, the drama of the aggressive male checked by the virtuous woman is paradoxically a reaffirmation of the patriarchal authority of the family" ("The Cult of Womanhood in Eighteenth-Century Thought," *Eighteenth-Century Studies* 10 [1976]: 30–31). *Pamela* is no more a full-scale assault upon the patriarchy than *Tom Jones* is. But Pamela is no more "helpless" than Sophia is. LeGates is correct that Pamela never achieves nor ever imagines that she achieves perfect equality with Mr. B. But we cannot fail to acknowledge how far Pamela has come. Compare her status as mater familias with the average servant's sexual bondage to the squirarchy. Pamela is an early domestic feminist who effects a substantial revolution by achieving as much respect and autonomy as she can within the purlieus of domesticity. We can hardly fault Pamela for not achieving at one stroke the full equality which we have still not attained two centuries later.

12. For Godwin and Richardson see Eric Rothstein, "Allusion and Analogy in the Romance of *Caleb Williams*," *University of Toronto Quarterly* 37 (1967): 18–30.

13. By 1842 Mary Shelley has added another sickly poet-type to her list, Alexander Andrew Knox. Like Shelley, "irritable" and prey to "great nervousness & distress" (*MSL* 2:166, 1 Oct. 1842; *MSL* 2:164, 17 Aug. 1842), Knox attracts Mary because his poetic spirit wars with his weak flesh. "Knox has an enlargement of the heart. . . . He ought to be kept quiet— but as he will write—& indeed in a certain sense he must—quiet he cannot have" (*MSL* 2:166, 1 Oct. 1842).

14. Effeminacy is distinct in Mary Shelley's mind and fiction from masculinity properly tempered by the feminine. When Perkin rejects an act as "womanly" (*Perkin Warbeck* 1:98), Mary sides with him. "Mewed up here with women [he declaims], the very heart of a Plantagenet will fail, and I shall play the girl at the sight of blood. . . . I, who am a Cavalier, Father, love rather to meet danger, than to avoid it like a woman or a priest. . . . I am not pleased to behold my sage self filed down into a woman's tool. . . . here are my unarmed hands; even a woman may bind them. . . . I would not be taken like an unarmed girl" (1:159, 264; 2:6; 3:229, 233).

Falkner echoes his sentiments: "I am not so weak and womanish that I need perpetual support. . . . Come, Neville, you must not take the matter in this girlish style; show yourself a man" (2:269; 1:233). For Lionel in a weak moment in *The Last Man*, "so effeminate an horror ran through my frame" (192).

15. Quoted by Dunn (123) from *To Lord Byron*, ed. George Paston and Peter Quennell (London: Murray, 1938), 208; Mary's next quotation is from Rennie (113). For Mary Shelley and Byron see Stuart Curran, "The Siege of Hateful Contraries: Shelley, Mary Shelley, Byron, and *Paradise Lost*," in *Milton and the Line of Vision*, ed. Joseph A. Wittreich (Madison: University of Wisconsin Press, 1975), 209–30; Paula R. Feldman, "Mary Shelley and the Genesis of Moore's *Life* of Byron," *SEL* 20 (1980): 611–20; Lovell (see bibliography, plus "Byron and Mary Shelley," *KSJ* 2 [1953]: 35–49, and "Byron, Mary Shelley, and Madame de Staël," *KSJ* 14 [1965]: 13); Nitchie; and Walling. For book-length studies of Byron and Shelley see Buxton; and Charles H. Robinson, *Shelley and Byron: The Snake and the Eagle Wreathed in Flight* (Baltimore: Johns Hopkins University Press, 1976).

16. Trelawny insists that "his softness of expression and mild bearing were deceptive, as you soon found out he was a resolute, self-sustaining man" (2:6). Medwin, having called Shelley at Eton "so strong and yet so feeble" (33), goes on to quote Hogg, who defines the adult Shelley in terms of both masculine traits—"a fire . . . a vivid and preternatural intelligence"—and feminine—"a softness and delicacy, a gentleness" (69). For Peacock, "delicate and fragile as he appeared, he had great muscular strength" (62). Captain Kennedy recalls a comparable blending, "an earnestness in his manner and such perfect gentleness of breeding" (Dowden 1:389). Williams attests to Shelley's "manners mild and amiable, but withal full of life and fun" (Dowden 2:406), while Rogers notes "his usual meek yet resolute manner" (Buxton 201). Biographers in the generations after Shelley's contemporaries have, of course, continued to discuss his androgyny. The best recent work is by Holmes and Brown.

17. Brown notes that "except for his translation of the *Symposium* (189D–190B), Shelley nowhere uses the term *androgyny*. Nevertheless the idea is implicit throughout his work, particularly in his portrayal of the sexes, with their harmonious blending of the traditionally masculine and the traditionally feminine. Moreover in his own person he most nearly incorporated this ideal. . . . All his life he retained a feminine gentleness and softness. . . . Yet there was a masculine side to Shelley too. . . . social independence, and a love of learning and the rigors of intellectual debate for their own sake. . . . This resulted in a lifelong androgynous merging of the traditionally masculine with the traditionally feminine" (225, 166). What Shelley admires in classical sculpture, Brown establishes convincingly, "is the epicene or androgynous element so prominent in the Greek aesthetic ideal" (21). The unsympathetic view of Shelley's androgyny is voiced by Aldous Huxley in *Point Counter Point* ("persuading himself and other people that he was Dante and Beatrice rolled into one" [ch. 10].

18. Noting that Shelley "saw that only a new type of human being combining the male and the female, could ultimately save the world" (19), Carpenter and Barnefield conclude that "he was thinking of a new type of human being (at present folded in sleep, but whose coming he perhaps fore-

saw)—a being having the grace of both sexes, and full of such dreams as would one day become the inspiration of a new world-order, yet of such a nature that its love would *not* be dependent (as, indeed, most loves now are) on mere sexual urge and corporeal desire, but would be a vivid manifestation of the universal creative life, in the body even as in the soul" (30).

CHAPTER TWO

1. For discussions of Shelley and Eros see Hoeveler; and Ross Greig Woodman, *The Apocalyptic Vision in the Poetry of Shelley* (Toronto: University of Toronto Press, 1966). Though Notopoulos does little with Shelley and Eros, he does detail the Platonic sources of Shelley's equation of body and prison. In the *Phaedrus*, Socrates calls the body "that living tomb which we carry about, now that we are imprisoned in the body, like an oyster in his shell" (250C). See also the *Phaedo* 62B, 67D, 82E; the *Cratylus* 400B–C; and Plotinus' *Enneads* 4.8.1,3,4. Notopoulos also confirms that Shelley was reading Plato intensely in the *Frankenstein* months of 1817–18.

Shelley's equation of body and prison affects his view of sexuality profoundly. "The heavy dead hulk / On the living sea rolls an inanimate bulk, / Like a corpse on the clay which is hungering to fold / Its corruption around it" ("A Vision of the Sea" 31–34); "More strength has Love than he or they; / For it can burst his charnel, and make free / The Limbs in chains" (*Epipsychidion* 404–6); "A spirit half-arisen / Shatters its charnel" ("Fragments Written for *Hellas*" 31–32); "The living grave I bear" ("Remembrance" 21); "The chains of clay that bound a soul" ("The Retrospect: Cwm Elan, 1812" 58). Holmes relates this view of body to Shelley's attitude toward his wife Harriet. "One may also perhaps detect a hint of dissatisfaction, if not actual disillusionment, with the intimate relationship that he should normally have been developing with his young and beautiful girl-bride, Harriet. There is a certain physical distaste, a Hamlet-like sneer at the fleshly fact that indicates this. . . . 'nor do I risk the supposition that the lump of organized matter which enshrines *thy* [Elizabeth Hitchener's] soul excites the love which that soul alone *dare* claim. Henceforth I will be yours, yours with truth sincerity & unreserve'" (85). Orgasm in *Islam* is described as "the sickness of a deep / And speechless swoon of joy" (2637–38). In "The Past" he asks, "Wilt thou forget the happy hours / Which we buried in Love's sweet bowers, / Heaping over their corpses cold / Blossoms and leaves, instead of mould?" (1–4). Even in the most perfect moment of sexual union in all of Shelley's poetry, woman is unsettling. "Cythna's sweet lips seemed lurid in the moon, / Her fairest limbs with the night wind were chill, / And her dark tresses were all loosely strewn / O'er her pale bosom:—all within was still, / And the sweet peace of joy did almost fill / The depth of her unfathomable look" (*Islam* 2668–73). Brown admits that Shelley "came increasingly to view the claims of the body as a distracting nuisance, even a pernicious obstacle in the way of the higher claims of the spirit" (63), but Brown wants to locate this reaction *after* 1819 and *Prometheus Unbound.* What I have tried to show is that Shelley's uneasiness with body is present from his earliest verse because it is basic to his psychological makeup.

Shelley's sexuality has inevitably attracted copious and conflicting commentary. Besides the Freudians (see Introduction, note 5), the major biographers, and Brown, see Edward E. Bostetter, "Shelley and the Mutinous Flesh," *TSLL* 1 (1959): 203–13; David Eggenschwiler, "Sexual Parody in 'The Triumph of Life,'" *Concerning Poetry* 5 (1972): 28–36; and Daniel Stempel, "Shelley and the Ladder of Love," *KSJ* 15 (1966): 15–23. Seraphia Deville Leyda sums up the positions of Clutton-Brock (Shelley the puritan hated the flesh), Strong (passion is a primary ingredient in Shelley's poetry), and Brooks (Shelley vacillated between physical and spiritual love) in her book *The Serpent Is Shut Out From Paradise* (Salzburg: Institut für Englische Sprache und Literatur, Universität Salzburg, 1972). For Shelley and homosexuality see note 7 to chapter 3.

2. For the vexed subject of will and necessity in Romantic thought, see Leslie Brisman, *Milton's Poetry of Choice & Its Romantic Heirs* (Ithaca: Cornell University Press, 1973), ch. 5; Kenneth Neill Cameron, "The Social Philosophy of Shelley," *Sewanee* 50 (1942): 457–66; William Royce Campbell, "Shelley's Philosophy of History: A Reconsideration," *KSJ* 21–22 (1972–73): 43–63; Michael G. Cooke, *The Romantic Will* (New Haven: Yale University Press, 1976); Frank B. Evans III, "Shelley, Godwin, Hume and the Doctrine of Necessity," *SP* 37 (1940): 632–40; Hughes; Albert J. Kuhn, "Shelley's Demogorgon and Eternal Necessity," *MLN* 74 (1959): 596–99; Gerald McNiece, *Shelley and the Revolutionary Idea* (Cambridge: Harvard University Press, 1963); Sister M. Eunice Mousel, "Falsetto in Shelley," *SP* 33 (1936): 587–609; John R. Reed, "Inherited Characteristics: Romantic to Victorian Will," *SIR* 17 (1978): 335–66, and "Will and Fate in *Frankenstein*," *Bulletin of Research in the Humanities* 83 (1980): 319–38. The distinction between "free acts" and "voluntary acts" is taken from Mousel. For Shelley's most necessitarian statements see his notes to *Queen Mab* (*CP* 809–11, 822), and his observation in the note to *Hellas* that "it appears that circumstances make men what they are" (*CP* 479).

Scholars studying Shelley from a philosophical viewpoint locate him within the Romantic debate over will and necessity. Imitating Godwin's fancy footwork around Hume, Shelley believes that although causation may be impossible to demonstrate, necessity is driving all creation toward perfection. And human will can foster this process. Shelley does not make his slippery position (espousing individual will when necessity is absolute) more precarious by insisting upon absolute freedom. Rather than "free acts"—performed by an agent who could do otherwise—Shelley settles for "voluntary acts"—performed with a knowledge of ends but without the capacity to do otherwise. Moreover, Shelley insists that even the voluntary acts of men are not limitless, as the end of act 3 and Demogorgon's final speech in *Prometheus Unbound* establish.

Mary learned much from Percy, even on the subject of will, because he by no means always espoused willfullness.

> Man who man would be,
> Must rule the empire of himself; in it
> Must be supreme, establishing his throne
> On vanquished will . . .
> ("Sonnet: Political Greatness" 10–13)

By vanquishing will, the individual does not annihilate it; he matures from the indulgence of active caprice to the heroism of passive endurance, from Eros to Agape. With "fearless resignation" the Wandering Jew in *Queen Mab* persists in "Mocking my powerless Tyrant's horrible curse / With stubborn and unalterable will" (7:81, 258–59). Passive will, moreover, need not lead to desolate hostility like that of Ahasuerus.

> Thus, gentle thoughts did many a bosom fill,—
> Wisdom, the mail of tried affections wove
> For many a heart, and tameless scorn of ill,
> Thrice steeped in molten steel the unconquerable will.
> (*Islam* 3528–31)

The courage to endure a vicious or ridiculous fate exempts man from even the ultimate tyrant. "Thou art a conqueror, Time; all things give way / Before thee but the 'fixed and virtuous will'" ("To Ireland" 25–26).

Mary's commitment to passive will ("I might be vanquished, but I would not yield," says her spokesman Lionel in *The Last Man* [207]) leads her to create situations like those in *Queen Mab* and *Islam*. Falkner endures "spasms of physical suffering; but his will [remains] unconquered" (2:191). Mary also shares another of Percy's beliefs—that passive will constitutes the standard for judging active will. Shelley's Count Cenci is malignant because his reigning principle is the will to power. "For Beatrice worse terrors are in store / To bend her to my will" (4.1.75–76). Yet Beatrice proves ultimately her father's daughter.

Instead of responding with the passive will which characterizes Agape and gives stature to Ahasuerus, Beatrice proceeds to validate her father's self-justifying claim that "'tis her stubborn will / Which by its own consent shall stoop as low / As that which drags it down" (4.1.10–12). While consistently deploring "the tyrannic will . . . a tyrant's will . . . your kingly will . . . The will of Europe's subtler son" ("Ginevra" 59; *Prometheus Unbound* 3.4.139; *Swellfoot the Tyrant* 1.1.33; *Islam* 3841–42), Shelley also criticizes those victims of tyranny who, like Beatrice, "think that ill for ill should be repaid" ("Marenghi" 2). All his life Percy opposes his passive will to that active power which institutions use against individuals and which presupposes that "the will of strength is right" (*Islam* 3269).

3. "Antitype" seems to suggest complementarity by establishing the oppositeness, the anti-ness, of the beloved, but Brown is correct that antitype in Shelley means "responding 'as an impression to the die'" (36). Shelley himself confirms Brown's interpretation when he calls Napoleon the "antitype" for Castruccio (*PSL* 2:353, 25 Sept. 1821).

4. Hogg seconds Trelawny here: "accession to his family did not appear to afford him any gratification, or to create an interest. He never spoke of his child to me, and to this hour I never set eyes on her" (2:462). Though Hogg elsewhere praises Shelley's affection for his children ("in Shelley the parental affections were developed at an early period to an unusual extent" [1:241]), he also maintains "in this most touching, melancholy letter only did Shelley even mention to me the children of his first marriage; and here he speaks of Ianthe merely incidentally, and rather to show his dislike for another, than his love of her" (2:517). Trelawny agrees with Hogg's negative

appraisal (quoting Shelley's own words that wise men have no children and describing a moment when the poet failed to recognize his own child [1:110]), though Peacock insists that Percy was a loving father (37). Peacock agrees with everyone, however, about Shelley's generally anti-domestic nature (44), quoting lines from *Childe Harold* that Shelley liked particularly: "On the sea / The boldest steer but where the ports invite; / But there are wanderers o'er Eternity, / Where dark drives on and on, and anch-er'd ne'er shall be." Trelawny insists that "he took no heed of the occurrences of daily life. . . . he grazed when he was hungry, anywhere, at any time. . . . to confine Shelley within the limits of conventional or any other arbitrary laws of society was out of the question" (1:157, 120, 170). Maintaining that "he was unconscious and oblivious of times, places, persons and seasons," Hogg parodies the golden rule in order to establish how far Shelley strayed from domestic orthodoxy. "He could follow no other laws than the golden law of doing instantly whatever the inclination of the moment prompted" (2:407, 426).

5. While Grylls calls the elopement "idyllic" (34), Gerson recognizes how close it was to becoming "a comedy of errors" (43). Percy's inadequacies continue as the elopement proceeds. "At Mumpf we cannot procure a boat . . . [the voiture] breaks down. . . . we walk to Rheinfelden. Unable to procure a boat, we walk" (*J* 12, 29 Aug. 1814). True to her express-repress tendency, Mary strives for the muting objectivity of third-person narration in her journal, but how can her dissatisfaction with the situation not carry over to the man managing that situation? "The filth of the apartment is terrible to Mary [she writes]; she cannot bear it all the winter. . . . Bed very uncomfortable. Mary groans. . . . It is Mary's birthday (17). We do not solemnize this day in comfort" (*J* 11, 24 Aug. 1814; *J* 12, 29 and 30 Aug. 1814). There are also joys, of course, freedom and adventure and first love. But once we have encountered Mary's barrage of graphic details—"beds were infinitely detestable. . . . a wretched apartment. . . . a dirty apartment of a nasty auberge. . . . the diligence is the most detestable of things. . . . we are horribly cheated" (*J* 7, 10 and 11 Aug. 1814; *J* 8, 12 Aug. 1814; *J* 14, 6 and 8 Sept. 1814) we can hardly agree with Cameron that "it appears to have been a happy, carefree trip" (17). We also cannot dissociate Percy entirely from the situation or from the novel Mary begins then, *Hate.*

6. The best sustained study of Mary's post-*Frankenstein* fiction is Nitchie's. For other work see Betty T. Bennett, "The Political Philosophy of Mary Shelley's Political Novels: *Valperga* and *Perkin Warbeck*," in *The Evidence of the Imagination*, ed. Donald H. Reiman et al. (New York: New York University Press, 1978) 354–71; Gareth W. Dunleavy, "Two New Mary Shelley Letters and the 'Irish' Chapters of *Perkin Warbeck*," *KSJ* 13 (1964): 6–10; Hugh J. Luke, Jr., "*The Last Man*: Mary Shelley's Myth of the Solitary," *Prairie Schooner* 39 (1965): 316–27; J. de Palacio, "Mary Shelley and the 'Last Man,'" *Revue de Litterature Comparée* 42 (1968): 37–49; Peck; Burton R. Pollin, "Mary Shelley as the Parvenue" *REL* 8 (1967): 9–21; Robert Lance Snyder, "Apocalypse and Indeterminacy in Mary Shelley's *The Last Man*," *SIR* 17 (1978): 435–52; Spark; Hartley S. Spatt, "Mary Shelley's Last Man: The Truth of Dreams," *Studies in the Novel* 7 (1975): 526–37; Lee Sterrenburg, "*The Last Man*: Anatomy of Failed Revolutions," *NCF* 33 (1978): 324–47; and Poovey 143–71.

7. Quoted by Feldman from a Moore letter ("Mary Shelley and the Genesis of Moore's *Life* of Byron," *SEL* 20 [1980]: 613).

8. For the argument that Shelley is portraying in the maniac his relations with Harriet and Mary see Cameron (262, 264, 304); and White (2:49). J. E. Saveson sees Byron's marital difficulties reflected in the maniac's plight ("Shelley's *Julian and Maddalo,*" *KSJ* 10 [1961]: 53–58).

9. Mary's condescension is gentle when the stakes are small: "you [Percy] were born to be a don Quixote and if that celebrated personage had ever existed except in the brain of Cervantes I should certainly form a theory of transmigration to prove that you lived in Spain some hundred years before & fought with Windmills. You were very good in this except in one thing—which was sitting up all night—which indeed you ought not to do especially when you are so fagged all day" (*NL* 27, 17 Jan. 1817). When the stakes are higher, when Percy is out with Claire, a street confrontation evokes from Mary a more biting response. "The other day as Clare & Shelley were walking out they beheld a little dirty blacksmith's boy running away from a tall long-legged man . . . Clare twitched S. & remonstrated— Don Quixote did not like to leave the boy in thrawl but deafened by the tall strider's vociferations & overcome by Clare's importunities he departed" (*NL* 132, 10 Mar. 1820). How like Shelley in both his delusions and his heroism is Mary's view of Don Quixote: "the idea of the crazed old gentleman who nourished himself in the perusal of romances till he wanted to be the hero of one, is true to the very bare truth of nature, and how has he followed it out? Don Quixote is as courageous, noble, princely, and virtuous as the greatest of the men whom he imitates: had he attempted the career of knight errantry, and afterwards shrunk from the subsequent hardships, he had been a crazy man, and no more; but meeting all with courage and equanimity, he really becomes the hero he desired to be" (Nitchie 196). Linking Shelley to "the amiable lunatic Don Quixote," Hogg says "I repeated to him the history of the injudicious and unfortunate interference of Don Quixote between the peasant, John Haldudo, and his servant, Andrew. Although he reluctantly admitted, that the acrimony of humanity might often aggravate the sufferings of the oppressed by provoking the oppressor, I always observed, that the impulse of generous indignation, on witnessing the infliction of pain, was too vivid to allow him to pause and consider the probable consequences of the abrupt interposition of the knight errantry, which would at once redress all grievances" (1:122–23). Percy read *Don Quixote* to Mary during the *Frankenstein* months, Bennett notes (*NL* 28).

CHAPTER THREE

1. I use James Rieger's edition of *Frankenstein* so that I can draw upon all three versions of the novel: the 1818 original, the corrections made by Mary Shelley in the Thomas copy of *Frankenstein* in 1823, and her extensive rewriting for the Colburn and Bentley edition of 1831. These various revisions present no consistent pattern that I can discover. (For recent discussions of textual variants see Rieger [*F* xliv], Ketterer, and Poovey.) Some changes add grist to my mill, others show Mary making less in 1831 of what I make much of in the 1818 text. She both plays up and tones down radical criticisms, and sometimes she seems to have forgotten or to have still not recognized the force of an image or action. Rather than insisting upon what

is manifestly untrue—that any one version of *Frankenstein* is the definitive edition—I will choose for the text of a particular scene the version which seems to me to contribute most to the overall coherence of the novel, recognizing full well how self-serving this could become. The 1818 edition is cited most frequently, largely because, I suppose, it reflects most directly the subversive forces which generated the project and which were dampened in Mary Shelley's later, more conservative years.

2. See Joseph Campbell (283), Eliade (115), O'Flaherty (310), and Singer (7, 51).

3. Knoepflmacher has noted the link of "Saville" and "civil" (107); Tropp sees Margaret as Mary Shelley's spokesperson and mentions their sharing the initials MS (15), but he does not discuss their common middle initial or the full presence and significance of Margaret in the opening frame.

4. In recent years critics studying Robert Walton have moved considerably beyond Spark's notion that he is "introduced merely for the purpose of recounting Frankenstein's story" (132). Hirsch emphasizes that Walton helps make the frame credible: Victor seems more believable because Robert is on the same quest. Also, Walton's growing belief helps to foster ours, while his diminished stature highlights Victor's superiority (140). Swingle agrees that Walton "functions in the novel to dissolve the particularity of Frankenstein's quest" (63). Wilfred Cude maintains, more problematically, that Walton "is objective," and gives us "an impartial view of Victor and his monster" ("Mary Shelley's Modern Prometheus: A Study in the Ethics of Scientific Creativity," *Dalhousie Review* 52 [1972]: 217). A second useful line on Walton is taken by critics who define his similarities to Victor. Bloom sees that Walton is a failed Promethean quester, like Victor (124, 128); Strevick, that Walton is like Frankenstein a dreamer who can't make his dreams coherent (230); Goldberg, that both men consider no price too high if they can achieve knowledge of the unknown (29); Levine, that both are lonely men, isolated by ambition and willing to endanger others (a 19); Kaplan and Kloss, that both men undertake adventures interdicted by their fathers, and both have deep ties to their sisters (134–35). The most extensive recent treatments of Walton are Hogle's and Poovey's.

5. See James O. Allsup, *The Magic Circle* (Port Washington, N.Y.: Kennikat, 1976); and Notopoulos. Shelley uses circles as an emblem of both inclusion and exclusion in "The Coliseum" (*JS* 6:303–4).

6. Scott (184). Nitchie believes that "the Shelley here portrayed in the person of Woodville is virtually perfect" (58), whereas Dunn sees Woodville as "ineffectual, lacking the passion and dynamism that might have stormed Mathilda's, and Mary's, dream" (202). Small sees "in Mathilda's complaints of the all-too perfect Woodville Mary's reproach to the unalterable benevolence of the Shelleyan exterior and lack of real feeling" (184).

7. Shelley's early response to the "inexpressibly attractive" schoolboy ("I remember in my simplicity writing to my mother a long account of his admirable qualities and my own devoted attachment. I suppose she thought me out of my wits" [Hogg 1:24]), his recurrent dream of this lad years later (*JS* 7:66), his ties to Hogg ("if I were free I were yours. . . . Oh, how I have loved you" [*PSL* 1:203, 10 Dec. 1811]), his obsession with male statues ("these sweet and gentle figures of adolescent youth in which the Greeks delighted" [*JS* 6:328]), and his refusal to admit that the Greeks actually prac-

ticed pederasty—these and much more material have inevitably sparked speculation about homosexuality. See Carpenter, Chesser, Merle, and Read. Brown in his discussion of Shelley's admiration of Greek sculpture says that "the pervasiveness of this response is testimony to the intensity with which the poet was temperamentally attracted to the Greek pederastic ideal and explains why he was so ready to believe that the Greek male in fact surpassed the female in beauty" (23).

8. Among various explanations of Victor and the monster as "doubles" or components of a single psyche—Bloom, Cantor, Hirsch, Hogle, Kaplan and Kloss, Ketterer, Kiely, Levine (b), Massey, Masao Miyoshi (*The Divided Self* [New York: New York University Press, 1969], 79–89), Seed, Small, Spark, and Tropp—the one closest to mine is Knoepflmacher's. "The Monster now assumes Victor's phallic aggression; and Victor becomes as tremulous and 'timid as a love-sick girl'" (106). Excellent as this insight is, the "now" indicates the difference between Knoepflmacher's sense of the novel and mine. "Now . . . and" makes the two events in the sentence seem causal, or at least sequential, when in fact the second event precedes the first by nearly one hundred pages. Victor becomes the love-sick girl on page 54, whereas the aggression referred to by Knoepflmacher occurs on page 149. In my view of causal sequence, Mary Shelley has Victor become effeminate *when the monster awakens*, because the creature embodies the creator's phallic drives. Victor, of course, does not *intend* to be rendered effeminate. He (at a deep level of the unconscious) expects to allow full expression to the feminine side of himself which he envisions joining with the projected masculine side. Effeminacy is Mary's work, her insistence that the halves of the psyche will polarize unless each finds complementarity in the two halves of an other.

Seeing the monster as Victor's male, passional side runs counter to two long-standing critical positions: that the creature is an intellectual force, and that he is feminine. Spark follows Church in viewing the "Monster firstly as representing reason in isolation. . . . a symbol of Mary's over-strained intellectual conscience" (137). That the monster has an intellectual side is as incontestable as that he has a feminine side; at issue is his specific function in relation to Victor. To equate the monster with intellect leaves Spark in the awkward position of having to account for such apparently passionate acts as his erotic killing of Elizabeth on the bridal bed and his pathological desire for revenge against Victor. "What passes for emotion . . . are really intellectual passions arrived at through rational channels" (149). The monster knows better. "I was the slave, not the master of an impulse, which I detested, yet could not disobey. . . . an insatiable passion" (218). How can such a slave of passion represent intellect when Victor as the slave of this "slave" says, "through the whole period during which I was the slave of my creature, I allowed myself to be governed by the impulses of the moment" (151)? Seeing the creature as animal passion fits not only with the text but also with tradition, for, as Small notes, what Prometheus botched in his creation of the male was precisely his "animal" side (48–49).

Any claims for the monster as male must acknowledge the ways in which he is female, as an expression of Mary Shelley's inner life and as a

potential androgyne with strong feminine traits. Critics who stress his feminine side are Gilbert and Gubar, Knoepflmacher, and Poovey. The unquestionable maleness of the creature physically is what allows him to express
the male extreme of Victor's unconscious. The maleness of the creature is
further confirmed by various elements of plot and characterization. Once
Robert Walton, for example, has engaged in a Shelley-like quest for a male
in the opening frame, Victor's pursuit of the monster continues that quest—
unconsciously before Elizabeth's death, purposively (though without real
self-knowledge) afterwards. Moreover, if Victor intuitively feels himself
feminine, this answers the Kaplan-Kloss question of why he does not create
the monstress and thus get rid of the monster. Victor wants not to be rid of
him, but to forestall any female who might preempt Victor himself with the
creature. Finally, the most sustained case for the monster's femininity is
Hirsch's argument that the creature is suffering from penis envy. Although
the proud possessor of a penis could, I feel, experience all the privations
which Hirsch attributes to the monster, Hirsch is properly directing attention to one of the most basic issues of *Frankenstein*, incompleteness.

9. Shelley's inclination to the feminine is indicated in various ways in
his art. As Moore notes, Shelley projects himself (though always with reservations) into that sympathetic father-killer, Beatrice Cenci (28), and into
Rosalind, who is suspected unjustly of adultery and atheism in *Rosalind
and Helen* (36–37). See also Carpenter (63). In *Epipsychidion*, Shelley's description of his interaction with the prostitute (if this is indeed who she is)
makes *him* female, pierced and penetrated. "Flame / Out of her looks into
my vitals came . . . A killing air . . . pierced like honey-dew / Into the core
of my green heart" (259–60, 262–63). Soon the phallic one is Emily: "All
other sounds were penetrated / By the small, still, sweet spirit of that
sound [her respiration]" (330–31). Shelley again is female: "I stood, and felt
the dawn of my long night / Was penetrating me with living light" (341–
42).

10. Among the few critics who recognize the orgasmic quality of the
moment are John C. Bean ("The Poet Borne Darkly: The Dream-Voyage
Allegory in Shelley's *Alastor*," *KSJ* 23 [1974]: 60–76); and Brown (58).

11. For stages of the *Alastor* debate see Olwen Ward Campbell (187–96);
Raymond A. Havens, "Shelley's *Alastor*," *PMLA* 45 (1930): 1098–1115;
Marion Clyde Wier, "Shelley's 'Alastor' Again," *PMLA* 46 (1931): 947–50,
and Havens' reply (950–51); Paul Mueschke and Earle Leslie Griggs,
"Wordsworth as the Prototype of the Poet in Shelley's *Alastor*," *PMLA* 49
(1934): 229–45; Marcel Kessel, Paul Mueschke and Earle Leslie Griggs,
"'The Poet in Shelley's *Alastor*': A Criticism and a Reply," *PMLA* 51
(1936): 302–12; Arthur E. Du Bois, "Alastor: The Spirit of Solitude," *JEGP*
35 (1936): 530–45; Evan K. Gibson, "'Alastor': A Reinterpretation," *PMLA*
62 (1947): 1022–45; Frederick L. Jones, "The Vision Theme in Shelley's
Alastor and Related Works," *SP* 44 (1947): 108–25; Albert Gerard, "*Alastor*,
or the Spirit of Solipsism," *PQ* 33 (1954): 164–77; Joseph Raben, "Coleridge
as the Prototype of the Poet in Shelley's *Alastor*," *RES* 17 (1966): 278–92;
Timothy Webb, "Coleridge and Shelley's *Alastor*: A Reply," *RES* 18 (1967):
402–11; W. H. Hildebrand, "Shelley's Early Vision Poems," *SIR* 8 (1969):
198–215; Luther L. Scales, Jr., "The Poet as Miltonic Adam in *Alastor*," *KSJ*

21–22 (1972–73): 126–44; Lloyd Abbey, "Shelley's Bridge to Maturity: From 'Alastor' to 'Mont Blanc,'" *Mosiac* 10 (1977): 69–84; Lisa M. Steinman, "Shelley's Skepticism: Allegory in 'Alastor,'" *ELH* 45 (1978): 255–69.

12. Hoeveler (82) quotes Franz von Baader from *La Notion D'Androgynie* by des Fontaines (Paris: Depot General, Le François, 1938), 139.

CHAPTER FOUR

1. Lest *The Assassins* be dismissed as a youthful extravagance, compare its ideal of "retiring from the intercourse of mankind" and Shelley's 1821 declaration, "I would be *alone* & would devote either to oblivion or to future generations the overflowings of a mind which, timely withdrawn from the contagion, should be kept fit for no baser object" (*PSL* 2:339, 15 Aug. 1821). Likewise the tension between Shelley's early pacifism and his bloodthirstiness in *The Assassins* continues throughout his life. In September of 1820 he tells Mary, "at Naples the constitutional party have declared to the Austrian minister that if the Emperor should make war upon them, their first action would be to put to death *all* the members of the royal family. A necessary, & most just measure when the forces of the combatants as well as the merits of their respective causes are so unequal!" (*PSL* 2:234, 1 Sept. 1820).

The only extended study of Shelley and *The Assassins* is Harold G. McCurdy's excellent "Shelley the Assassin" (*Georgia Review* 27 [1973]: 182–93). The most recent discussion of it, David Seed's "Shelley's 'Gothick' in *St. Irvyne* and after" (in *Essays on Shelley*, ed. Miriam Allott [Totowa, N.J.: Barnes & Noble, 1982], 62–63), does not follow McCurdy in recognizing either the unpleasant aspects of the Assassins' philosophy or their appearance in Shelley's life.

2. Most discussions of Shelley's politics have concentrated on its radical aspects. See, for example, R. Anthony Arthur, "The Poet as Revolutionary in *The Revolt of Islam*," *Xavier University Studies* 10 (1971): 1–17; Roland Bartel, "Shelley and Burke's Swinish Multitude," *KSJ* 18 (1969): 4–9; Kenneth Neill Cameron, "The Social Philosophy of Shelley," *Sewanee* 50 (1942): 457–66, and "Shelley and Marx," *Wordsworth Circle* 10 (1979): 234–39. An excellent start toward redressing this imbalance is made by Donald H. Reiman in his "Shelley as Agrarian Reactionary" (*KSMB* 30 [1979]: 5–15). Holmes also discusses reactionary and counterrevolutionary tendencies that coexist with the revolutionary spirit of *The Revolt of Islam* (400–401). Olwen Ward Campbell quotes Charles MacFarland's perception that Shelley could never be taken for anything but "a true thoroughbred English gentleman" (154). Hughes quotes Hogg's contention that Shelley "was in theory wholly a republican, but in practice so far only as it is possible to be one with due regard to the sacred rights of a scholar and a gentleman" (54). Shelley was in fact quite like Byron in his capacity to combine ardent liberal emotions with thoroughly conservative inclinations. He told Mary, after all, that should he die she was to give Percy Florence the education of a gentleman, first public school and then university.

3. I have put the somewhat inchoate passage from Claire's journal (184) into order. The original reads:

> Caricature for poor ⟨Dear⟩ S. He looking very sweet & smiling. a little ⟨Child playing⟩ Jesus Christ playing about the

room He says. Then grasping a ⟨sm⟩ small knife & looking
mild—I'll quietly kill that little child. Another. Himself &
God Almighty . . .

Confirming Claire's intuitions, Thornton Hunt remembers his childhood play with Shelley being "broken off by my terror at his screwing up his long and curling hair into a horn, and approaching me with rampant paws and frightful gestures as some imaginative monster. . . . he took a pleasure in frightening me. . . . Sometimes, but much more rarely, he teased me with exasperating banter. . . . I was tortured" (186, 187).

4. Small establishes that it is impossible to tell how many of the Promethean legends Mary knew. His examination of the links of various legends to *Frankenstein* (48–67) is the best work done on this aspect of the novel. Lederer shows how Prometheus can be seen as an emblem of the Greco-Judaic tradition's denial of woman. In the Greek legends, Prometheus creates man without woman; in the Talmudic version of the Genesis story, Michael creates Adam from the dust at Jehovah's command, again without woman. See also William H. Hildebrand, "On Three Prometheuses: Shelley's Two and Mary's One," *The Serif* 11 (1974): 3–11. Among many discussions of Prometheus in the nineteenth century see Bloom; Frye; Peter Thorslev's chapter "Satan and Prometheus" in *The Byronic Hero* (Minneapolis: University of Minnesota Press, 1962), plus his bibliography which includes important items on Shelley. For the claim that Faust, not Prometheus, is the central Romantic figure see Hume. In *Proserpine* Mary refers to "impious Prometheus" (act 1).

5. James Rieger, "Dr. Polidori and the Genesis of *Frankenstein*," *SEL* 3 (1963): 461–72. Mary Shelley's insistence upon *Frankenstein* as *hers* shows through her ostensibly self-effacing response to Sir Walter Scott's praise for the novel. "I am anxious to prevent your continuing in the mistake of supposing Mr. Shelley guilty of a juvenile attempt of mine" (*NL* 71, 14 June 1818).

6. The bizarre repetition of names in Shelley's life has often been noted. Beside all the Elizabeths—mother, sister, Hitchener, and "Eliza" Westbrook—there are the two Harriets, Grove and Westbrook. Fuller among others has speculated that the fact that *Queen Mab* is dedicated to "Harriet******" suggests that although Shelley ostensibly intends his wife, the actual dedicatee is Harriet Grove (133).

7. The extremely close tie between Percy and Mrs. Shelley lasts until he does away to school. (Hogg perceptively notes that Shelley's early verse features poems "with a good deal about sucking in them" [1:267]). What happens then between Percy and his mother is unclear. Dowden insists that, although Percy felt Mrs. Shelley had "turned traitor" (1:189) after his marriage to Harriet, "his mother and sisters were anxious to welcome him and Harriet to Field Place" (1:364) in April of 1813. Later in that year "Shelley's mother privately acquainted him with all that went on, and Harriet received friendly letters from her husband's sisters" (1:391). Captain Kennedy confirms that in 1813 "Mrs. Shelley often spoke to me of her son; her heart yearned after him with all the fondness of a mother's love" (Dowden 1:388). Why, then, does Shelley suddenly believe so emphatically the charge of adultery that he had laughed at earlier? Certainly he feels both rejected by Mrs. Shelley and desirous of a mother substitute. Of Elizabeth Hitchener's

aunt he says in 1812, "I already reverence her as a Mother" (*PSL* 1:162, 28 Oct. 1811)—though he has never met the woman. When Harriet refuses to nurse Ianthe and Percy tries to suckle the baby himself, he is doing with regard to mothers what in chapter 5 we will see him do with regard to father—incorporating the parental role within himself so he can go it alone. And Shelley definitely does go it alone. One of the most chilling aspects of his whole biography is the silence which soon and permanently settles around his mother and sisters. Shelley writes them no letters; he mentions them very rarely.

Victor-Percy's reaction to mother-woman as body-sensuality-death is part of an age-old male response studied by many scholars in many disciplines. For some helpful work and excellent references see Karen Horney's "The Dread of Woman" and other essays collected in *Feminine Psychology* (New York: Norton, 1967); Lederer; Erich Neumann, *The Great Mother* (Princeton: Princeton University Press, 1963); Karl Stern, *The Flight from Woman* (New York: Farrar, Straus, Giroux, 1965). Frye notes that "in Shelley, as in Blake, the mother, especially the Mother Earth of *Prometheus Unbound*, usually represents a state of imperfection which has yet to be transcended" (113).

8. I use the Thomas emendations here: the 1818 text is factually inaccurate, since it has the newlyweds retiring to "the inn" when in fact they go to Evian to stay at the Frankensteins' house there.

9. For discussions of Victor's sexual anxiety on the wedding night see Brooks (213), Kiely (165), Joseph (109), Levine (b 9).

10. The issue of the living dead is recurrent in both Mary and Percy. In *Perkin Warbeck* we are told that when good fortune smiles "Warwick ceased to be the dead alive" but that when gloom descends again the queen calls herself "a dead-alive" (3:290, 335). Lionel bravely asserts in *The Last Man* that "we may not enchain ourselves to a corpse" (237). Closest to *Frankenstein* is the moment in *Lodore* when "the child of the wilderness and the good lady of Longfield, were like a living and dead body in conjunction" (2:151). In Shelley we find "I [Rosalind] walked about like a corpse alive!" (*Rosalind and Helen* 312) and "Lumps neither alive nor dead" (*The Witch of Atlas* 135).

CHAPTER FIVE

1. Mary Shelley's respect for her mother is obvious and considerable. She reads and rereads Mary Wollstonecraft throughout the early years with Percy. For Mary and her mother see Gilbert and Gubar; Mary Jacobus, "Is There a Woman in this Text?" *New Literary History* 14 (1982): 117–41; Poovey; Rubenstein; and Janet M. Todd, "Frankenstein's Daughter: Mary Shelley and Mary Wollstonecraft," *Women and Literature* 4 (1976): 18–27.

2. Elsewhere in *Lodore*, Ethel's "affection for her father gathered strength from the confidence which existed between them. He was the passion of her soul, the engrossing attachment of her loving heart" (1:235). Probably most revealing, in the extreme care with which it is phrased, is the continuation of this passage. "Her heart was bent upon pleasing him, she had no thought or pursuit which was not linked with his participation. There is perhaps in the list of human sensations, no one so pure, so perfect, and yet so impassioned, as the affection of a *child* for its parent, during that brief interval

when *they* are leaving childhood, and have not yet felt love. There is something so *awful* in a father. His words are laws, and to obey them happiness. Reverence and a desire to serve, are mingled with gratitude; and duty, without a flaw or question, so second [sic] the instinct of the heart, as to render it imperative. Afterwards we may love, in spite of the faults of the object of our attachment; but during the interval alluded to, we have not yet learnt to tolerate, but also, we have not learned to detect faults. All that a parent does, appears an emanation from a diviner world" (1:235–36; my italics). Mary and Percy discuss incest—one of Shelley's premier themes—in 1818 and 1819. Medwin believes that Mary planned a father-daughter incest play, based on Alfieri's *Myrrha* (252).

3. Dussinger is probably hardest on Alphonse (42–47); see also Hill (345–46), Hirsch (128), and Knoepflmacher (104–5). Small goes too far in the opposite direction. "Frankenstein . . . never shows anything for his father but pious regard" (193). There are unquestionably oedipal aspects to Victor's behavior. Murphy emphasizes oedipal elements in Shelley's early work. The father who ruins a young man's mother appears in *Zastrozzi* and in "Revenge." Even here, however, one needs caution. Father-killing in *Zastrozzi* is, Murphy says, "a simple matter and actually takes place outside the story's action" (29). The very fact that the killing occurs offstage precludes its being a simple matter. Shelley's more mature work features the father as blighter of his children's lives. In *Rosalind and Helen* (1818), the lovers reach "the altar stair / When my father came from a distant land, / And with a loud and fearful cry / Rushed between us suddenly" (290–93). *The Cenci*, of course, allows Shelley unlimited expression of anti-paternal sentiment. "Such merriment again / As fathers make over their children's graves. . . . tortured me from my forgotten years, / As parents only dare . . ." (1.3.124–25; 3.1.72–73). Wilt wisely rejects any simple oedipal interpretation of such materials. "A Freudian might see in the whole progress of Frankenstein via the dream a wish to join his dead mother in the grave; but . . . the Gothic adds an extra dimension, a profound resentment of the sources of one's being, especially the female sources, stemming from the desire to be one's own source—and goal" (65).

4. Freud's fullest discussion of the negative oedipus occurs in chapter 3 of *The Ego and the Id* (*SE* 19:28–39); it also permeates his analysis of the Wolf-Man (*SE* 17:7–122).

5. "Dostoevsky and Parricide," in *Sigmund Freud: Collected Papers* (New York: Basic Books, 1959) 5:232. The subsequent quotations are from: Régis Durand, " 'The Captive King': The Absent Father in Melville's Text," in Davis, 70; Jean-Michel Rabaté, "A Clown's Inquest into Paternity: Fathers Dead or Alive, in *Ulysses* and *Finnegans Wake*," in Davis, 88; Sadoff 38; Barickman 169; Irwin 119; Sadoff 45. Useful for understanding fathers is Ernest Jones' "The Phantasy of the Reversal of Generations," in *Papers on Psycho-Analysis* (Boston: Beacon, 1961), 407–12. For self-generation in Shakespeare see C. L. Barber's " 'Thou That Beget'st Him That Did Thee Beget': Transformation in 'Pericles' and 'The Winter's Tale,' " *Shakespeare Survey* 22 (1969): 59–67. Among other authors concerned with self-generation, Dickens has elicited particularly good analyses. See Lawrence Jay Dessner, "*Great Expectations:* The Ghost of a Man's Own Father," *PMLA* 91 (1976): 436–49; Albert D. Hutter, "Nation and Generation in *A Tale of*

Two Cities," *PMLA* 93 (1978): 448–62; Branwen Bailey Pratt, "Dickens and Father: Notes on the Family Romance," *Hartford Studies in Literature* 8 (1976): 4–22. For fathers in American literature see Eric J. Sundquist, *Home as Found* (Baltimore: Johns Hopkins University Press, 1979); for continental literature see Tony Tanner, *Adultery in the Novel* (Baltimore: Johns Hopkins University Press, 1979).

6. Harold Bloom, "Freud's Concepts of Defense and the Poetic Will," in *The Literary Freud,* ed. Joseph H. Smith (New Haven: Yale University Press, 1980), 6. Bloom's most extended discussion of Shelley and origins is "Shelley and his Precursors," in *Poetry and Repression* (New Haven: Yale University Press, 1976), 83–111. See also *The Anxiety of Influence* (New York: Oxford University Press, 1973) and *A Map of Misreading* (New York: Oxford University Press, 1975). Self-generation in Shelley is discussed by Leslie Brisman in *Romantic Origins* (Ithaca: Cornell University Press, 1978).

7. In his persuasive study of the psychological forces shaping *Prometheus Unbound,* Leon Waldoff sees Shelley caught between oedipal rage at father and guilt at that rage. Shelley's solution, according to Waldoff, is to give "hate . . . guiltless expression through moral assertiveness" ("The Father-Son Conflict in *Prometheus Unbound:* The Psychology of a Vision," *The Psychoanalytic Review* 62 [1975]: 92). Aggressive feelings merge, and then emerge as moral superiority. A related psychology is at work, Irwin notes, in Thomas Sutpen. "The son tries to overcome the mastery of the personal father while maintaining the mastery of fatherhood—a mechanism in which the personal father dies without the son's having to kill him" (99).

8. Interestingly, Shelley's first poetic persona, the Margaret Nicholson whose poems "Fitzvictor" supposedly edits in Percy's second volume of verse, is another woman from the past who expresses homicidal inclinations toward authoritative males. She is, Shelley tells us, "that noted Female who attempted the life of the King in 1786" (*CP* 861).

9. For recent viewpoints on *The "Cenci"* (and bibliographies of earlier work) see Sara M. Miller, "Irony in Shelley's *The Cenci,"* *University of Mississippi Studies in English* 9 (1968): 23–35; Wasserman 84–128; Stuart Curran, *Shelley's "Cenci"* (Princeton: Princeton University Press, 1970); Justin G. Turner, *"The Cenci,* Shelley vs. the Truth," *American Book Collector* 22 (1972): 5–9; Arline R. Thorn, "Shelley's *The Cenci* as Tragedy," *Costerus* 9 (1973): 219–28; P. Jay Delmar, "Evil and Character in Shelley's *The Cenci,"* *Massachusetts Studies in English* 6 (1977): 37–48; Fred L. Milne, "Shelley's *The Cenci:* The Ice Motif and the Ninth Circle of Dante's Hell," *Tennessee Studies in Literature* 22 (1977): 117–32; Ronald L. Lemoncelli, "Cenci as Corrupt Dramatic Poet," *English Language Notes* 16 (1978): 103–17; James D. Wilson, "Beatrice Cenci and Shelley's Vision of Moral Responsibility," *Ariel* 9 (1978): 75–89; James B. Twitchell, "Shelley's Use of Vampirism in *The Cenci,"* *Tennessee Studies in Literature* 24 (1979): 120–33.

10. The one critic to notice that the deaths proceed in the order of increased intimacy is Frank H. McCloskey ("Mary Shelley's *Frankenstein,"* in *The Humanities in the Age of Science,* ed. Charles Argoff [Rutherford, N.J.: Fairleigh Dickinson University Press, 1968], 137). Seed suggests that "since he is ultimately responsible for all their deaths we could see Frank-

enstein progressively killing off more and more humanizing aspects of his self" (332). Seed does not, however, go on to explain how Alphonse as the last of the family fatalities might be the most humane aspect of Victor's self. Tropp argues that Frankenstein is destroying rivals for his parents' love (20–27). Ketterer, moving out from Tropp, suggests, I think quite incorrectly, that sibling rivalry explains why Alphonse is *not* murdered. "He dies 'naturally' of grief" (64). Ketterer goes on to recognize Victor's "ambivalence" toward Alphonse, but does not see the father killed by the son. More generally, Cantor maintains that "something in Frankenstein wants to kill anyone who comes close to him so that he can maintain his willful isolation" (118).

11. Sigmund Freud, "Remembering, Repeating and Working-Through (Further Recommendations on the Technique of Psycho-Analysis II)," *SE* 12;145–56.

CHAPTER SIX

1. The dangerous aspects of True Woman have been studied recently from a variety of viewpoints. Alexander Welsh associates the angel with death (*The City of Dickens* [London: Oxford University Press, 1971]), as Auerbach does with the demon. Sadoff focuses on father-killing daughters in Dickens and Eliot. The extent to which Charlotte Brontë's punitive dealings with male characters are in fact therapeutic for the males has been widely discussed. For women and sensationalism see my section on the sensation heroine in Helsinger, Sheets, and Veeder (3:122–45); plus Elaine Showalter, "Subverting the Feminine Novel: Sensationalism and Feminine Protest," in *A Literature of their Own* (Princeton: Princeton University Press, 1977), 156–81; and Winifred Hughes, *The Maniac in the Cellar* (Princeton: Princeton University Press, 1980). Father-daughter incest is the subject of two very different recent authors, Gallop (see particularly chapter 5), and Judith Lewis Herman (*Father-Daughter Incest* [Cambridge: Harvard University Press, 1981]). See also Marjorie B. Leonard, "Fathers and Daughters: The Significance of 'Fathering' in the Psychosexual Development of the Girl," *International Journal of Psychoanalysis* 47 (1966): 325–34; and Michael E. Lamb, Margaret Tresch Owen, and Lindsay Chase-Lansdale, "The Father-Daughter Relationship: Past, Present, and Future," in *Becoming Female*, ed. Claire B. Kopp and Martha Kilpatrick (New York: Plenum, 1979), 89–112. Fathers' relations with daughters (and sons) contemporary with Mary Shelley are studied by Frank Swinerton in *A Galaxy of Fathers* (London: Hutchinson, 1966).

2. Dowden finds in Mary Shelley herself "an expression at once of sensibility and firmness" (1:418). In *The Last Man* Mary features women who in crises are "more eager and resolute than their male companions" (277). That women at such moments need not fear "unsexing" themselves is clear from *Falkner*. "She [Elizabeth] looked beautiful as an angel, as she spoke; her independent spirit had nothing rough in its texture. It did not arise from a love of opposition, but from a belief, that in fulfilling a duty, she could not be opposed or injured" (2:226–27). Thus Mathilda's mother can manifest "an understanding that receives the name of masculine for its firmness and strength while in her feelings she was gentle and susceptible" (quoted by Nitchie from MS B of Mary's fragment "The Fields of Fancy," 97). And

Euthanasia can determine "to preserve a firmness and sweetness, that might sustain her, and soften him" (*Valperga* 3:236).

3. Biographers and critics have often noted Lord Dillon's testament to Mary Shelley's bifurcation—"your writings and your manner are not in accordance. I should have thought of you—if I had only read you—that you were a sort of my Sybil, outpouringly enthusiastic, rather indiscreet, and even extravagant; but you are cool, quiet, and feminine to the last degree. . . . Explain this to me" (Mrs. Marshall 2:197). Nitchie (10) and Grylls (xv) confirm what Mary knows is particularly true of herself after Percy's death. "One . . . leads as it were an internal life, quite different from the outward and apparent one!" (*J* 183, 19 Oct. 1822).

4. Mary Shelley makes the same criticisms of women in real life. "She [Gabrielle Wright] shewed & still shews herself ready to sacrifize all—even her lover's safety, to her wilful desires" (*NL* 306, 12 Jan. 1823). *Lodore* dramatizes Cornelia's "self-will" (1:190); *Perkin Warbeck* presents "vain, heedless, self-willed Lady Jane" (2:191). Mary is, however, careful to distinguish true willfulness in woman from that legitimate insistence upon rights which males characteristically deride as petulance. When Euthanasia refuses to surrender her castle and her political beliefs to Castruccio's lust for power, he avoids the moral force of her argument by saying, "I know that the wisdom of all ages tells us, that women will have their will; I had hoped to find you superior to the foibles of your sex . . . you are as headstrong as a girl of fifteen, who hopes to cover her head with the nuptial veil" (*Valperga* 2:246–47). Even so excellent a male as Villiers in *Lodore* accedes to Ethel while joking in conventional fashion: "having deprived you of every other luxury, at least, you shall have your will; which, you know, compensates for everything with your obstinate sex" (3:48).

5. Thornton Hunt too allows for no playfulness when he links Mary and his father: "both persons being very sensitive in feeling, quick in temper, thoroughly outspoken, and obstinantly tenacious of their own convictions" (196).

6. Knoepflmacher defines Mary Shelley's predicament well. She must recognize that she shares with the Prometheans a "desire for knowledge" and a capacity for "perseverance" which threaten to overdevelop the masculine side "of a personality that had developed . . . without a feminine or maternal model" (105).

7. Knoepflmacher links William to Mary and to Godwin's son by Mrs. Clairmont. For other interpretations of Mary's choice of the name William see Spark ("when she began to feel her intellect grow under her new task, she automatically identified the child with her threatened emotions" [138]).

8. Although no critic has examined this speech as a covert attack upon Justine, Wolf does note what a terrible comforter of Justine Elizabeth is (119). Visiting Justine in prison after the servant has confessed, Elizabeth seems entirely concerned with her own grief. What must the doomed Justine feel when the first words out of her adored Elizabeth's mouth are "Oh, Justine! . . . why did you rob me of my last consolation. I relied on your innocence; and although I was then very wretched, I was not so miserable as I am now" (81). Justine's response confirms what the courtroom speech has in fact shown—that Elizabeth is of the devil's party. "Do you also join with

my enemies to crush me?" (81). Elizabeth soon apologizes, but her focus remains upon herself: "I never can survive so horrible a misfortune" (82). *Justine* is the one forced into the role of comforter. "I will try to comfort you" (82).

9. That some of Mary Shelley's most admirable characters evince the traits she shares with Victor indicates her awareness that we all are implicated in Prometheanism, and that she has little right to indignation. Lionel in *The Last Man* "was least miserable" when he "could, absorbed in reverie, forget the passage of the hours" (332). After Perkin's death Katherine "conversed with [him] only in her nightly dreams . . . 'I court sleep because he wanders into my dreams'" (*Perkin Warbeck* 3:13, 322). Ethel and her aunt in *Lodore* find that the dead Lodore "visited their dreams by night" (1:283). Mary also displays other aspects of the weakness which she faults in Prometheans. She can disavow responsibility for her plights ("we have been pursued by so much ill luck" [*MSL* 1:85, 24 Nov. 1819]) and can echo Percy's self-pity when she does accept responsibility. "I have fabricated only misery for myself" (*MSL* 1:370, 14 Feb. 1828). Mary sounds like Robert Walton descanting upon what he sees in his "friend" and what he finds in Victor Frankenstein. "Genius . . . guided my thoughts. I conversed with him; rectified my errors of judgment" (*J* 180, 2 Oct. 1822). Like both Robert and Percy, Mary can say "I have no friend" (*J* 180, 2 Oct. 1822).

10. Mary Shelley may tell Jane Williams that "however devotedly one may love a woman, she can never support, defend, & protect as a man" (*MSL* 2:5, 28 June 1828), but she knows that women, even viewed conventionally, were created with resources of strength in times of duress. Thus in her fiction Mary shows women supporting both men (Perkin Warbeck "tried to raise himself, and she [Monina] bent down to support him. . . . she received him as he fell, and, supporting him to a bank, called aloud" [1:234]) and each other (Monina "rushed forward, supporting the faltering Queen" [3:223]). She also insists that self-support is necessary for both genders: "He [Castruccio] supported himself with courage" (*Valperga* 3:268); "yet a little longer, my Elizabeth, support yourself" (*Falkner* 2:262). *Falkner* repeatedly demonstrates woman's ability to act under duress (2:153, 284).

11. Mary Shelley's obsession with indecisiveness is demonstrated by the frequency of its recurrence in her fiction. *The Last Man* mirrors her Rome experience. " 'Why [asked Lionel] adhere to a plan whose dilatory proceeding you already disapprove?' 'Nay,' replied he [Adrian], 'it is too late now. A month ago, and we were masters of our selves; now,— . . . a man died of the plague last night!'" (289). Mary's most explicit self-indictment occurs in *Falkner*, where she portrays the True Woman who is destroyed by the Byronic man. "She [Alithea] had a good deal of timidity in her character. She was so susceptible to pain, that she feared it too much. . . . this terror of meeting anything harsh or grating in her path, rendered her too diffident of herself—too submissive to authority—too miserable, and too yielding" (1:195). Robert Dale Owen, seeing Mary Shelley as she did Fanny Wright, describes her as "dependent for happiness on loving encouragement, needing a guiding and sustaining hand" ("Frances Wright, General Lafayette, and Mary Wollstonecraft Shelley" *AM* 32 [1873]: 457). For her part, Mary repeats her belief in a woman's need for male support when she discusses Jane

Williams' relationship with Hogg. "How I envy you—a dear man person—on whom . . . one can repose as one's support in life" (*MSL* 2:4, 28 June 1828).

She rejects any thought of an intimate relation with Trelawny because support requires the man's undivided attention. "I must have the entire affection, devotion, and, above all, the solicitous protection of any one who would win me. You belong to womankind in general, and Mary Shelley will *never* be yours" (*MSL* 2:49, 26 July 1831). Mary defines her relation with Percy in terms similar to those she used with Jane and Fanny. "I have lost my support . . . my tree of life is felled" (*NL* 317, 28 Feb. 1823). Over and over her letters return to her "unsupported situation. . . . in all this [raising Percy Florence] I had no one friendly hand stretched out to support me" (*MSL* 2:73, 16 Jan. 1833; 119, 27 Jan. 1837). For herself, "I was always a dependent thing—wanting fosterage and support" (*MSL* 2:98, 11 June 1835). Still more revealingly she confesses to her journal that since Shelley's death "I have found strength in the conception of its [her heart's] faculties. . . . But I have found less strength of self-support" (189, 19 Mar. 1823).

12. Besides Ellis's belief that Elizabeth's and Justine's "model behavior similarly lowers their resistance to the forces that kill them" (133), Swingle claims that "trusting him [Frankenstein] instead of becoming suspicious of his peculiar behavior. . . . they [Elizabeth and Henry] die without knowing what hit them" (62). Jacobus agrees: "at best, women are the bearers of a traditional ideology of love, nurturance, and domesticity; at worst, passive victims" (132). Wexelblatt associates Elizabeth exclusively with the super-ego. She is "clearly identified with the first set of values, the 'enervating' ones [of traditional ethics] that do the censoring [of the unconscious]" (109).

13. Burton R. Pollin suggests that "Safie" comes from "Sophie" in Rousseau's *Emile* ("Philosophical and Literary Sources of *Frankenstein*," *Comparative Literature* 17 [1965]: 97–108). Pollin leaves unexplained why Mary, if she had wanted to echo "Sophie," didn't use that name or the more traditional Turkish "Sophia."

CHAPTER SEVEN

1. The Mary Shelley quotation is from *MSL* 2:98, 11 June 1835; the Somerville is quoted by E. C. Patterson from unpublished Somerville papers ("The Case of Mary Somerville: An Aspect of Nineteenth-Century Science," *Proceedings of the American Philosophical Society* 118 [1974]: 274); Wollstonecraft, 70; the George Eliot is from her "Woman in France: Madame de Sable" (*Essays of George Eliot*, ed. Thomas Pinney [New York: Columbia University Press, 1963], 56).

2. Mary Shelley's reservations about traditional education we have seen with Ethel in *Lodore*. For woman's obligation to compensate self-sacrificingly for and to her man, see *Valperga* (3:64, 178–83, 236, 248). For the limits of an exclusively maternal existence—Mary associates this view of woman with Catholicism—see *Falkner* 2:61. Moreover, Mary dislikes housework and prefers to have her domestic ideal realized by servants and nannies.

These and other reservations, however, do not prevent Mary Shelley from being on the whole overwhelmingly sympathetic with the traditional view of woman. *Falkner,* for example, goes on to celebrate maternity (2:63–64). Self-sacrifice is eulogized not only here (1:110, 138, 146, 264; 2:93), and in *The Last Man* (127, 266), but also in Katherine's devotion to the beset Perkin Warbeck. Home is Mary Shelley's unquestioned ideal. "When I would picture happiness upon earth, my imagination conjures up the family of a dweller among the fields" (*Valperga* 1:53). *Perkin Warbeck* constantly contrasts the vanities of court life with the basics of domestic life (1:20; 2:300; 3:88–92). *Valperga* also sounds this theme, of course, with Castruccio Castracani.

3. Kiely's chapter is difficult to be fair to because its assertions of Victor's ultimate heroism alternate with excellent insights which lead to a very different and, I feel, much better reading of *Frankenstein:* "The controlling perspective is that of an earthbound woman. . . . the [*Alastor*] poet appears to luxuriate in the forbidden and fruitless act" (161, 163). That "Frankenstein's presumption is not in his attempt to usurp the power of the gods . . . but in his attempt to usurp the power of women" (164) is wittily put, but Mary Shelley does not make so neat a division between God and woman. God is on woman's side because together they constitute the natural. What is unnatural with regard to procreation offends against both.

Other critics who share Kiely's sense of Victor's ultimate heroism are Alan Rodway; Wilfred Cude, and Massey. Rodway concludes that "on the whole the reader's sympathy is urged for Frankenstein, not the unhappy monster" (*The Romantic Conflict* [London: Chatto & Windus, 1963], 60). Believing that "Victor is following in the footsteps of the noble Titan" Cude concludes that "the modern Prometheus represents the best in mankind. . . . the error of the scientist can only have dreadful consequences if the rest of society proves to be irresponsible" ("Mary Shelley's Modern Prometheus: A Study of the Ethics of Scientific Creativity," *Dalhousie Review* 52 [1972]: 219, 224). Massey finds that "Frankenstein is now acknowledged to be 'the select specimen of all that is worthy of love and admiration among men'" (131). Recently Seed has argued for the unheroic quality of Victor. "The novel denies any grandeur either to Frankenstein's ambition or to his enterprise. . . . any mythic parallels further reduce the stature of the action by showing ironically how far it is from the heroic or truly spiritual" (329, 340).

4. According to Scott, "Walton is moved by Victor's final speech, yet rejects its male goals of 'glory and honour' (p. 213)" (200). There is no rejection of glory and honor on page 213 of *Frankenstein.* What Walton says is: "I had rather die, than return shamefully,—my purpose unfulfilled. Yet I fear such will be my fate; the men, unsupported by ideas of glory and honour, can never willingly continue to endure their present hardships."

5. Poovey agrees basically with Knoepflmacher. Associating Walton with Felix De Lacey as "the domesticated male" (131), Poovey finds in Robert the "ability to deny his selfish desire and to replace it by concern for others. . . . Frankenstein's narrative resolves Walton's internal conflict and restores to him the domestic affection which has been all along the innate 'groundwork of [his] character'" (132, 137). Johnson agrees. "Walton assures his sister that he has not really left the path she would wish for him, that he still resembles *her*" (3).

6. Rieger points out the northward course of the wedding journey to the south (83–84).

7. Tropp believes that rejecting the monster proves Walton's moral growth (80–82). For other viewpoints, see Levine (a 22), and Swingle (55). Critics who see the monster actually perishing are Griffin (171) and Rieger (82).

8. Scott 200. Tropp also evokes Dante, saying that *Frankenstein* is "meant, like Dante's poem, to show the way to salvation" (83).

Bibliography of Works Cited

TEXTS OF THE SHELLEYS

Mary Wollstonecraft Shelley

F   *Frankenstein; or The Modern Prometheus.* Edited by James Rieger. Indianapolis: Bobbs-Merrill, 1974. Reprint Chicago: University of Chicago Press, 1982. (The abbreviation *F* will be used only when passages from *Frankenstein* might be confused with passages quoted from other works.)

Mathilda. Written in 1819 but unpublished until this edition. Edited by Elizabeth Nitchie. Chapel Hill: University of North Carolina Press, 1959.

Proserpine & Midas. Written in 1820 but unpublished until this edition. Edited by A. Koszul. London: Milford, 1922.

Valperga; or, The Life and Adventures of Castruccio, Prince of Lucca. London, 1823.

The Last Man. London, 1826. Reprint Lincoln: University of Nebraska Press, 1965.

The Fortunes of Perkin Warbeck. London, 1830.

Lodore. London, 1835.

Falkner. London, 1837. Reprint Folcroft, Pa.: Folcroft, 1975.

MSL   *The Letters of Mary W. Shelley.* Edited by Frederick L. Jones. Norman: University of Oklahoma Press, 1946.

J   *Mary Shelley's Journal.* Edited by Frederick L. Jones. Norman: University of Oklahoma Press, 1947.

NL   *The Letters of Mary Wollstonecraft Shelley.* Edited by Betty T. Bennett. Baltimore: Johns Hopkins University Press, 1980, 1983.

Percy Bysshe Shelley

JS   *The Complete Works of Percy Bysshe Shelley.* The Julian Edition. Edited by Roger Ingpen and Walter E. Peck. London: Ernest Benn Limited; New York: Scribner's, 1926–30. Reprint New York: Gordian, 1965.

CP   *The Complete Poetical Works of Percy Bysshe Shelley.* Edited by Thomas Hutchinson. London: Oxford University Press, 1943. (All

Shelley poems except "The Wandering Jew," on which Medwin may have collaborated, are quoted from this edition.)

PSL   *The Letters of Percy Bysshe Shelley.* Edited by Frederick L. Jones. London: Oxford University Press, 1963.

EIGHTEENTH- AND NINETEENTH-CENTURY WORKS

Arnold, Matthew. "Shelley." In *The Complete Prose Works of Matthew Arnold.* Edited by R. H. Super. Vol. 4. Ann Arbor: University of Michigan Press, 1960.

Austen, Jane. *Northanger Abbey.* London: Oxford University Press, 1965.

Clairmont, Claire. *The Journals of Claire Clairmont.* Edited by Marion Kingston Stocking. Cambridge: Harvard University Press, 1968.

Dowden, Edward. *The Life of Percy Bysshe Shelley.* 2 vols. London, 1886.

Emerson, Ralph Waldo. *Journals and Miscellaneous Notebooks.* Edited by William H. Gilman. Cambridge: Harvard University Press, 1960–82.

Farnham, Eliza W. *Woman and Her Era.* New York, 1864.

Fielding, Henry. *The History of Tom Jones, A Foundling.* New York: Random House, 1950.

Godwin, William. *Caleb Williams.* Edited by David McCracken. New York: Norton, 1977.

Hogg, Thomas Jefferson. *The Life of Percy Bysshe Shelley.* 2 vols. London, 1858.

Hunt, Thornton. "Shelley." *AM* 11 (1863): 184–204.

Lewis, Matthew Gregory. *The Monk.* Edited by Louis F. Peck. New York: Grove, 1952.

Marshall, Mrs. Julian. *The Life and Letters of Mary Shelley.* London, 1889.

Medwin, Thomas. *The Life of Percy Bysshe Shelley.* Edited by H. Buxton Forman. London: Oxford University Press, 1913.

Melbourne, Lord. *Memoirs.* London, 1878.

Melville, Herman. *Pierre; or, The Ambiguities.* Evanston, Ill.: Northwestern University Press, 1971.

Merle, Joseph Gibbons. "A Newspaper Editor's Reminiscences." *Fraser's Magazine* 23 (1841): 699–710.

Mill, John Stuart, and Harriet Taylor Mill. *Essays on Sex Equality.* Edited by Alice S. Rossi. Chicago: University of Chicago Press, 1970.

Peacock, Thomas Love. *Thomas Love Peacock: Memoirs of Shelley and Other Essays and Reviews.* Edited by Howard Mills. London: Hart-Davis, 1970.

Rennie, Eliza. *Traits of Character.* London, 1860.

Trelawny, Edward John. *Records of Shelley, Byron and the Author.* 2 vols. London, 1878.

Wollstonecraft, Mary. *A Vindication of the Rights of Woman.* Edited by Charles W. Hagelman, Jr. New York: Norton, 1967.

Wordsworth, William. *The Poetical Works of Wordsworth.* Edited by

Thomas Hutchinson and Ernest de Selincourt. London: Oxford University Press, 1936.

MODERN WORKS

Auerbach, Nina. *Woman and the Demon.* Cambridge: Harvard University Press, 1982.

Barickman, Richard, Susan MacDonald, and Myra Stark. *Corrupt Relations.* New York: Columbia University Press, 1982.

Bloom, Harold. "Frankenstein, or the New Prometheus." *Partisan Review* 32 (1965): 611–18. Reprinted in *The Ringers in the Tower,* 119–29. Chicago: University of Chicago Press, 1971. Also reprinted as the afterward to Bloom's edition of *Frankenstein,* 212–23. New York: Signet, 1965.

Bowerbank, Sylvia. "The Social Order vs. The Wretch: Mary Shelley's Contradictory-Mindedness in *Frankenstein.*" *ELH* 46 (1979): 418–31.

Brooks, Peter. "'Godlike Science–Unhallowed Arts': Language, Nature, and Monstrosity." In Levine and Knoepflmacher, 205–20.

Brown, Nathaniel. *Sexuality and Feminism in Shelley.* Cambridge: Harvard University Press, 1979.

Buxton, John. *Byron and Shelley: The History of a Friendship.* London: Macmillan, 1968.

Cameron, Kenneth Neill. *Shelley: The Golden Years.* Cambridge: Harvard University Press, 1974.

Campbell, Joseph. *The Hero with a Thousand Faces.* Princeton: Princeton University Press, 1949.

Campbell, Olwen Ward. *Shelley and the Unromantics.* London: Methuen, 1924. Reprint London: Russell & Russell, 1966.

Cantor, Paul A. "The Nightmare of Romantic Idealism." In *Creature and Creator,* 103–32. New York: Cambridge University Press, 1984.

Carpenter, Edward, and George Barnefield. *The Psychology of the Poet Shelley.* London: Allen & Unwin, 1925. Reprint Folcroft, Pa.: Folcroft, 1976.

Chabot, C. Barry. *Freud on Schreber.* Amherst: University of Massachusetts Press, 1982.

Chesser, Eustace. *Shelley and Zastrozzi: Self-Revelation of a Neurotic.* London: Gregg/Archive, 1965.

Chodorow, Nancy. *The Reproduction of Mothering.* Berkeley: University of California Press, 1978.

Church, Richard. *Mary Shelley.* London: Howe, 1928.

Cott, Nancy F. "Passionlessness: An Interpretation of Victorian Sexual Ideology, 1790–1850." *Signs* 4 (1978): 219–36.

Crompton, Margaret. *Shelley's Dream Women.* London: Cassell, 1967.

Crumpacker, Laurie. "Four Novels of Harriet Beecher Stowe: A Study in Nineteenth-Century Androgyny." In *American Novelists Revisited,* edited by Fritz Fleischmann, 78–106. Boston: Hall, 1982.

D'Arcy, M. C. *The Mind and Heart of Love.* Cleveland: World, 1956.

Davis, Robert Con, ed. *The Fictional Father.* Amherst: University of Massachusetts Press, 1981.

de Rougemont, Denis. *Love in the Western World.* New York: Harcourt, Brace, 1940. Revised edition New York: Pantheon, 1956.

Dinnerstein, Dorothy. *The Mermaid and the Minotaur.* New York: Harper & Row, 1976.

Douglas, Ann. *The Feminization of American Culture.* New York: Knopf, 1977.

Dunn, Jane. *Moon in Eclipse.* London: Weidenfeld and Nicholson, 1978.

Dussinger, John A. "Kinship and Guilt in Mary Shelley's *Frankenstein.*" *Studies in the Novel* 8 (1976): 38–55.

Eliade, Mircea. *The Two and the One.* New York: Harper & Row, 1965. Reprint Chicago: University of Chicago Press, 1979.

Ellis, Kate. "Monsters in the Garden: Mary Shelley and the Bourgeois Family." In Levine and Knoepflmacher, 123–42.

Fleck, P. D. "Mary Shelley's Notes to Shelley's Poems and *Frankenstein.*" *SIR* 16 (1967): 238–54.

Freedman, Estelle. "Separation as Strategy: Female Institution Building and American Feminism, 1870–1930." *Feminist Studies* 5 (1979): 512–29.

Freud, Sigmund. *The Standard Edition of the Complete Psychological Works of Sigmund Freud (SE).* 24 vols. Translated by James Strachey. London: Hogarth, 1953–74.

Frye, Northrop. *A Study of English Romanticism.* New York: Random House, 1968. Reprint Chicago: University of Chicago Press, 1983.

Fuller, Jean Overton. *Shelley: A Biography.* London: Cape, 1968.

Gallop, Jane. *The Daughter's Seduction.* Ithaca: Cornell University Press, 1982.

Gerson, Noel B. *Daughter of Earth and Water: A Biography of Mary Wollstonecraft Shelley.* New York: Morrow, 1973.

Gilbert, Sandra M., and Susan Gubar. *The Madwoman in the Attic.* New Haven: Yale University Press, 1979.

Girard, René. *Desire, Deceit, & the Novel.* Baltimore: Johns Hopkins University Press, 1965.

Glut, Donald F. *The Frankenstein Legend.* Metuchen, N.J.: Scarecrow, 1973.

Goldberg, M. A. "Moral and Myth in Mrs. Shelley's *Frankenstein.*" *KSJ* 8 (1959): 27–38.

Griffin, Andrew. "Fire and Ice in *Frankenstein.*" In Levine and Knoepflmacher, 49–73.

Grylls, R. Glynn. *Mary Shelley: A Biography.* London: Oxford University Press, 1938.

Helsinger, Elizabeth K., Robin Lauterbach Sheets, and William Veeder. *The Woman Question: Society and Literature in Britain and America, 1837–1883.* 3 vols. New York: Garland, 1983.

Hill, J. M. "Frankenstein and the Physiognomy of Desire." *American Imago* 32 (1975): 332–58.

Hirsch, Gordon D. "The Monster Was a Lady: On the Psychology of Mary Shelley's *Frankenstein.*" *Hartford Studies in Literature* 7 (1978): 116–53.

Hoeveler, Diane Long. "The Erotic Apocalypse: The Androgynous Ideal in Blake and Shelley." Ph.D. diss., University of Illinois at Urbana-Champaign, 1976.

Hogle, Jerrold E. "Otherness in *Frankenstein:* The Confinement/Autonomy of Fabrication." *Structuralist Review* 2 (1980): 20–48.

Holmes, Richard. *Shelley: The Pursuit.* New York: Dutton, 1975.

Hughes, A. M. D. *The Nascent Mind of Shelley.* London: Oxford University Press, 1947.

Hume, Robert D. "Exuberant Gloom, Existential Agony, and Heroic Despair: Three Varieties of Negative Romanticism." In *The Gothic Imagination,* ed. G. R. Thompson, 109–27. Pullman, Wash.: Washington State University Press, 1974.

Irwin, John T. *Doubling and Incest/Repetition and Revenge.* Baltimore: Johns Hopkins University Press, 1975.

Jacobus, Mary. "Is There a Woman in This Text?" *NLH* 14 (1982): 117–41.

Johnson, Barbara. "My Monster/My Self." *Diacritics* 12 (1982): 2–10.

Joseph, Gerhard. "Frankenstein's Dream: The Child is Father of the Monster." *Hartford Studies in Literature* 7 (1975): 97–115.

Kahn, Coppélia. *Man's Estate.* Berkeley: University of California Press, 1981.

Kaplan, Morton, and Robert Kloss. "Fantasy of Paternity and the Doppelganger: Mary Shelley's *Frankenstein.*" In *The Unspoken Motive.* New York: Free Press, 1973.

Ketterer, David. *Frankenstein's Creation: The Book, The Monster, and Human Reality.* ELS Monograph Series, no. 16, Victoria, B.C., 1979.

Kiely, Robert. *The Romantic Novel in England.* Cambridge: Harvard University Press, 1972.

Killham, John. *Tennyson and 'The Princess'.* London: Athlone, 1958.

Kinkead-Weekes, Mark. *Samuel Richardson: Dramatic Novelist.* Ithaca: Cornell University Press, 1973.

Knoepflmacher, U. C. "Thoughts on the Aggression of Daughters." In Levine and Knoepflmacher, 88–119.

Lederer, Wolfgang. *The Fear of Women.* New York: Grune & Stratton, 1968.

Levine, George. a) "*Frankenstein* and the Tradition of Realism." *Novel* 7 (1973): 14–30. Revised and reprinted in *The Realistic Imagination,* 24–34. Chicago: University of Chicago Press, 1981.

————. b) "The Ambiguous Heritage of *Frankenstein.*" In Levine and Knoepflmacher, 3–30.

Levine, George, and U. C. Knoepflmacher, eds. *The Endurance of Frankenstein.* Berkeley: University of California Press, 1979.

Lovell, Ernest J., Jr. "Byron and the Byronic Hero in the Novels of Mary Shelley." *University of Texas Studies in English* 30 (1951): 158–83.

Marshall, William H. "The Father-Child Symbolism in *Prometheus Unbound.*" *MLQ* 22 (1961): 41–45.

Massey, Irving. *The Gaping Pig.* Berkeley: University of California Press, 1976.

Massingham, H. J. *The Friend of Shelley: A Memoir of Edward John Trelawny.* New York: Appleton, 1930.

Moers, Ellen. "Female Gothic." In Levine and Knoepflmacher, 77–87. Originally published in *The New York Review of Books,* 21 March 1974, 24–28. Also in *Literary Women,* 90–99. New York: Doubleday, 1976.

Moore, Thomas Verner. *Percy Bysshe Shelley.* Princeton: Psychological Review Company, 1922.

Murphy, John V. *The Dark Angel.* Lewisburg, Pa.: Bucknell University Press, 1975.

Nitchie, Elizabeth. *Mary Shelley.* New Brunswick, N.J.: Rutgers University Press, 1953.

Norman, Sylva. *On Shelley.* London: Oxford University Press, 1938.

Notopoulos, James A. *The Platonism of Shelley.* Durham: Duke University Press, 1949.

Nygren, Anders. *Agape and Eros.* Philadelphia: Westminster Press, 1953. Reprint Chicago: University of Chicago Press, 1982.

O'Flaherty, Wendy Doniger. *Women, Androgynes, and Other Mythical Beasts.* Chicago: University of Chicago Press, 1980.

Peck, Walter Edwin. "The Biographical Element in the Novels of Mary Wollstonecraft Shelley." *PMLA* 38 (1923): 196–219.

Pivar, David J. *Purity Crusade.* Westport, Conn.: Greenwood, 1973.

Poovey, Mary. "My Hideous Progeny: Mary Shelley and the Feminization of Romanticism." *PMLA* 95 (1980): 332–47. Reprinted in *The Proper Lady and the Woman Writer.* Chicago: University of Chicago Press, 1983.

Rank, Otto. *The Double.* Trans. and ed. by Harry Tucker, Jr. Chapel Hill: University of North Carolina Press, 1971.

Read, Herbert. *In Defense of Shelley and Other Essays.* London: Heinemann, 1936.

Rieger, James. *The Mutiny Within.* New York: Braziller, 1967.

Rubenstein, Marc A. " 'My Accursed Origins': The Search for the Mother in *Frankenstein.*" *SIR* 15 (1976): 165–94.

Rubin, David. "A Study of Antinomies in Shelley's *The Witch of Atlas.*" *SIR* 8 (1969): 216–28.

Sadoff, Dianne F. *Monsters of Affection.* Baltimore: Johns Hopkins University Press, 1982.

Scott, Peter Dale. "Vital Artifice: Mary, Percy, and the Psychopolitical Integrity of *Frankenstein.*" In Levine and Knoepflmacher, 172–202.

Seed, David. " 'Frankenstein'—Parable of Spectacle?" *Criticism* 24 (1982): 327–40.

Singer, June. *Androgyny: Toward a New Theory of Sexuality.* New York: Anchor/Doubleday, 1976.

Small, Christopher. *Ariel Like a Harpy*. London: Gollancz, 1972.

Smith, Daniel Scott. "Family Limitation, Sexual Control, and Domestic Feminism in Victorian America." In *Clio's Consciousness Raised*, ed. Mary Hartman and Lois W. Banner, 119–36. New York: Harper, 1974.

Spark, Muriel. *Child of Light*. Handleigh, England: Tower Bridge, 1951.

Strevick, Philip. "*Frankenstein* and Comedy." In Levine and Knoepflmacher, 221–39.

Swingle, L. J. "Frankenstein's Monster and its Romantic Relatives: Problems of Knowledge in English Romanticism." *TSLL* 15 (1973): 51–65.

Tropp, Martin. *Mary Shelley's Monster*. Boston: Houghton Mifflin, 1977.

Walling, William A. *Mary Shelley*. New York: Twayne, 1972.

Wasserman, Earl R. *Shelley: A Critical Reading*. Baltimore: Johns Hopkins University Press, 1971.

Webb, Timothy. *Shelley: A Voice Not Understood*. Atlantic Highlands, N.J.: Humanities, 1977.

Weissman, Judith. "A Reading of *Frankenstein* as the Complaint of a Political Wife." *Colby Library Quarterly* 12 (1976): 171–80.

Wexelblatt, Robert. "The Ambivalence of *Frankenstein*." *Arizona Quarterly* 36 (1980): 101–17.

White, Newton Ivey. *Shelley*. 2 vols. New York: Knopf, 1940.

Wilt, Judith. *Ghosts of the Gothic*. Princeton: Princeton University Press, 1980.

Wolf, Leonard. *The Annotated Frankenstein*. New York: Potter, 1977.

JOURNALS

AM	*The Atlantic Monthly*
AQ	*American Quarterly*
ELH	*English Literary History*
JEGP	*Journal of English and Germanic Philology*
KSJ	*Keats-Shelley Journal*
KSMB	*Keats-Shelley Memorial Bulletin*
MFS	*Modern Fiction Studies*
MLN	*Modern Language Notes*
MLQ	*Modern Language Quarterly*
N&Q	*Notes and Queries*
NCF	*Nineteenth-Century Fiction*
NEQ	*New England Quarterly*
NLH	*New Literary History*
PQ	*Philological Quarterly*
REL	*Review of English Literature*
RES	*Review of English Studies*
SEL	*Studies in English Literature*
SP	*Studies in Philology*
SIR	*Studies in Romanticism*
TSLL	*Texas Studies in Literature and Language*

Index